INTERFACE DESIGN for Learning

Design Strategies for Learning Experiences

DORIAN PETERS

To Rafa and the Coconuts. You shaped the path.

Interface Design for Learning

Design Strategies for Learning Experiences

Dorian Peters

New Riders
www.newriders.com

To report errors, please send a note to errata@peachpit.com

New Riders is an imprint of Peachpit, a division of Pearson Education.

Project Editor: Michael J. Nolan
Development Editor: Margaret Anderson/Stellarvisions
Production Editor: Rebecca Winter
Copy Editor: Gretchen Dykstra
Indexer: Joy Dean Lee
Proofreader: Patricia J. Pane
Cover Designer: Charlene Will
Interior Designer: Claudia Smelser
Compositor: Danielle Foster

ISBN 13: 978-0-321-90304-4
ISBN 10: 0-321-90304-8

9 8 7 6 5 4 3 2 1

Printed and bound in the United States of America

Acknowledgements

From my parents came the writing, Michael's vision was the door,
Margaret kept me floating, and Glenn will make it soar;
Claudia, Danielle, and Charlene, gave it life with their design,
And the family all around me gave me heart and made it shine,
Patricia, Gretchen, Becky gave it a worthy slap and polish,
but it started the day two Peters took me in,
and it's all of these guys I'd like to acknowledge.

Table of Contents

Preface

For a decade now I've been marveling at the fact that, despite the eLearning explosion across industry and education, the thousands of designers responsible for creating these learning environments face a conspicuous lack of help. Of course, we thrive on the wealth of knowledge available from user experience and web design, but learning really is unique, and design for learning requires specialized knowledge. That's why I decided it was high time for a book.

Over the last ten years I've spent time reading, researching, writing, and practicing interface design for learning—finding needles in haystacks of educational research. Working at a research center for computer-supported learning has meant that my days (and sometimes nights) resound with the latest findings on how to help people learn.

At this nexus of education and digital design is a font of valuable information: evidence-based guidance about which design decisions help or hinder learning. My hope is that by channeling this into a book for fellow designers, I'll not only learn a whole lot myself, but also meet a need, inject a bit of inspiration into the field, and at the end of the day, help people learn a little bit better with technology.

I also hope this is just a kickoff to a vibrant new community of practice, and that together we can expand our body of knowledge and best practices until digital learning becomes nothing short of a human-made wonder of the world.

FROM USERS TO LEARNERS

You wouldn't be crazy to think this book was only for people developing "educational technologies." But that would belie the reality that we engage in learning processes all the time, throughout our day and throughout our lives. It would also miss the point that social media and open content have seen many of the boundaries around learning and expertise bust wide open.

Experts are watching as people all over the world learn from one another informally because now they can. By aggregating the services made available via the internet (from social networks to multiplayer games to multimedia content), we're inhabiting "personal learning environments," curated and directed by our own needs, interests, and styles.

In their article "Learner-Centered Design," Sherry Hsi and Elliot Soloway suggest that even common applications like spreadsheet software should support not just the task, but learning while doing the task.

We need to raise our expectations for what computationally based technologies can support. We need to address the real issue of our times: nurturing the intellectual growth of children and adults, supporting them as they grapple with ideas, unleash and train their imaginations, and develop all manner of expertise.

In this dynamic new world, every technology designer should consider how people use software to learn and how it could be better designed for users as learners.

ABOUT THE BOOK

Where exactly will this book take you? First we'll do a round of speed dating with the big names in learning theory and psychology (Chapter 2, "How We Learn"). Then we'll tour the wilderness of online learning from the conventional to the experimental (Chapter 3, "A View of the eLearning Landscape"). After that, we'll pop some core principles into our kit (Chapter 4, "Basic Principles A–Z") just before we make a beeline for the practical stuff: design strategies.

Chapters 5–10 deal with specific areas of interface design for learning: emotion, social learning, educational games, and so on. Each of these chapters has two parts: the backstory and strategies. The backstory includes research and core principles that form a foundation for the strategies that follow.

To seal the deal, I've thrown in a set of heuristics, lists, and resources in Chapter 11, "The Learning Interface Designer's Toolkit," that may save you time and money, or just inject some extra finesse when you need it. With all this at hand, you'll be suited up and ready to design incredible learning experiences in no time.

Oh, one last thing—the insights in this book, like all strategies, are context dependent. As Jeff Johnson put it, design rules can be funny in that they "may be ambiguous or require subtle interpretation of context or contradict other guidelines." He also notes that presenting design rules with the science at their core makes them easier to adapt to different settings. That's why I preface each set of strategies with the scientific rationale behind them, so you can decide how best they apply in your situation. If you want to dig into a source or read a paper I've cited, all references are listed at the end of each chapter. And the essential library of books I've turned to repeatedly, and to which I owe much, are listed in a bibliography at the back of the book.

Introducing IDL

Say hello to interface design for learning

Bill Gates has claimed that in under a decade the best education will come from the web. If that ship's setting sail, designers need to get on board.

Digital learning today brings us some of the best and worst learning experiences available. I have yet to meet anyone who adores his learning management system, but I've met many who have had inspirational learning experiences online. I've bought children's software with interfaces so bad they didn't see five minutes of use, but also watched kids spend enchanted hours engaged with online reading programs. I've seen beautiful educational games that taught nothing at all, and eLearning courseware that turned dry-as-dust skills training into award-winning interactive learning. In each and every case, the interface design has played some part in the success or failure of the experience.

Welcoming interface design for learning (IDL) as a field in its own right means that we can finally start building a body of shared knowledge and best practices specific to this area. This book takes an ambitious step toward laying the groundwork for this new discipline. In it, you'll learn from principles and discoveries in psychology, human-computer interaction, and the learning sciences that can inform the practice of interface design for learning. You'll read examples and case studies, and uncover a set of evidence-based strategies for successful learning interfaces.

interface Design for Learning (IDL)

Does interface design affect learning?

In 2010, Expedia made a single design change to a web form and its profits increased by an equivalent of $12 million a year overnight. No joke (see the full story at zdnet.com). If that's what better design can do for profits, imagine what it can do for learning.

If you're a designer of eLearning, you've probably been asked to make content more "appealing" or "sexy." Part of our job as learning interface designers is to communicate that appeal is the tip of the proverbial iceberg. As an industry, we need to move beyond shallower notions of design and come to terms with the fact that it holds immense power. It really can make or break a learning experience.

Research has now proven that multimedia and interface design affects how users learn. The myth of visual design as an optional extra (which is still alive in too many dark corners) is in desperate need of busting. The hard fact is that how you create graphics, sequence interaction, display information, use animation, and design for social presence and emotion will impact how users learn. This is interface design. And this is where a new subdiscipline is ready to step in and change the game.

But you certainly don't have to take my word for it. The following chapters roll out the proof. Evidence-based practice means making decisions, as much as possible, based on what has been demonstrated in research and practice, rather than on speculation. There's a significant and growing amount of educational research on interface design decisions that help and hinder learning. There's also a wealth of design best practices that can inform education. This book pulls together much of this multidisciplinary research and practice into one package you can use to improve your design.

What makes interface design for learning different?

You may be wondering what makes a learning experience so special that it needs its own subdiscipline. I mean, what makes this book different from any of the user interface (UI) or user experience (UX) design books already out there? Here are just a few of the things I believe make *Interface Design for Learning* unique:

- **Education joins the party:** There are decades of research in education and the "learning sciences" that designers have yet to plunder. Should we really be designing learning without this knowledge?

- **User goals meet instructional goals:** Traditional UX centers on user goals, balancing them with business goals. Learning centers on instructional goals that users may or may not be aware of. Tasks that a user seeks to accomplish are important, but they are only one consideration among many. While user-centered design is often about supporting task completion, learner-centered design is about transforming the user.

- **Learning is multiscale:** Learning designers must manage user and instructional goals at very different scales, for example, at the level of subtask, task, activity, class, course, and possibly even degree or career.

- **Learning changes user needs:** In *The Cambridge Handbook of the Learning Sciences*, Chris Quintana and colleagues highlight a distinction between user-centered and learner-centered design: "Developing new understanding is the central goal for learners. If learner-centered software is at all successful, a learner's understanding will grow and change significantly while using the software and thus the software will have to change with them."

- **Desirable difficulty:** In general, good interface design aims to remove obstacles and improve efficiency. In learning design, information might deliberately be obscured or a procedure deliberately slowed to leverage the instructional benefits of reflection, effort, or even "productive failure." As MIT design professor John Maeda puts it, "Giving students a seemingly insurmountable challenge is the best motivator to learn." However, the mere operation of the interface shouldn't be the cause of irrelevant challenge or distraction. Steve Krug's timeless tenet "Don't make me think" remains sacred. Usability bloopers are not *desirable* difficulty. Intrinsic challenge is linked to the learning activity itself, and designed in deliberately.

- **Quiet design:** One of the best things an interface can do for learning is stay out of the way. A restrained and targeted use of visual elements is especially important to learning—overuse of color and other visual elements has been shown to decrease learning outcomes.

- **Emotions for learning:** Learning evokes a unique palette of emotions that we can skillfully tap into through interface design. In addition to those emotions commonly valued in UX (like pleasure, delight, and curiosity), learning experiences can benefit from calm, happiness, small amounts of stress, frustration, and a state of flow.

- **Control over experience:** UX can seek total control. As Jesse James Garrett notes in *The Elements of User Experience,* "No aspect of the user's experience with your product happens without your conscious explicit intent." Learning researchers take a very different view. Far from seeking to determine every detail of a learner's experience, they embrace the uniqueness and flexibility of individual experience. Educational technology researchers Peter Goodyear and Lucila Carvalho emphasize that "we may be able to design the thing which is experienced, but we can't design the experience itself." This is an important distinction, because it lets us consider the impact of the many undesignable elements during needs analysis. Things like prior knowledge, social resources, location constraints, available tools, or preconceptions all affect learning. By focusing on the things that we *can* design, and taking into consideration the things that we can't, we can create optimal conditions for learning. Acting as facilitators, we find that the best design philosophy is one that sees the learner and the environment as adaptive and evolving through experience.

Getting the language straight

You may already be aware that there's an alarming amount of ambiguity surrounding terms used at the intersection of learning and technology. Terms like *eLearning* and *online learning* are defined in many different ways, depending on whom you ask or what you're reading.

In this book, I use *eLearning* as an umbrella term for learning experiences that involve digital technology. I use the terms *learning technologies* and *educational technologies* interchangeably to refer to digital systems and software designed specifically to support learning.

I find that the term *interface design for learning* (IDL) gives focus to a range of design concerns related to learning. These are only now beginning to get the attention they require if we're going to see eLearning come of age.

When I use *interface design for learning* in this book, I'm referring to the design of the following aspects of digital learning experiences:

- Multimedia and visual design (graphics, video, animation, audio)
- Information design and architecture (structure, labels, navigation)
- Usability
- Screen-based interaction

THE LEARNING EXPERIENCE

The term *user experience* was coined by design psychology hero Don Norman, and it refers to a holistic and human-centered approach to the design of web or software environments. (You can read an interview with Norman at adaptive-path.com.) User experience designers rely on a wealth of methods, processes, and deliverables, from personas and card sorting to task flows and maps. UX draws from, and coordinates, a large number of different fields, famously visualized in Dan Saffer's map of UX disciplines (**FIGURE 1.1**).

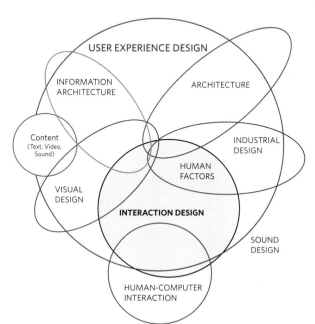

FIGURE 1.1 The disciplines of user experience design by Dan Saffer (Courtesy of Dan Saffer).

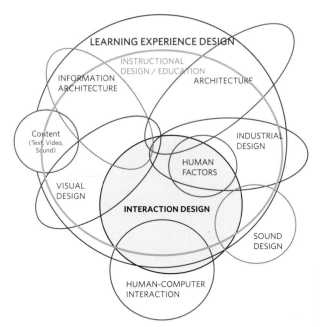

FIGURE 1.2 The disciplines of user experience design by Dan Saffer, reconceived for learning experience design.

If we imagine user experience design reconceived as learning experience design (LX), the most conspicuously missing element is instructional design, as informed by educational research (**FIGURE 1.2**).

Realistically, instructional design should inform every step of the design process. Most obviously, instructional design is central to the content and task design of a learning experience. But it's also relevant to information architecture and interaction design, including decisions about learner control over content, activities, and navigation.

Therefore, we can think of the learning experience as an umbrella term for the various elements that create an environment in which someone has an opportunity to learn something.

While in much of design we aim to craft a user experience that meets business or communication goals, in learning experience design, the goal is to help someone learn something. More technically, that's about improving what folks in education call *learning outcomes* and the quality of the learning experience. A big part of LX is designing the interface in a way that supports and enhances the cognitive and affective processes involved in learning.

What kind of designer are you?

The word *design* has a very different meaning in education than it does in the web profession. In the field of education, design refers to the creation of curricula and learning activities. It's what teachers do. It's also what instructional designers of eLearning do. They create and assemble content (worksheets, books, and so on) and orchestrate combinations of activities (writing, brainstorming, role-playing) to help students learn things. There are a number of good books for professionals on instructional design (Julie Dirksen's *Design for How People Learn* being one of them.)

For most web professionals, design involves devising, prototyping, and creating multimedia objects and environments. These environments and resources are designed to facilitate activity (which we call interaction or behavior), but it isn't the activity itself we're generally devising.

eLearning deals with both areas of design: the design of the educational content and activity, as well as the design of the digital environment/resources to support it. For example, a learning interface designer might take content created by a teacher or instructional designer, and transform it into an online resource by applying principles of effective communication and multimedia design.

While there will certainly be areas of overlap between instructional design and interface design for learning, this book focuses on the latter.

- **Interface design for learning:** User interface design intended to support learning objectives.
- **Learning design/instructional design:** The design of content and activities created to support learning objectives.

It's also useful to think in terms of the team. Just as a user experience team may include a manager, developers, interface/interaction designers, information architects, and content strategists, a learning experience team might include a similar group of people with the addition of instructional designers, subject-matter experts (SMEs), and learning interface designers, where, ideally, all members of the team have some knowledge of pedagogy and the distinctions of designing for learning.

WARNING: TERMINOLOGY MAY CAUSE BLINDNESS

If you're an old hand at interface design but new to education, it's worth noting the differences in how terms are used in this field. Corporate eLearning professionals frequently use the word *training* to refer to their learning programs, but some researchers and school educators cringe and equate it with animal training and behavioral conditioning. Likewise, use a term like *technology-enhanced learning and teaching* in the commercial world and they may label you an academic fuddy-duddy.

The term *instructional design* is more likely to be used in commercial eLearning, whereas *learning designer* or *educational designer* is common elsewhere. This is because instructional design is seen as a specific theory in education, but has come to be used as more of a general term in industry. In this book, I use *instructional design* because it's more easily distinguished from other types of design for learning.

There will be other variations as the field matures, and there are no hard and fast rules. The key is to take note of the preferred terms in your environment and not assume that they're interchangeable.

The layer cake of eLearning design

Interface design for learning experiences generally comes in one of three layers (**FIGURE 1.3**).

Multimedia Content — Graphics, video, audio, animation objects; info & interaction design

Interface Styling — Look & feel, interface elements, customization, information design

System Design — Architecture, interaction design, default interface elements and look & feel

FIGURE 1.3 The three layers of interface design for learning: system design, interface styling, and multimedia content. Learning interface designers may work on one or a combination of these levels depending on the project.

- **System design:** If you're a designer working as part of an EdTech development team in a startup, an open-source community, or a research group, you may be involved in creating the underlying system design for an eLearning technology. This may include creating the basic information architecture, interaction design, and primary interface.

- **Interface styling:** The second layer applies where the look and feel of a learning system can be redesigned in the form of interface skins or themes. This restyling lets designers who use and configure the software tailor it to brand styles or unique learning scenarios, or improve on the default interface based on new findings.

- **Multimedia content:** If you're working in an organization with closed systems and prepackaged visual standards, you may be unable to make changes to the other two levels. For example, you might create course materials for a company learning system, or configure a class space for a university. Don't feel disempowered by the restrictions—the design of multimedia content (like explanatory graphics, video, and animation) has considerable impact on learning. Also relevant at this layer are decisions about course configuration. You may not be able to restyle learning spaces, but you can organize and configure content within them. In these cases, the decisions you make about course architecture, navigation, and information design will also have impact.

The rest of this book takes on issues and strategies that influence design in each of these three layers. Because IDL is distinguished from other forms of interface design by having learning as its goal, some of the expertise and knowledge of the instructional designer should overlap with that of the learning interface designer (and vice-versa). That's why, in the next chapter, we'll take a jaunty foray into the learning theory that has shaped formal and informal education over the past 150 years.

SOURCES

Garrett, Jesse James. 2011. *The Elements of User Experience: User-Centered Design for the Web and Beyond*, 2nd ed. Berkeley, CA: New Riders.

Goodyear, Peter and Lucila Carvalho. 2013. "The Analysis of Complex Learning Environments." In *Rethinking Pedagogy for a Digital Age: Designing for 21st Century Learning*, 2nd ed., edited by Helen Beetham and Rhona Sharpe, 49–63. New York: Routledge.

Heath, Nick. November 1, 2010. Expedia on How One Extra Data Field Can Cost $12M. ZDNet. http://www.zdnet.com/expedia-on-how-one-extra-data-field-can-cost-12m-3040153863.

Hsi, Sherry and Elliot Soloway. 1998. "Learner-Centered Design: Addressing, Finally, the Unique Needs of Learners." In *CHI 98 Conference Summary on Human Factors in Computing Systems* (pp. 211–212). ACM. http://portal.acm.org/citation.cfm?id=286697.

Johnson, Jeff. 2010. *Designing with the Mind in Mind: Simple Guide to Understanding User Interface Design Rules*. Amsterdam/Boston: Morgan Kaufmann Publishers/Elsevier.

2

How We Learn

A whirlwind tour of essential learning theory with a who's who of big names in educational psychology

Learning theory and interface design

Designers need to understand how people learn in order to develop learner-centered software ... learning sciences must be integrated into software design.

—QUINTANA, ET AL., in "Learner-Centered Design," *The Cambridge Handbook of the Learning Sciences*

If you work in education, you're probably familiar with terms like *constructivism* and names like Piaget. In employee training, instructional designers make reference to Bloom's taxonomy or Mayer's work on multimedia learning. Learning theory can be decidedly academic, but that's only because learning is a complex thing. Theories provide explanations for how and why we do things, and in order to design interfaces for learning that are genuinely effective, you need a basic understanding of how we learn new things.

Interestingly, different theories of how we learn can dramatically affect how a learning technology is designed. For example, will an eLearning program be designed with a single-user linear architecture, or will it be open-ended and collaborative? That depends on your theory of learning.

This chapter is by no means comprehensive—there's no way to condense 150 years of science and philosophy into a few pages. Instead, it presents the main theories at the core of twentieth and twenty-first century learning with a focus on those that crop up consistently in both corporate and school-based eLearning strategies.

So sit back and let's dig into the essentials and academic name-dropping that will guarantee your success at any geek party of educational psychologists.

ARE YOU MORE OF A VESSEL OR A BUILDER?

First, an esoteric interview question: Would you consider yourself an empty vessel or a construction worker? One basic distinction between how teachers and researchers think about learning has to do with whether they see learners as empty vessels into which knowledge is poured, or as active builders of their own knowledge. Therefore, instruction becomes about how to best transfer knowledge to a learner's brain *or* how to best facilitate opportunities for learners to construct their own knowledge.

In the first instance, the teacher is often described as a "sage on the stage," and in the second, a "guide on the side." Page-turner and multiple-choice courseware generally comes from the knowledge transfer department. An open space with various tools for learners to seek out information, develop ideas, and share them with others comes out of the construction department.

Taking this a step further, your view of learners depends on your view of knowledge. Is knowledge a collection of objective facts about the world that can be transferred? If so, your view is *objectivist*. If you see human knowledge as something dynamic that's continually being adapted and constructed by people individually and socially, then your view is *constructivist*.

As you'll see, the theories summarized in this chapter are like siblings (complete with shared history and the proverbial rivalry) and they overlap in many ways. It's not my intention to suggest that one theory is better or more accurate than another; nor are there clear boundaries between them.

Surely different perspectives on learning are valuable for different reasons and within different contexts, and no single theory is ideal for every situation. I value the notion that by using different perspectives in complementary ways, we can achieve the best of all worlds.

Moreover, theories themselves are steps in a journey of discovery, not an end in themselves. With each step we broaden our understanding of what learning is, but we'll always have more to discover.

Behaviorism: Learning as the science of behavior change

Behaviorism, the first major theory of learning, was born in the second half of the nineteenth century from animal behavioral studies. Behaviorism embraced what was the reasonably new concept of "science." Behaviorists were adamant that the scientific method could and should be applied to the study and practice of learning and teaching.

In order to be scientifically precise about something as psychological and complex as learning, behaviorists claimed that only observable "overt action" (that is, behavior) was worth studying because it's the only thing we can see, and therefore measure empirically.

Furthermore, they believed that the inner workings of the mind were too airy-fairy for real scientists to consider. They didn't think that thoughts had much to do with causing behavior and instead claimed that all behavior was triggered by external stimuli.

In bringing a scientific approach to the study of learning for the first time, behaviorists sought to measure, predict, and manipulate patterns of behavior, using the now-familiar notion of *stimulus-response* for research and training.

BEHAVIORAL CONDITIONING

The first big daddy of behaviorism is the celebrated Russian physiologist Ivan Pavlov (1849–1936). Perhaps even more famous than Pavlov himself are his dogs. Knowing that dogs salivate in the presence of food, Pavlov conducted a legendary experiment in which he repeatedly rang a bell just before each mealtime. After a while, the dogs began to salivate in response to the bell itself, even when food never came. The dogs were *conditioned* to salivate in response to the bell.

In this well-known experiment, Pavlov demonstrated the discovery that animals, including humans, could be conditioned to behave in certain ways on cue, by training one stimulus to trigger another (**FIGURE 2.1**). This is now known as *classical conditioning*.

At the turn of the twentieth century, American psychologist Edward Thorndike (1874–1949) developed the notion of *operant conditioning*. Rather than working with the involuntary behaviors of classic conditioning (like salivating), Thorndike dealt with behaviors over which we have control. He also developed the conclusion, known as the law of effect, which basically states that behaviors associated with pleasure and comfort are more likely to be repeated ("Mmmm, I'll eat there again."), whereas those associated with displeasure are less likely to be repeated ("Brrr, no more sledding in my underwear.").

FIGURE 2.1 From *Saturday Cartoons* by Mark Stivers. © 2003 Mark Stivers.

Thorndike's studies formed the groundwork for the second big daddy of behaviorism, American psychologist B. F. Skinner (1904–1990). Skinner's methods for operant conditioning relied on reinforcement and punishment, with an emphasis on positive reinforcement. Of course Skinner didn't invent the ideas of punishment and reward, but he conceptualized them scientifically and conducted experiments to determine how to use them most effectively, based on various schedules of frequency.

REINFORCEMENT AND PUNISHMENT

The notions of positive and negative reinforcement are probably familiar to you, but the latter is often misunderstood. *Positive* and *negative* don't mean pleasant or unpleasant, but rather whether something is being added or removed (+ or –).

Positive reinforcement is easy to remember, as it refers to providing something nice as a reward for a desired behavior, like a dog getting a treat for rolling over. *Negative reinforcement* is still a reward because it involves removing something bad, like removing a dog's muzzle when it stops growling.

Positive punishment is about adding something unpleasant, like clapping near the dog's ears when it barks. *Negative punishment* involves removing something pleasant, like not letting the dog sleep inside after it pees on the carpet. Both positive and negative reinforcement increase the likelihood of a behavior, while punishments decrease it.

I use animal examples here, mainly because they're easy to understand and dogs are cute, but indeed Skinner conducted his experiments largely on nonhuman subjects (he especially liked rats and pigeons). Many critics of behaviorism refer to the problematic nature of research on lab pigeons being applied to children in schools, and regard it as unsuited to supporting the breadth and complexity of human learning. Nevertheless, it remains one of the most easily recognized strategies at work in education today—even on the web (**FIGURE 2.2**).

As politically incorrect as punishment has become for learning since the days of rulers on knuckles to "encourage" correct behavior, behaviorist learning strategies continue to permeate our experience online and off. Fortunately, the methods are now less sadistic on the whole.

For example, schoolchildren are still sent to detention (positive punishment) or excluded from playground games (negative punishment) for misbehaving.

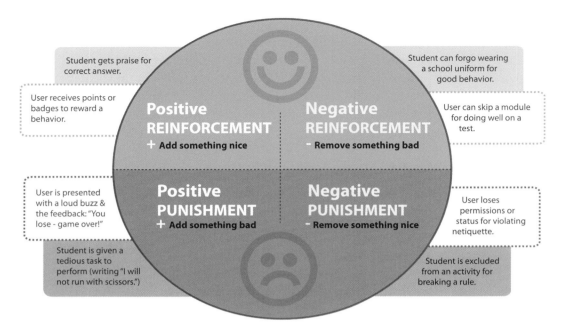

Student gets praise for correct answer.

User receives points or badges to reward a behavior.

Student can forgo wearing a school uniform for good behavior.

User can skip a module for doing well on a test.

Positive REINFORCEMENT
+ Add something nice

Negative REINFORCEMENT
− Remove something bad

Positive PUNISHMENT
+ Add something bad

Negative PUNISHMENT
− Remove something nice

User is presented with a loud buzz & the feedback: "You lose - game over!"

User loses permissions or status for violating netiquette.

Student is given a tedious task to perform (writing "I will not run with scissors.")

Student is excluded from an activity for breaking a rule.

FIGURE 2.2 Behaviorist learning strategies involve the use of rewards and punishments.

But reinforcement and punishment need not be as dramatic as they sound. Something as simple as a teacher's smile or frown can motivate a child.

The consequences online can be as subtle as wording or color choice. When Flickr praises you for uploading your photos "Good job!" or the Blackboard Learning Management System displays a confirmation in bright green that says "Success!" as if it's celebrating with you for posting to a forum, you're experiencing a type of positive reinforcement.

Games and gamification often rely heavily on rewards. The so-called "Foursquare technique" consists of providing a series of positive reinforcements in the form of badges, points, levels, and leaderboards. Many of the most widely used eLearning programs and educational apps employ rewards like these to motivate learners (**FIGURE 2.3**).

Critics of ill-founded attempts at gamification caution that these motivators are limited because they're entirely extrinsic, that is, the learner's motivation to achieve a goal is based on external motivators (buttons and badges) rather than on what she's actually learning. We'll look at motivation in depth in Chapter 7, "Learning Is Emotional."

FIGURE 2.3 Behaviorism is modernized in gamification. Gamify is one of a number of companies that sell software for adding rewards like points, badges, and coupons to any product.

BEHAVIORISM AND ELEARNING

Behaviorism has inspired many of the best-known eLearning styles and technologies, from early computer-assisted instruction (CAI) to present-day page-turners and drill-and-practice games. Behaviorist technologies typically have explicit and discrete steps and are therefore suitable for automation. **FIGURE 2.4** shows an example of an early "teaching machine" based on the behavioral approach.

CAI, for example, provides guided individual learning and was initially designed for military training and language learning. CAI can also refer to software that

FIGURE 2.4 The Pressey Testing Machine, a behaviorist learning technology created in 1924, offered multiple-choice exercises.

Benjamin Bloom and his taxonomy

Bloom's Taxonomy, a classification of learning objectives edited in 1956 by American educational psychologist Benjamin Bloom (1913–1999), makes a regular appearance in seminars on instructional design. Bloom was interested in applying scientific structure, akin to the classification of animals and plants, to learning goals in order to support educational design and assessment.

While Bloom envisioned a series of three taxonomies, it's his cognitive taxonomy that was completed and which has been so widely applied. (The others were affective and motor-sensory.) It attempts to classify all possible cognitive learning objectives into six categories: knowledge, comprehension, application, analysis, synthesis, and evaluation. These are arranged in order of lesser to greater cognitive complexity.

In 2001, Bloom's six categories were revised, leading to the following revamp.

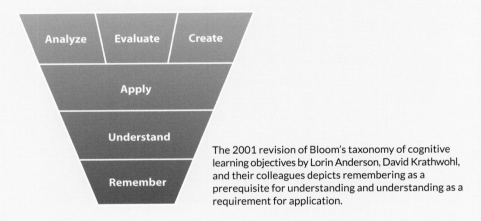

The 2001 revision of Bloom's taxonomy of cognitive learning objectives by Lorin Anderson, David Krathwohl, and their colleagues depicts remembering as a prerequisite for understanding and understanding as a requirement for application.

Critics of Bloom's taxonomy point out that many complex tasks involve many different processes going on in parallel. Tasks should not be created for only one cognitive process, but should aim to combine several of them.

involves a series of branching steps designed by an instructional designer to ensure that the learner moves onto the next step only when ready, or gets diverted to further instruction depending on the accuracy of her response. Following a behaviorist view, the learner would be asked to provide definitions verbatim.

Bloom's taxonomy and behaviorist training approaches are prevalent in the modern workplace. For the same reason that early CAI suited military training, the promise of low-cost efficiency and objectives structured around predictable behaviors remains appealing for many types of job skills training today.

Learning based on behaviorism tends to focus on rote learning through drill and practice exercises. The learner ("the empty vessel") is required to memorize then reiterate information to show learning. In CAI, learning material is often presented in small, isolated chunks of knowledge with little emphasis on connecting the pieces.

Cognitivism: Mind as computer

Just because we can't see something easily enough to measure it doesn't mean it isn't important. Behaviorism could not explain all the situations in which our actions stem from the workings of our mind—not just our environment. This gap in behaviorism led to the development of the theory of *cognitivism* in the 1950s. Dismissing the behaviorists' view of the mind as an inaccessible black box, proponents of cognitive theory looked for ways to understand the mind itself and found their answer in the emerging field of computer science.

Cognitivism is based on the idea that the human brain can be understood as a computer that processes information. Artificial intelligence pioneer Marvin Minsky put it graphically when he described the mind as "a meat machine." Cognitivists sought to model the brain accurately on the assumption that this would help design instruction for more complex behavior, like problem solving and decision making, than behaviorism allowed.

COGNITIVE LOAD—WE CAN ONLY TAKE IN SO MUCH AT A TIME

Studies of the limitations of short-term memory, the human equivalent of a computer's RAM, produced the famous 7 ± 2 rule of working memory capacity, referred to as Miller's Law (after George Miller, the psychologist who formulated it).

Robert Gagné and instructional design

Theory longs to be applied. It's the models, strategies, and approaches used for teaching that allow learning theories to take shape in the real world.

The most popular collection of eLearning models and strategies in eLearning can be herded under the umbrella of *instructional design* (ID), a field with a multitude of practices founded on behaviorist and cognitivist theories of learning. A central structure of ID is frequently summed up by the acronym, ADDIE, which stands for analysis, design, development, implementation, and evaluation.

The beginnings of instructional design can be traced to the efforts of psychologists who were recruited to develop training programs for the military during World War II. Their work finally earned a name in the 1960s, when it was tagged with various labels, including instructional design, instructional systems design, and systematic instruction. By the late 1970s, forty different models for systematically designing instruction had been defined. Through the 1980s, ID was widely used in business, industry, and military training.

One of the most influential practitioners of ID was American instructional psychologist Robert Gagné (1916–2002). His book, *The Conditions of Learning*, published in 1965, was based on behaviorist strategies; later editions evolved into cognitive information processing. Like Benjamin Bloom, Gagné developed a taxonomy of learning outcomes, which he classified into five categories: intellectual skills, cognitive strategy, verbal information, attitude, and motor skills. Each of these is linked to a set of conditions of learning that form the basis of his theory of instruction.

Gagné also provided strategies for facilitating these learning outcomes in the form of nine events of instruction intended to help transfer knowledge into learner memory.

GAGNÉ'S NINE EVENTS OF INSTRUCTION

1. Gain attention.
2. Inform learners of objectives.
3. Stimulate recall of prior learning.
4. Present the content.
5. Provide learning guidance.
6. Elicit performance (practice).
7. Provide feedback.
8. Assess performance.
9. Enhance retention and transfer to the job.

Having such a tidy guide for effective learning has made Gagné's work popular, particularly in professional development.

The idea is that the mind can keep only about seven items in working memory at any one time, for example, the digits in a phone number. When faced with more than that, the brain manages by chunking: aggregating the information into about seven chunks. More recently, researchers have put the actual limit at 4 ± 2.

Following on this growing understanding of working memory, Australian educational psychologist John Sweller developed the concept of *cognitive load* to describe the limitations of working memory while trying to learn something.

What has followed is a wealth of advice on how to free the mind for learning by reducing cognitive load, or more specifically, *extraneous cognitive load*—complexity that is not important for the learning task, but is added by the design or technology, for instance, hard-to-read text or poorly written instructions.

Cognitive load theory is also at the core of Richard E. Mayer's work on multimedia learning that comprises possibly the largest collection of research-based principles that deal specifically with multimedia design issues in education (see sidebar).

SCHEMAS

Cognitivists assert that we learn better when we can connect new information to things we already know; they call the existing mental framework for something a *schema* (or mental model). In Chapter 5, "Learning Is Visual," we'll look at examples of visuals that support the integration of new knowledge via links to existing knowledge, including representational images, comparative images, and advance organizers.

Schemas provide a structure to which we can attach new information. Schemas are dynamic and change as we interpret new experiences and adapt our understanding accordingly.

COGNITIVISM AND ELEARNING

Cognitivism's love affair with computer science made it an ideal candidate as a theory for educational technology. In 1970, Jaime Carbonell suggested that, through dialogue with a student, computers could act as *teachers* and not just *tools* for learning. Rather than just the predetermined questions, answers, and predefined pathways that made up behaviorist CAI technologies, Carbonell envisioned "programs that know what they are talking about, the same way human teachers do."

CAI programs soon evolved into the more complex intelligent tutoring systems (ITS). Ideally, an ITS adapts to an individual student's performance automatically by drawing on the knowledge incorporated into its database. It's also intended to transfer lesson content to the learner, just as topic knowledge might be passed from tutor to student.

ITSs have become more and more sophisticated; some experimental examples even have the capacity to detect and respond to learners' emotional states. But, for a variety of reasons they have not been widely adopted. We'll look at ITSs more closely in the next chapter.

THE COGNITIVE SCIENCES

In the last two decades of the twentieth century, cognitive psychology expanded into the more multidisciplinary field of the cognitive sciences. Studies carried out by those working in the cognitive sciences brought many new understandings of learning to the table, including new ideas about knowledge, learning, and problem solving.

For example, key to cognitive science study is the idea that the mind develops "representations" or knowledge structures, such as concepts, beliefs, facts, procedures, or models. Cognitive science also helped uncover the importance of reflection to learning and to expert behavior. Studies found that experts in a field (as opposed to novices) were better at the reflective practices of criticizing and planning their work. Thus novices must develop these abilities if they wish to evolve into experts.

Cognitive science has given learning theory an injection of sociocultural perspective as well. Socioculturalists study learning outside schools and outside Western culture. Their work has revealed that, outside schools, learning almost always takes place within a complex social environment and therefore, it can't be fully understood as a mental process taking place only within the boundaries of the mind. The learner's physical and social environment must also be considered. These results fueled the theory of situated cognition (described below) and align with the descriptions of learning provided by constructivism.

Richard E. Mayer and multimedia learning

Many researchers turn to cognitive load theory to explain how we learn, but there's one standout for professionals in the area of multimedia learning: Richard E. Mayer. Based on cognitive load theory and findings from the cognitive sciences, Mayer and his colleagues developed the *cognitive theory of multimedia learning*. This theory is based on three assumptions:

1. We process visual and auditory information through separate channels (dual-channel processing).

2. We are limited in the amount of information we can take into either channel at once.

3. When we're engaged in active learning, we're not passively receiving information. Instead, we a) pay attention, b) organize incoming information (picking and choosing what's important), and c) integrate incoming information with other knowledge. We do all this in order to build a mental model of the key parts and relationships of the information we're presented with.

These assumptions have implications for the design of multimedia learning environments and resources, and Mayer has spent over fifteen years testing specific guidelines for multimedia learning design from the perspective of this theory. Specifically, he's studied the relative superiority of different combinations of text, graphics, video, and audio for different learning contexts. His research has led to the development of a number of research-based multimedia learning design principles, many of which (but not all) pertain specifically to interface design.

MAYER'S PRINCIPLES OF MULTIMEDIA LEARNING

- Multimedia principle
- Contiguity principle
- Modality principle
- Coherence principle
- Personalization principle
- Redundancy principle

- Segmenting principle
- Pre-training principle
- Signaling principle
- Voice principle
- Image principle
- Individual differences principle

We'll look at the application of these principles to interface design in more detail in the strategies throughout this book. For an in-depth discussion, see *e-Learning and the Science of Instruction: Proven Guidelines for Consumers and Designers of Multimedia Learning* by Ruth Clark and Richard E. Mayer.

Constructivism: Knowledge as built by the learner

Inventions are obviously human constructions. (And note that it is the inventive idea or design that is patented, not its physical embodiment.) But if an idea for controlling the flight of an airplane is a human construction, why not a theory that explains flight? With recognition of this parallelism, the final stone was in place for a full-blown constructivism that recognizes all kinds of intellectual products as human constructions: theories, algorithms, proofs, designs, plans, analogies, and on and on.

—MARLENE SCARDAMALIA and CARL BEREITER in "A Brief History of Knowledge Building"

Unsurprisingly, more than a few people were dissatisfied with the idea that humans are just like computers and can be programmed as such. In fact, the fundamental notion that knowledge is objective and flows from teacher to student proved unconvincing to a growing contingency. And thus we come to *constructivism*.

Constructivists argue that when we learn, we're not simply empty sponges absorbing facts, but rather we're constructing our own knowledge of the world based on personal experiences and reflection on those experiences. Therefore, knowledge, rather than being an objective matchup with reality, is an individual's interpretation and construction based on a unique collection of past experiences, prior knowledge, and ways of interpreting things. This philosophy of knowledge spawned the classic constructivist learning theory.

In a learning experience based on constructivist ideas, the learner might be asked to describe something in her words, rather than being given a verbatim definition. Constructivist instruction also aims to build on the learner's existing knowledge, for example, by connecting new concepts to related everyday experiences. Certain everyday experiences and prior knowledge will contradict new knowledge. As such, learning new concepts requires *restructuring* elements of existing concepts (conceptual change) rather than just accumulating knowledge in a vessel.

While classic constructivism emphasizes individual knowledge construction, *sociocultural constructivism* (see sidebar on Lev Vygotsky) emphasizes the importance

Jean Piaget and the stages of human development

Jean Piaget (1896–1980) originated the first of two primary perspectives on constructivism: *cognitive constructivism*. A Swiss-born psychologist and biologist, Piaget was as committed to the scientific method as B. F. Skinner or Ivan Pavlov but to a very different end. He dedicated his life to a biological explanation of knowledge and did groundbreaking work on the study of child development.

Piaget saw human learning as a series of stages in which we construct new logical structures—each more sophisticated than the last—as we move from birth to adulthood. He suggested that everyone moves through the same four stages of development around the same age:

PIAGET'S STAGES OF DEVELOPMENT

1. **Sensorimotor** (commonly birth to 2 years): We construct our understanding of the world based on information from our senses and movement.
2. **Pre-operational** (commonly 2–7 years): We are self-centered and can act on objects and represent them with words and symbols, but we cannot fully think through our actions.
3. **Concrete operational** (commonly 7–11 years): We can use logic to solve actual nonabstract problems and we discover that viewpoints beyond our own exist.
4. **Formal operational** (commonly 12+ years): We can think abstractly, hypothesize, and draw conclusions.

of interaction with others—be they teachers, experts, or peers—to the learning process. While engaging with others, we take part in a process of idea negotiation and interpretation. In this process, we all construct meaning together.

Constructivist learning theories permeate much contemporary work in education research and have much to contribute to collaborative online learning. While it can be tricky to get a sound grasp of constructivist ideas, probably because we were largely raised on objectivist thinking, we begin to see how familiar constructivist ideas actually are when we consider learning outside of institutions.

Learning that occurs throughout life, in workplace teams or as part of daily life, seems to be more easily described by constructivist theory. When we debate with friends, integrate new experiences as we travel, or negotiate our way around problems and new ideas, we're constructing new knowledge.

Lev Vygotsky and the zone of proximal development

Russian psychologist Lev Vygotsky (1896–1934) described the second major perspective on constructivism: learning is definitively social. Vygotsky reacted to Piaget's individualist approach and stressed the importance of the social-cultural context of human learning. He argued that, rather than individual development leading to learning, learning leads to individual development and is contingent on the use of language and interaction with others.

He also developed the notion of the *zone of proximal development* (ZPD). A learner's ZPD consists of activity beyond her current level of development but within her potential level. It ranges from easy tasks that can be solved individually to complex tasks that can be solved only with the help of others, such as a parent, teacher, or more capable peer. A learner can solve far more complex problems with others than she could alone, and as she moves through her ZPD, she learns to solve these problems without support.

This translates to an approach in which the instructor supports the learner in achieving her goal *independently* by supporting her with the necessary language and concepts along the way. The instructor facilitates the learner's move through the zone of proximal development—from what she knows to what she needs to know in a course or lesson. Scaffolding (explained in Chapter 3, "A View of the eLearning Landscape") is a common teaching strategy used for this approach.

Passing through the zone of proximal development. Cartoon by José Montaño (Courtesy of the artist).

As a student, I never had anything against the didactic approach of lectures, or even the odd bit of rote memorization, but the experiences I remember with the greatest fondness involved active, constructive learning with others, such as doing science experiments, role-playing money markets, or engaging in fieldwork. These are also the experiences I associate most with conceptual breakthroughs.

Piaget explained that we learn by a combination of assimilation and accommodation. Put simply, we either make sense of something new and add it to our existing knowledge (assimilation), or, our understanding gets disrupted by new information, throwing us off balance (disequalibration). When we're thrown off balance, we have to adjust our existing understanding (accommodation) in order to regain equilibrium.

KNOWLEDGE BUILDING

Knowledge building in an educational context was first introduced by Marlene Scardamalia and Carl Bereiter, who define it as "the creation and improvement of knowledge of value to one's community." It moves the focus from individual to community. Many see it as unique to—and critical for—the knowledge age in which we live, an age in which the collaborative construction of new ideas, tools, and improvements is central to the economy.

Knowledge building is founded on twelve principles, among them *real ideas and authentic problems, improvable ideas,* and *idea diversity.* For a full list of the twelve, see Scardamalia and Bereiter's paper, "A Brief History of Knowledge Building," in the *Canadian Journal of Learning and Technology.*

CONSTRUCTIVISM AND ELEARNING

Constructivist theory is most evident in more recent incarnations of eLearning and educational technologies. When you think of computer-based training, you might imagine an individual in front of a screen clicking through courseware designed to impart information and test for retention. In contrast, a constructivist technology might provide tools for group discussion and knowledge building like wikis, collaborative media-making tools, discussion forums, or chat rooms.

There are also web-based technologies specifically designed to support knowledge building and knowledge communities such as Knowledge Forum and Cohere. 3-D worlds that let learners engage in virtual fieldwork experiences, explore virtual environments, make hypotheses, collect various types of data, and propose solutions draw on constructivist learning theory as well.

Connectivism, ecologies, and twenty-first century learning

The gradual embedding of digital connectedness into every aspect of our lives has changed us so dramatically that some argue twentieth-century learning theory is no longer enough. As we change and our environments change, the way we learn is also changing. Researchers like George Siemens, Linda Harasim, and Stephen Downes have proposed new theories for understanding learning that take into account the needs and realities of the knowledge age. As Siemens writes:

> Technology is altering (rewiring) our brains. The tools we use define and shape our thinking .... Many of the processes previously handled by learning theories can now be off-loaded to, or supported by, technology. Know-how and know-what is being supplemented with know-where (the understanding of where to find knowledge needed).

In the mid-2000s, Siemens proposed a theory of *connectivism,* which describes learning as being centered on the building of connections. It states that our ability to connect to new knowledge is more important than how much we actually already know.

Connectivism addresses the idea that knowledge is shifting and growing at an unprecedented rate, and that much of our own knowledge is being off-loaded to technologies so that the information that was once mostly inside our heads is now distributed onto devices and across the internet. As such, it focuses on the meta-skills that help learners evaluate, distinguish, and select valuable information from a sea of data. Connectivism also describes learning as a nonlinear process that includes using technology, forming networks, and recognizing patterns across fields.

From the stimulus-response of behaviorism, through the journey into the mind with cognitivism, and the expansion into subjectivity and collaboration with the cognitive sciences and constructivism, we finally head into a future of networking and connections. If our understanding of learning is growing broader and deeper, then we may have finally hit a large enough metaphor with the notion of learning as an ecology.

ECOLOGIES OF LEARNING

John Seely Brown uses the ecology metaphor to refer to the emergence of learning ecologies that have reached global scales since the advent of the web. The traditional boundaries around learning and expertise are bursting wide open. We are now learning with and from others within our own *personal learning environments* that integrate internet technologies like social media to make instant connections to content, activities, and people possible anytime and from anywhere via increasingly portable devices.

Ecology is a useful metaphor in that it reflects the complexity and interdependence of the many components necessary for successful learning environments. Furthermore, by definition, it emphasizes the environment and the importance of material, social, and cultural concerns to a complete understanding of how learning works.

In *Living and Learning with New Media*, Mizuko Ito and her colleagues use the metaphor of ecology "to emphasize that the everyday practices of youth, existing structural conditions, infrastructures of place, and technologies are all dynamically interrelated." It's a way of acknowledging that we can't realistically extract either technology or learning from the great web of our life experience any more than we can understand an elephant by looking only at its trunk.

The concept of *situated learning* acknowledges the importance of real-world context, and places learning within the authentic situation to which it pertains. For example, if you learn about vegetables in a garden, or role-play professional activities in a professional setting, you're engaged in situated learning. Learning on the job, internships, and apprenticeships are also situated learning opportunities.

Though situated learning can be applied at any level, Jean Lave and Etienne Wenger introduced it as a method for adult learning that takes place within what they term a *community of practice.* Their definition of a community of practice is a group of people who share a craft or profession. They argue that much adult learning can occur as part of activity within a community of practice, in which more knowledgeable peers act as teachers, and learners co-construct knowledge by problem solving in groups.

Of course the garden, the office, or the operating room aren't always available to learners, which has led many to look to technology to fill the gap. With its capacity to create realistic simulated environments, technology has a unique potential to provide the realistic context that can be so helpful to successful learning.

Certainly computers can provide excellent environments for engaging in real activity. Educational technologies like Scratch (http://scratch.mit.edu), Toon-Talk (www.toontalk.com), and the Logo programming language are intended to teach computer science concepts by showing students as young as 5 or 6 how to program. These are based on Seymour Papert's theory of *constructionism* (not to be confused with constructivism), which emphasizes the pedagogical value of learning by constructing objects that includes learning by doing, tinkering, and making.

Adult learning is sometimes spoken about as *lifelong learning,* a term that communicates the point that learning does not happen only at school between kindergarten and a degree, but is something that continues informally, as well as formally, throughout our lives.

Informal learning is generally understood as learning that is not externally structured by, for example, educational institutions or structured courses. We learn informally on the job and among friends.

As an eLearning interface designer, you might be designing tools for informal learning (for example, collaboration space to support people learning from one another in a workplace) or for formal learning (for example, structured multimedia course materials with specific objectives.)

THE LEARNING SCIENCES

The modern, big-picture understanding of learning, which has been colorfully described as ranging from "neurons to neighborhoods," requires expertise from an impressive variety of disciplines. While new knowledge has frequently come from psychology and education research, many working on learning in the twenty-first century do so as part of a newish discipline (born in the late 1980s) called "the learning sciences."

The learning sciences combine work from educational psychology, computer science, anthropology, sociology, information sciences, neuroscience, design studies, and just about any field that can inform learning. The learning sciences draw on both cognitive and constructivist theories and they focus on learning as it happens in the complex real world, as opposed to the controlled conditions of a laboratory.

A US National Research Council report titled "How People Learn" brought this "new science of learning" into the mainstream. It described a new understanding of what's necessary for effective learning in the knowledge age, based on recent interdisciplinary research, and included five key requirements (paraphrased from *The Cambridge Handbook of the Learning Sciences*):

- **Support deep conceptual understanding**. Expert knowledge includes facts and procedures, but acquiring these isn't enough. Facts and procedures are useful only when a person knows when and how to apply them, and how to adapt them to new contexts.

- **Focus on learning, not just teaching.** Students can gain deep conceptual understanding only by actively participating in their own learning process. The learning sciences focus on students' learning processes as well as teachers' instructional techniques.

- **Create learning environments.** The role of schools is to support students in becoming competent adult experts. This includes learning facts and procedures, but also gaining the deeper conceptual understanding necessary for real-world problem solving.

- **Build on learners' prior knowledge**. Students learn best from experiences that build on their existing knowledge, which includes working with both accurate and flawed preconceptions.

- **Support reflection.** Learners benefit from opportunities to express their developing knowledge and to analyze their current state of understanding, whether through discussion or the creation of artifacts like papers, reports, or media.

Technology plays a major part in the learning sciences. The focus is on how technology can be used to support the requirements listed above. For example, technology environments designed to support reflection as well as virtual worlds used for science or historic inquiry all emerge from work in the learning sciences.

From stimulus-response to networked ecologies, our understanding of learning has clearly come a long way in the last 150 years. And without a doubt, we still have much to discover.

This was a lot of ground to cover in one chapter. But I hope that, if this information was new to you, you now have a broader concept of how we learn and what can help us learn better.

Drawing from what all these learning theories have taught us, education researcher Peter Goodyear sums up the main design components that impact learning as the design of good learning tasks, the design of physical and digital resources and spaces for learning, and the design intended to evoke convivial learning relationships. In other words, we can think about learning experiences as comprising

- Learning tasks
- Physical/digital environment
- Social relationships

Learning interface designers play a critical role in each of these. In the first case, we contribute through best practices in interaction design; in the second, through informed design of the digital learning space as well as the multimedia resources provided; and in the third, we employ interface/interaction design strategies that support and inspire helpful social interaction. In the second half of this book, you'll find strategies to inform your design in each of these areas.

Designing for experience

Although we talk a lot about experience design in our field, many researchers are quick to point out that the term is misleading. We can design content for experience, but each user's experience is hers alone and will be a unique combination of many undesignable things, like behaviors, reactions, environmental influences, social context, prior knowledge, attitudes, and goals that are uniquely hers. Some users will even use the provided tools in entirely unexpected ways. The environment affects the user, but the user also changes the environment.

However, our inability to design experience is a good thing. It is the undesignable aspects that allow people to adapt, personalize, and create as they learn; learners can be partners in their own instruction. It's also important we consider (rather than neglect) the undesignable aspects of experience during the design process in order to be effective.

This is a good reminder of why good design is iterative; it involves testing as well as collaboration with (and regular feedback from) users. In the context of learning, this feedback can come from industry-standard web methods, but also from instructional evaluation strategies. The work of good digital designers and teachers is never done.

What we can do is design *content, environments,* and *conditions* for experience, and they can make all the difference. We can work diligently to guide and facilitate, to prevent errors, and to increase the likelihood of a positive experience and better learning outcomes.

In other words, we can design *for* experience.

Go further

- Linda Harasim's book *Learning Theory and Online Technologies* is an excellent resource for exploring learning theory as it relates to educational technologies.
- Learning-theories.com is a helpful hub of definitions and resources.
- In case you're thinking that eLearning is new, check out Wikipedia's timeline of virtual learning environments which starts in 1728 (http://en.wikipedia.org/wiki/History_of_virtual_learning_environments).
- I owe thanks to Beat Schwendimann for helping ensure the academic integrity of this chapter. I also recommend his blog (http://proto-knowledge. blogspot.com) and his Educational Theories Brain Map, a network of theories, models, philosophies, and key individuals, with handy summaries and definitions for each concept (http://tinyurl.com/kjtn5fh).

SOURCES

Anderson, Lorin W., and David R. Krathwohl, eds. 2005. *A Taxonomy for Learning, Teaching, and Assessing: A Revision of Bloom's Taxonomy of Educational Objectives*. New York: Longman.

Clark, Ruth C., and Richard E. Mayer. 2008. *E-Learning and the Science of Instruction: Proven Guidelines for Consumers and Designers of Multimedia Learning,* 2nd ed. San Francisco: Pfeiffer.

Goodyear, Peter, and Lucila Carvalho. 2013. "The Analysis of Complex Learning Environments." In *Rethinking Pedagogy for a Digital Age: Designing for 21st Century Learning,* 2nd ed., edited by Helen Beetham and Rhona Sharpe, 49–63. New York: Routledge.

Harasim, Linda. 2011. *Learning Theory and Online Technologies*. New York: Routledge.

Ito, Mizuko, Heather Horst, Matteo Bittanti, danah boyd, Becky Herr-Stephenson, Patricia G. Lange, C. J. Pascoe, and Laura Robinson. 2009. *Living and Learning with New Media: Summary of Findings from the Digital Youth Project*. Chicago: MIT Press.

Mayer, Richard E. 2005. "Principles for Reducing Extraneous Processing in Multimedia Learning: Coherence, Signaling, Redundancy, Spatial Contiguity, and Temporal Contiguity Principles." In *The Cambridge Handbook of Multimedia Learning*, edited by Richard E. Mayer, 183–200. New York: Cambridge University Press.

Mayer, Richard E. 2005. "Principles of Multimedia Learning Based on Social Cues: Personalization, Voice, and Image Principles." In *The Cambridge Handbook of Multimedia Learning*, edited by Richard E. Mayer, 201–214. New York: Cambridge University Press.

Quintana, Chris, Namsoo Shin, Cathleen Norris, and Elliot Soloway. 2006. "Learner-Centered Design: Reflections on the Past and Directions for the Future." In *The Cambridge Handbook of the Learning Sciences,* edited by R. Keith Sawyer, 119–34. New York: Cambridge University Press.

Sawyer, R. Keith. 2006. *The Cambridge Handbook of the Learning Sciences*. New York: Cambridge University Press.

Scardamalia, Marlene, and Carl Bereiter. 2010. "A Brief History of Knowledge Building." *Canadian Journal of Learning and Technology/La revue canadienne de l'apprentissage et de la technologie* 36(1): 1–15.

Siemens, George. January 2005. "Connectivism: A Learning Theory for the Digital Age." *International Journal of Instructional Technology and Distance Learning*.

3

A View of the eLearning Landscape

A stroll through the surprising diversity of digital learning experiences, and a sneak peek at the future of learning interfaces

This chapter surveys the range of experiences that can be dubbed eLearning or EdTech. As mentioned in Chapter 1, "Introducing IDL," there's still an extraordinary amount of ambiguity surrounding terms in the eLearning field. Since my goal is to help designers speak the local language and navigate the landscape, I've favored the most commonly used terms and included mention of alternatives when helpful.

Think of the headings in this chapter more as signposts than as dividers, because there is much overlap.

Standard technologies

From learning management systems to ePortfolios, standard technologies come in many flavors and are used across industries.

Learning management systems

At the foundation of most formal eLearning strategies sits the learning management system (LMS). Fairly ubiquitous, if much maligned for the user experience they provide, these educational technology workhorses handle administrative tasks, store and deliver learning content and resources, and host a variety of tools that allow for different types of interaction among students and instructors.

Moodle calls itself a course management system (CMS); Sakai, a collaboration and learning environment; and Blackboard, an educational technology plat-form. Most people refer to all of these systems as LMSs. On occasion, LMSs are categorized as virtual learning environments (VLEs), but in this book, VLE is reserved for 3-D, immersive environments, which we'll get to later.

From the learner's perspective, an LMS provides portals to class information, forums for discussion, quizzes, activity content, personalized learning plans, chat rooms, wikis, and more. On the instructor's side, it offers administrative tools, grouping, gradebooks, and a means to create an online space for a partial-ly or entirely online course. From the manager's perspective, it tracks certifica-tion, delivers performance support, and handles enrollments.

LMSs are sometimes linked to learning content. For example, OpenClass is an LMS built on Google Apps that was released for free by Pearson Education. In a similar way, Blackboard partnered with content provider McGraw-Hill (**FIGURE 3.1**).

On the off chance that you've never been inside an LMS, register for one of the free courses available at open course sites like Udacity.com or EdX.com. I can especially recommend the free Stanford human-computer interaction (HCI) course at Coursera.com. Massive open online courses (MOOCs) are often only about six weeks long, doing homework is optional, and you'll get a taste of one style of distance education and one flavor of LMS.

Virtual classrooms

LMSs are sometimes referred to as virtual classrooms, but the term *virtual classroom* is more accurately used to describe a space for *synchronous interac-tion*—online social interaction that occurs in real time. In contrast, *asynchronous interaction* lets users participate in a staggered way on their own time with tools like forums and e-mail.

Virtual classrooms support live lectures (or webinars) and live discussion via au-dio and video chat. They may have tools for learners to raise their hands, clap, ask questions, or create notes or diagrams collaboratively. They also offer tools for the instructor to pass the microphone, create polls, or share screens and media.

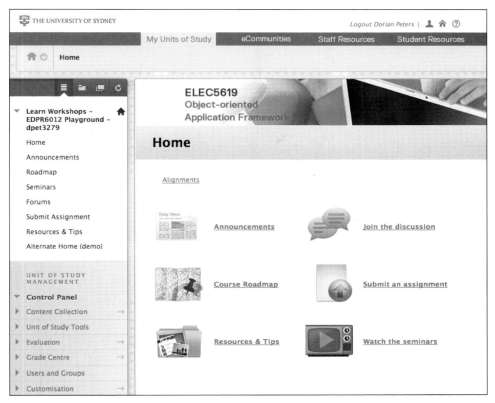

FIGURE 3.1 This course home page in the Blackboard Learn LMS shows interface design at the styling and multimedia layers. I began with a Blackboard default template, but redesigned the course site architecture and created an icon-based menu.

LEARNING OBJECTS AND REPOSITORIES

While LMSs manage many of the practicalities of the learner experience, learning content management systems (LCMSs) are focused on the authoring and delivery of learning content. This content can be designed and packaged as stand-alone "learning objects" and stored in a learning object repository until it's requested, either as a lesson on its own, or as a component of a series of objects that together make up a larger course (**FIGURE 3.2**).

It's like a big Lego dispenser. You can add new blocks to it if you're an instructor, and if you're a learner, it dispenses a block of learning to you when you need it, or a unique combination of blocks designed to help you build your skills.

FIGURE 3.2 A clean and attractive interface for an eLearning content management system (Courtesy of Deanna Mitchell, The Learning House).

This modular approach to training was popular in the early 2000s, when there was an explosion of excitement around the possibility of breaking learning experiences down into discrete, reusable, easy-to-manage resources (objects) that could be shared and recycled to save time and money (**FIGURE 3.3**). They could be shared across companies for workers to call on when needed, or across communities of teachers to save curriculum design time.

Significant investment led to the creation of large commercial and public repositories like Merlot (www.merlot.org), Ariadne (www.ariadne-eu.org), and the National Digital Learning Resources Network (http://ndlrn.edu.au).

It soon became clear that if these objects were to be reusable and shareable, it was necessary to develop interoperability standards that included metadata rules for finding the objects in a database. This led to the development of standards like the shareable content object reference model (SCORM) and the IMS learning design specification.

The boundary between LMSs and LCMSs is more like a spill than a line. There are now LMSs that include authoring tools and LCMSs that manage performance, as well as integrated systems.

FIGURE 3.3 A learning object for use in a Japanese language curriculum (Courtesy of Education Services Australia Limited).

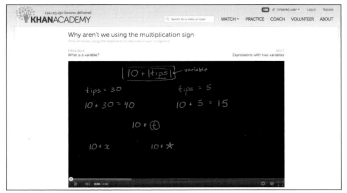

FIGURE 3.4 A math demonstration from the Khan Academy.

One interesting example of learning objects gone MOOC is the well-known Khan Academy (www.khanacademy.org). What started as a motivated math teacher putting up simple YouTube videos on various high school math concepts has exploded into a free education empire. The Khan Academy offers free learning content in multiple subject areas to millions of users around the world (including Bill Gates's children, according to one article in *The Telegraph*).

Teachers now use resources like those created by the Khan Academy to enable a new approach to teaching: the *flipped classroom* (**FIGURE 3.4**). In a flipped classroom, students watch lecture videos at home, and do practice work in class. The idea is that with lectures taken care of, the teacher has more time to give students individualized instruction in person.

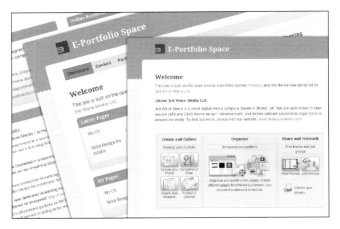

FIGURE 3.5 A beautiful theme designed by 3rd Wave Media for the Mahara open source ePortfolio (Courtesy of elearning. 3rdwavemedia.com).

EPORTFOLIOS

ePortfolios are systems for organizing and sharing evidence of learning, work, achievements, and qualifications. They can be used to show off capabilities to employers, or for assessment and feedback in a degree program (**FIGURE 3.5**).

ePortfolios aren't just extended resumes, however. An ePortfolio used over the duration of a course or degree program lets a student reflect on his progress and on how his ideas and strategies have changed over time (see sidebar). For more information on how ePortfolios are used, see the infokit provided by JISC, a UK expert organization on digital technologies for education (www.jiscinfonet.ac.uk/e-portfolios).

Online learning

The term *online learning* has been used as a catchall for any kind of learning experience that involves the web. It has consistently come in at least four different flavors: online collaborative learning, online distance education, online courseware (OC), and more recently, MOOCs.

Online collaborative learning (OCL) is founded on a constructivist theory of learning. It focuses on knowledge building and group work. *Online distance education* (ODE) brings the correspondence courses of the past into the twenty-first century by moving correspondence online. It involves a large amount of self-study, but also guidance and feedback from remote tutors.

Let's look at MOOCs in more detail.

ePortfolios and the double life

Encumbered with brass instruments and thick folios of sheet music, instructors at the Sydney Conservatorium of Music have to juggle a degree in music with a degree in teaching. ePortfolios help make this double life possible.

Elizabeth Gresser, a conservatorium graduate who now teaches music in the United Kingdom, recalls how using an ePortfolio helped her and her classmates merge their otherwise split personalities:

"Many of us were highly involved and heavily practicing musicians and performers outside the classroom. Rather than seeing ourselves as two different 'selves'—the practicing musician and the music teacher—the e-folio system allowed us to document our involvement in both of these spheres."

Unsurprisingly, she highly valued the audio/video support for reflection offered by this type of technology:

"As we progressed through the semesters, the e-folio started to grow with us. As our thoughts on music pedagogy and educational philosophy were developing, we could document these experiences by contributing to diary reflections, or by uploading evidence, such as videos of performances. The e-folio system proved to be an effective tool for reflection."

Far beyond being mere brag books or certification folders, ePortfolios can support not only recruitment, but also learning itself by providing a center of gravity for reflection, metacognition, and personal growth. Gresser was so impressed with the reflective experience provided by ePortfolios that she has since shared her experience publicly with other educators.

"This e-process would ultimately shape not only knowledge and understanding, but the quality of the educational interactions we would take into our classrooms in the future."

MASSIVE OPEN ONLINE COURSES

Massive open online courses (MOOCs) are generally university-level courses that would normally be run institutionally for a group of, say fifty, but are instead opened up to the world, often for free. They hung around quietly beginning in about 2007, but gained celebrity status when Stanford professor and computer science guru Sebastian Thrun quit his day job to start a company that would give away education for free. At that point, MOOCs stormed the press and set university administrators into bouts of panic.

As the hype clears, we see that MOOCs are a unique and valuable contribution to educational offerings. From the learner's perspective, MOOCs represent open education from reliable sources. So who's complaining? Of course, "open" doesn't mean free and some MOOCs charge a fee.

MOOCs can't provide everything a structured university education does, like personalized expert feedback, physically situated practice, face-to-face communication skills, consequences for not engaging, or binge drinking (yet). However, they do allow anyone with a computer and some time to:

- Improve skills (take an engineering course from an academic celebrity at MIT)
- Study a topic of special interest (finally do that class in songwriting)
- Shift career focus (upskill on SaaS with a Harvard course)
- Expand understanding of a topic (see sustainable energy explained by academics)
- Spread the reach of the latest educational perspectives (experience a Princeton lecture or a P2PU course on social innovation from a phone in India or an internet café in Mozambique)

There are small business owners out there whose lives may be changed by a free course in business growth from the University of Virginia, or perhaps a course in equine nutrition will equip gauchos in Argentina with new methods to keep their horses healthy (well, OK, they need to have a computer and speak English). Undoubtedly, this new wave of online education provides a level of access to university-level learning never seen before.

Of course, having to design a course for 160,000 (the number that registered for Thrun's course) is bound to be different than designing a course for thirty or even 200. For one thing, you can't grade all those assignments. For another, you can't answer all those questions. Also, university students are dedicated participants, unlike the thousands of full-time workers experimenting with a MOOC on the side, so dropout rates are sky-high and course length is often shorter than a full semester.

MOOCs pose an educational design challenge and some academics get involved just to explore the space and learn from the experience. Others are dedicated believers in a connectivist philosophy that suggests that our education system will only be truly successful when it's freely available to all anywhere, anytime. Others point out that a company like Thrun's Udacity will be collecting incomparable amounts of user data that's a mega-treasure for researchers and businesses alike.

This young addition to the eLearning family is bound to look very different in its adolescence and later life. The best way to get your head around MOOCs now is to do them. So get MOOCing.

OER AND EDUCATION FOR ALL

For many, the future of eLearning is far more about philosophical changes than it is about technology. Education philosopher Ivan Illich (1926–2002) envisioned a world in which education, rather than being bound within closed institutions, was available for everyone anywhere, through connections between people. His vision became an inspiration for many dedicated to the notion of a global community of learners benefiting from open access. Take the dedicated folks at One Laptop per Child (OLPC), a nonprofit that aims to "empower the world's poorest children through education" by providing them each with "a rugged, low-cost, low-power, connected laptop," or UNESCO's Education for All initiative (**FIGURE 3.6**).

FIGURE 3.6 Children in a refugee camp in Gaza learning from computers provided by One Laptop per Child (Image from the OLPC website).

Eighty-four years of lifelong learning and counting

Settled into her cozy home office in the mountains, dogs nestled at her feet, Patricia Thomas tackles her next digital information assignment. She admits that outlining an information architecture in Google Sites hasn't been easy at age eighty-four, but she's never shied away from a challenge.

A thick binder of diplomas on her bookcase preserves the relics of a life spent constantly learning. During her forty-five years of nursing, she worked as a midwife in England, attended the daughter of a noble family in Sardinia, got special training in child protection, and later qualified as a veterinary nurse. With no sign of becoming complacent, she now runs a rural bed-and-breakfast in Australia's Blue Mountains and is getting a degree in library sciences on the side.

Her remote location has not derailed her learning quest, as she interacts online with her teachers at Charles Sturt University. She publishes assignments to her own Google site, accesses resources using Moodle, and receives feedback via e-mail. When she gets stuck, she picks up the phone.

But she makes no bones about how hard it's been. Technical hang-ups and a lack of human interaction are daily sources of frustration, and when support is thin, she describes the experience as a "survival of the fittest." Yet she persists, owing in part to key moments of support along the way from teachers and staff who have provided encouragement just when she needed it most.

For many college students—most sixty years her junior—getting a degree is about getting a job, but Thomas's experience is a reminder that the rewards of learning can be more profound:

"Learning how to do something well, and using those skills to achieve something new, helps one to feel one is still a useful member of society. One experiences a feeling of pride."

Her educational endeavors have helped her through difficult times and provide solace when the practicalities of later life weigh heavy:

"The involvement of study removes one from the awareness of daily bodily pain, lack of mobility, the specter of reduced income, and other frustrations of everyday life."

And when her friends ask her why on earth she would so doggedly persist in such a difficult pursuit? Her answer is revealing:

"They conclude I am continuing the studies to keep my brain cells active. I do not bother to explain it is for my self-worth. These studies provide me with experience, and a high level of pleasure when a successful grade is achieved, a sense of euphoria .... It is clear learning is an adventure."

There's also a growing movement in the creation and sharing of free open educational resources (OER) at websites like Wikiversity (www.en.wikiversity.org), Jorum (www.jorum.ac.uk), and Connexions (www.cnx.org).

At Connexions, like Wikiversity, anyone can contribute a learning module. However, the Connexions system also allows a second layer of contribution: "instructors" can take content in the system and sequence it into a book or lesson, thus creating a new kind of resource. Learnist (www.learni.st) is similar to Wikiversity; however, it's created by a for-profit company and is described as a social learning service. Some services focus on curation and others on creation, but the running theme is freely available instructional content.

Skills training and workplace eLearning

From compliance training and performance support to team-based help via social networks, eLearning in the workplace is found at the office, in the field, and on the go.

ELEARNING COURSEWARE AND STAND-ALONE PROGRAMS

Like ODE, computer-based or online courseware generally consists of a package of content structured and designed to convey information required for a learner to meet particular training objectives. It frequently leaves the learner on his own, without peer or tutor interaction. This has the advantage of making it doable anytime, anywhere. From modules on employee induction to workplace health and safety, the online courseware approach is very familiar to corporate, government, and military employees.

The learning design of eLearning courseware determines whether the experience is mostly a book onscreen that displays information to be memorized, or whether the screen is a conduit for activity that draws on prior knowledge, challenges misconceptions, and supports the learner in building comprehension and knowledge.

JUST-IN-TIME TRAINING AND PERFORMANCE SUPPORT

Not all workplace eLearning is delivered via courseware. *Just-in-time training* (JiTT) is provided at the moment in which the skills or information to be learned are needed in action (**FIGURE 3.7**).

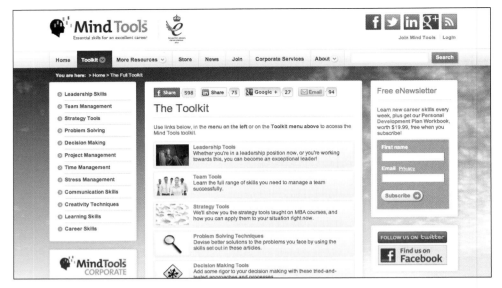

FIGURE 3.7 Mind Tools provides just-in-time management training to subscribers via learning content, short courses, and access to a community.

Take, for example, a keyboard shortcut map, a worksheet in a tax filing program, or flight time information provided just as you're organizing a trip on a travel site. Each of these is something you could, in theory, be "trained" in before attempting the task, but instead, tools are designed to pop up mid-task, just when you need them. JiTT resources can take the form of job aids, reference materials, or demo videos that often are accessible through mobile devices.

Researchers have found that performance support is most effective when it is *intrinsic*, that is, when it's included directly within the interface of the task at hand, such that workers perceive it as part of the system.

Mobile performance support tools provide references, checklists, job aids, text messages, and social networks to support people on the job. They can even use QR codes to contextualize support.

Designers of performance support tools talk about the five moments of need, developed by Bob Mosher and Conrad Gottfredson:

1. When learners are learning something new (for the first time)
2. When they need to learn more
3. When they're applying what they've learned

4. When they have to solve problems that arise

5. When they have to change or learn a new way of doing something

Performance support tools are most obviously applicable to the last three.

Imagine that you're in the middle of an assignment. You get to square roots and realize you've forgotten how to do them, so you look up the square root lesson at the Khan Academy (mentioned above). In this scenario, the Khan Academy is a kind of performance support for high school students (or adults who forgot their high school math) and it falls in the applying phase. Similarly, if you're a plumber searching via iPad for the correct placement of a water distributor, you're using on-the-job performance support.

SOCIAL LEARNING AND COMMUNITIES OF PRACTICE

Although much workplace learning is individual, the incorporation of more social and constructivist approaches is gaining ground. This is in part because social media have such an impact on our lives, but, according to Linda Harasim, it's also intended "to reduce high drop-out rates, to better motivate and engage learners and to better emphasize understanding over retention of facts."

Companies use enterprise social networks like Yammer, tibbr, or the open source ELGG to facilitate team building and information sharing across dispersed offices, to host exercises, to conduct polls or other learning events, and for just-in-time information sharing. Companies may also provide discussion forums, blogs, or wikis to support collaboration and social learning. All these tools can allow workers to find, create, and share content, expertise, and job aids with one another.

When social learning in an organization is successful, it facilitates a community of practice. According to Etienne Wenger, who originated the idea with fellow researcher Jean Lave, a *community of practice* (CoP) is a group of people "who share a concern or a passion for something they do and learn how to do it better as they interact regularly."

Whether it's a group of gardeners, a UX book club, or a discussion forum for franchise managers of a national restaurant, if members of a community are interacting specifically to help one another do what they do better, then it's a community of practice. Wenger references the legendary Parisian gatherings of the French impressionists as a community of practice (www.ewenger.com).

Would Monet and his crew be meeting on a social network today? If so, would that be with or without the absinthe?

School support and K–12 tools

Many of the technologies mentioned above are already in use in classrooms from kindergarten through high school (K–12). It can start with a tech-savvy teacher installing Moodle, or with a national government initiative like Australia's "digital education revolution," when it rolled out smartboards and then laptops in classrooms nationwide.

Some schools provide education partially or entirely online in order to serve students living in remote areas (**FIGURE 3.8**). These schools support students who frequently change location, like actors and musicians; they support home-schooling; and they provide an alternative for students who have dropped out of traditional schools.

Aside from learning technology that's used in the classroom, there's an abundance of technology designed for children to use when they're not in class, to support their interests or improve their academic performance. Gamification thrives in this environment and can be found in hundreds of apps, DVDs, and websites for kids.

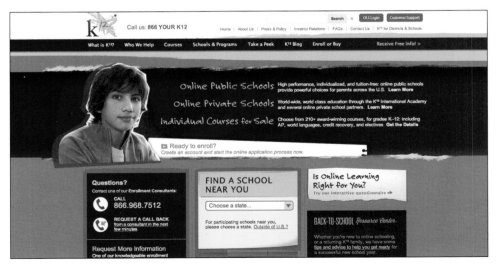

FIGURE 3.8 K12.com is a portal to online primary schools and high schools.

It seems that plenty of parents are willing to spend money on educational games or other digital tools to improve their children's grades, so catalogues of learning software, from high-quality productions to those with a painfully 1980s feel that lack evidence of any user testing, reach homes via backpacks with regularity.

Others hit toy store shelves, linked to specialized hardware like the LeapFrog Leapster GS, modeled after the Nintendo DS but with an educational spin. Similar are the "learning tablets" such as the LeapPad and InnoTab, which are like simplified, sturdy iPads that are limited to learning games and kid-safe activities. These devices frequently track user activity so kids can share achievements with parents and parents can see what they've been learning.

LEARNING OBJECTS, ONLINE PRACTICE, AND HOMEWORK SUPPORT

eLearning for kids usually focuses on standard school subjects like English, math, history, and science. Some programs are specifically designed to meet the requirements of particular curriculum standards, which is a major sell for teachers.

For example, BrainPOP (www.brainpop.com) provides multimedia lessons, including videos and games, in multiple subject areas; its resources are aligned with US teaching standards (**FIGURE 3.9**). BBC Bitesize does the same for the UK

FIGURE 3.9 BrainPOP offers multimedia curriculum content.

Playing to learn in second grade

On arriving home from school, second-grader Frankie drops his bag and races to the living room. "Can I do Reading Eggs?" he nags. He's an active kid who'd play football all day if he could, yet he'll also happily spend dedicated time practicing his literacy skills on a laptop.

But when asked about his top ten favorite video games, up against the slew of entertainment games on the market, Reading Eggs doesn't quite make the cut. Two educational games do manage to slip in down the end of the list: Marble Math and Dr. Seuss Band. Actually, he also mentions Wordle, which certainly has learning value for someone his age, even though it's not marketed as a learning game.

His top three are Hay Day, Minecraft, and Sonic & SEGA All-Stars Racing. The racing game hardly comes as a surprise for a boy his age, but the farm and world-building games speak to the educational potential of some entertainment apps. In fact, a sizable education community has formed around Minecraft. (Try a Google search for "Minecraft and education" to tap in.)

When I rephrase the question slightly and ask Frankie what his favorite *learning* games are, he immediately knows what I mean and unleashes a slew of names of math games. He tells me his favorite school subjects are Greek myths, math, and science. When I ask him what he likes best about his favorite games, he gestures and alludes to the physicality of it: "It's fun to keep moving your hands."

Does he think he's learned anything from playing these games? His answer is matter of fact: "Pluses and times tables and counting money."

Finally, I appeal to his creativity and pose him a hypothetical challenge: "If you could make up your own learning game, what would it be about?" With little more than a second's thought he replies:

"It would be about monsters! And you'd have to create your own monsters and battle with other people's and the computer's monsters, and you pass levels and you have to make better monsters cause it gets harder."

And what would you learn from that?" I ask. Again, his response is lightning fast:

"You'd have to make pluses and times and math to control the monster's power. Like you'd have to answer 1+1 and then you could tell it what you wanted your monster to do. Well, not 1+1, that would be too easy. But something harder. That would be really fun."

curriculum. Espresso Education (www.espresso.co.uk) provides a subscription service to teachers and schools, and its content aligns with UK standards.

Entertainment providers like PBS KIDS (www.pbskids.org) and the BBC (www.bbc.co.uk/schools) are great places to look for examples of educational games and resources.

Some eLearning programs use multiplayer global competition to motivate kids to practice and improve their skills, such as Mathletics (www.mathletics.com), a widely used math skills program that allows children in different countries to compete against one another online.

Navigating the anything-goes web for high-quality learning resources can be daunting for teachers and learners, so a number of sites act as curators of existing resources. For example, Teachers' Domain (www.PBSLearningmedia.org) makes it easier for teachers to leverage the high-quality programs developed by public broadcasting, such as Nova, Nature, and Frontline, in the classroom.

LEARNING BY DOING AND MAKING

Artificial intelligence pioneer Seymour Papert has been a major influence in education owing to his strong belief in constructionism, which emphasizes the role of object creation. He invented a programming language called Logo that allows even young students to learn by actively programming.

Papert's constructionist philosophy is evident in modern software like Scratch (http://scratch.mit.edu), Alice (www.alice.org), and the Cargo-Bot app, which enable learners age 4 to 100 to learn by programming. According to the makers of Scratch, "As young people create and share Scratch projects, they learn important mathematical and computational ideas, while also learning to think creatively, reason systematically, and work collaboratively" (**FIGURE 3.10**).

Lego has merged its classic block-building with sensors, motors, and programming to allow kids to create working robots (http://mindstorms.lego.com).

Learning by making has as much potential for adults as it does for kids and melds gracefully with the maker movement, which broke well into the mainstream in 2011. Now YouTube videos, Pinterest boards, and websites on how to make everything from kids costumes and shabby chic headboards to USB chargers and robots permeate the web.

FIGURE 3.10 A collection of kid-created media objects programmed in Scratch. These examples are all Virtual Pet projects.

MOBILE APPS FOR KIDS

After early adopters languished in lines around the block to be among the first to own an iPad, it didn't take long for their kids to realize this thing was meant for them. A few device generations later, kids have taken over our handhelds. Parents still gaze in wonder as their toddlers manipulate their touchscreens, summoning videos, music, and cameras at their command. As adults, we had to retrain ourselves to move from mice to touchscreens but, in reality, the touchscreens are easier and more intuitive to use, making them an instant hit with kids.

Parents have tuned into the potential for tablets to be portable learning devices, and today the world of educational apps is a universe that just keeps expanding. Apple alone has over 20,000 educational apps for its devices. There are even apps that review educational apps (www.kindertown.com). And the industry is showing no signs of slowing down.

Seeing an opportunity, companies like MEEP! and nabi have created kid-tailored tablets. These Android-based tablets are as capable as their adult counterparts, but they're designed to be safer, cheaper, and more educational.

If you're looking for inspiring interfaces in the world of digital education, children's apps are definitely the place to look. The sheer number of educational apps can be overwhelming, but there's also inspiration in the diversity of approaches.

The creativity of e-books like Sesame Street's *The Monster at the End of This Book* or whimsical apps like the Singing Alphabet bring joy to the hearts of big kids, too. Alien Assignment gets kids moving around by taking them on scavenger hunts in the real world. Operation Math Code Squad lets a team of up to four kids join forces around an iPad to solve math missions.

Apps like Phlip leverage the accelerometer for getting kids to shift and shake to move puzzle pieces, while others like Picture Me Dinosaur make use of the camera to cast kids in their own storybook. Helicopter Taxi augments reality with superimposed characters and flying objects. Kids can even contribute data to scientists around the world with apps like Project Noah. And scientists are sharing, too: Shark Net hooks future marine biologists up to live shark data so they can track real great whites in real time on their tablets. It's pretty remarkable stuff (**FIGURES 3.11** through **3.14**).

You can browse the gallery of educational apps in multiple ways:

- **Libraries.** Search libraries like iTunes or Google Play.
- **Reviewers.** Turn to the many top ten lists and review sites.
- **Producers.** Go direct to providers like PBS KIDS, or companies like Mindshapes, Toca Boca, or Busy Bee Studios. Even the legendary IDEO has partnered with Sesame Street and Fisher Price to make educational apps.
- **Curators.** Browse a specialized storefront or curated space like Kindertown (www.kindertown.com), which has an app and website that let you browse by age, price, device, or skills taught. YogiPlay (www.yogiplay.com) curates educational apps, and collects play data and uses it to customize recommendations and report children's activity to parents.

FIGURE 3.11 The elegant Write My Name app by NCSOFT helps children learn to trace letterforms. The company's Injini project creates educational apps and assistive apps for children with special needs.

FIGURE 3.13 With Shark Net, shark enthusiasts of all ages can track real sharks across the oceans, read their bios, and explore their 3-D shape. Opening the app is like plunging into the deep as the watery blue and media-rich cockpit puts you face to face with real sharks in the world. As you get to know Bite-head and Little John, you can choose to use your in-app purchase power to donate to their cause. Created by EarthNC, this example of data turned into learning is pretty darn cool.

FIGURE 3.12 Hickory Dickory Dock by Mindshapes teaches children how to tell time. Its attractive and imaginative interface no doubt appeals to children's fondness for a certain wizard.

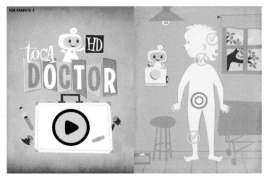

FIGURE 3.14 Toca Doctor, designed by Toca Boca, has irresistible style with its vintage take on a medical-themed puzzle game for preschoolers. This is an excellent example of how well a limited color palette can work, even for kids.

Educational games

Sure, some games are violent and have characters with bust-to-waist ratios that put Barbie to shame, but the game world isn't all first-person shooters. In fact, the game world is also a wonderland of mind-blowing creativity. Games can be visually stunning or visually simplistic, fast-paced or self-paced, realistic or abstract, colorful or black and white, serious or quirky. They can be about adventures and entrapment, building things or destroying things, working alone or in a team. And they almost always require problem solving (**FIGURE 3.15**). As with films, there are big budget blowouts and cult indie classics. From skills apps, to augmented reality to alternative reality, the educational games world is a mighty one. We'll talk about them in more detail in Chapter 8, "Multimedia and Games," and Chapter 9, "Learning Is Mobile."

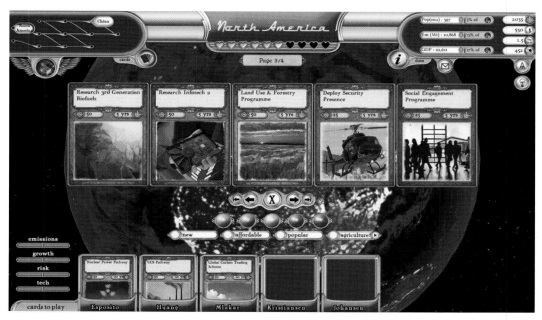

FIGURE 3.15 The award-winning Fate of the World, created by British indie games producer Red Redemption, is a global simulation strategy game that allows players to act out various climate change calamity scenarios.

Intelligent tutoring systems

As mentioned in Chapter 2, "How We Learn," intelligent tutoring systems (ITSs) are designed to automatically adapt to individual performance using knowledge incorporated into the database (**FIGURE 3.16**).

Many supporters of ITS are working to engage technology in a solution to close the gap. The gap, in the United States, for example, is the significant gap in test scores and academic achievement between low- and high-income students; white and minority students; students with home computers, broadband, and money for human tutoring, and those without. Teachers and tutors in low-income schools face classrooms of forty children with myriad disciplinary and social challenges, all performing below grade level. The question isn't whether we should make computer tutors so we can get rid of the human ones, but whether we should make computers that can help students learn because students and teachers could really use the help. That's where a virtual coach can provide extra support.

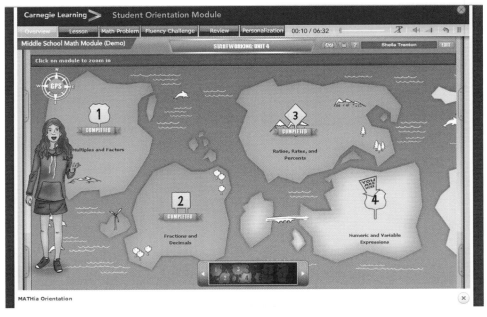

FIGURE 3.16 Carnegie Learning creates tutoring systems for middle and high schools. This screen is from the orientation module for MATHia, part of the Carnegie Learning Math Series.

Informal learning and infographics

Informal learning is not externally structured by, for example, institutions, teachers, or courses. It can happen in public spaces, on the web, or among friends as part of a community of practice.

From TED Talks by the world's greatest thought leaders (www.ted.com), to foreign language podcasts, to web services that bring scientific data to life in your living room, informal digital learning opportunities are forming ecosystems of learning that let us learn throughout our lives.

Second Story has been engaged in gorgeous and educational multimedia storytelling for two decades (**FIGURE 3.17**). From interactive walls and sculptural pieces to museum installations and kiosks, the company's portfolio gives a sense of what eLearning beyond traditional screens can look like (www.secondstory.com).

Media publishers like the BBC and *The New York Times* are also producers of multimedia assets that facilitate educational exploration of issues like sustainability or gun control. Head to their sites for excellent examples of interactive infographics. We'll look at infographics more carefully in Chapter 5, "Learning Is Visual."

FIGURE 3.17 This interactive wall celebrates the history and significance of the New York marathon (Courtesy of Second Story Interactive Studios).

Learnability and nano-learning

Learnability, or the ease with which people can learn how to use software, can be supported in many ways. Some software encourages engagements with full-screen tutorials. Other programs or apps use hints or microinteractions, or demonstrate possible actions as you begin to engage.

When you log in to a software system and it shows you how to use a new feature, or you're offered a mini-tutorial, you're presented with a kind of nano-learning experience. While this isn't generally included under the umbrella of eLearning, it's a particularly prevalent category, and just like other types of eLearning, these experiences

- Are discrete and intentionally designed
- Occur via technology
- Can benefit just as much from principles for effective eLearning interface design

The Mendeley example in **FIGURE 3.18** employs a number of useful strategies in a small space:

- It points to the benefit ("get you up and running quickly").
- It displays user time/effort required by indicating progress within a short sequence ("1 of 4").
- It makes it optional with a No Thanks button. Note, however, that the design of this button has fewer clicking signifiers—the other button looks more enticingly clickable.

Interface designers for software of any kind are likely to confront moments for which a knowledge of design for learning is relevant. As these tiny learning

FIGURE 3.18 Mendeley gently offers an interface tour at the bottom of the screen.

experiences become an increasingly popular approach to learnability support, they may far outnumber our encounters with other kinds of digital learning. So let's not neglect the little things.

The future of eLearning

Significant changes coming for education are predicted each year in the New Media Consortium's Horizon Report (http://horizon.nmc.org). In the past few years, the NMC has spotlighted things like educational games, wearable technologies, personal learning environments, and learning analytics.

Designers and developers are increasingly working with multitouch, tangible, natural, or augmented reality interfaces, along with context-aware, socially aware, or emotion-aware systems.

South Africa–based interaction designer Mike Wolf provides a compelling vision of the future personal learning environment in his blog:

Imagine a learning environment that harnesses a host of distributed activities ... which can be selected or booked by learners according to their self-guided, teacher-guided, and data-informed learning paths. Activities like reading a blog or a book on Google Books, signing up for a math class, visiting a museum, or doing an internship at a local company would be logged in the learning path, acknowledged, and credited. Traditional schools would focus on producing good content and exciting projects that could be individually booked by learners, instead of trying to fit everything into one curriculum. The system would be equipped with powerful data-mining tools, which would dynamically evaluate and visualize the impact of personal learning decisions and activities.

Of course, a technology doesn't have to be EdTech to be useful for learning. In 2012, *Edudemic* published a list of the top twenty-five most used mobile apps for education, and the majority were standard software like Twitter, Dropbox, and Bento—not eLearning programs. Some would argue that the best way to learn is by using the very technology used by professionals in the area in which you're learning, rather than by turning to dedicated separate tools. As learning gradually merges with working and living, expect interface design for learning to integrate into the design of just about everything.

Go further

To further explore the wide and colorful world of digital learning experiences, check out these resources:

- Learning designer Cathy Moore has pulled together an impressive list on her blog: http://blog.cathy-moore.com/resources/elearning-samples.
- Plumb the depths of iTunes, Google Play, and other app directories.
- Articulate and Adobe Captivate both showcase industry eLearning work created with their tools.
- A growing database of serious games and simulations is listed at clarkchart.com.
- Check out the work of producers like BBC and PBS, as well as eLearning Studios like Second Story, Allen Interactions, and Upside Learning.
- I regularly post interesting examples on my blog at www.InterfaceDesignForLearning.com.

SOURCES

de Bertodano, Helena. 2012. "Khan Academy: The Man Who Wants to Teach the World." *The Telegraph*, September 28. http://www.telegraph.co.uk/education/educationnews/9568850/Khan-Academy-The-man-who-wants-to-teach-the-world.html.

Gottfredson, Conrad, and Bob Mosher. 2012. "Are You Meeting All Five Moments of Learning Need?" *Learning Solutions Magazine*, June 18. http://www.learningsolutionsmag.com/articles/949/.

Harasim, Linda. 2011. *Learning Theory and Online Technologies*. New York: Routledge.

Wolf, Michael. 2013. "Interaction Design for Learning." *Design Talk*, February 12. http://www.formula-d.co.za/blog/2013/02/12/interaction-design-for-learning/.

4

Basic Principles A–Z

A crash course in basic concepts from psychology, education, and human-computer interaction essential to the design of learning interfaces

Accessibility

Most interface designers are well versed in the World Wide Web Consortium's guidelines for web accessibility and in the various country-specific requirements, but abiding by these regulations is critical when it comes to education.

While it might not be immediately obvious, a well-designed, accessible learning experience helps everyone down the road. For example, kids and teens typically use secondhand equipment—special plug-ins and heavy download times can be frustrating. Programs like Flash aren't available on all devices and may be blocked by corporate firewalls. Beautiful virtual worlds designed for classroom use may fail to run on classroom computers.

Native speakers of all languages and learners of all ages are accessing online learning from every country on the planet. The biggest reason to ensure that your designs comply with accessibility guidelines is so you can be sure to reach all your learners.

Check out the WAI-ARIA guidelines for detailed and definitive advice on making widgets, navigation, and behaviors accessible. If you need some inspiration, see the Thare Machi sidebar.

AFFORDANCES AND SIGNIFIERS

An affordance is something about an object that allows it to be used for a certain action. So a knob affords twisting and a cord affords pulling. Chat rooms afford fast, live social interaction, whereas forums afford longer-term, considered discussion. In the digital world, we talk a lot about affordances, but we really mean *perceived* affordances. After all, no matter what we do on a computer, we're performing the same set of physical actions every time (clicking a mouse or moving a finger), so perceived affordances are aspects of the design of things like buttons, links, and interactions that communicate their purpose to the user.

But get it right, and the rewards are unsurpassed. A photo caption on the website reads:

"Our troika of recently returned Associates found a family living in a slum just feet from the tracks but sleeping under a mosquito net as a result of watching our lesson 'Bednets Can Save Lives' in the Bengali language."

Thare Machi Education is making life-changing and life-saving messages accessible in audio-visual format in the languages of the developing world. Check out the company's amazing work at www.tme.org.uk.

The notion of affordances was originally proposed by psychologist James Gibson in the 1970s, and Don Norman helped to popularize the concept with modern designers. Norman has since acknowledged that the term has met with much confusion in the virtual world. As such, he has suggested the term *signifier* as a replacement. In the 2013 revision of his classic tome, *The Design of Everyday Things*, Norman explains, "Affordances define what actions are possible. Signifiers specify how people discover those possibilities: signifiers are signs, perceptible signals of what can be done. Signifiers are of far more importance to designers than are affordances." Certainly, this is most obviously true in virtual design.

Here are some of the most common online examples of signifiers:

- Underlined text signals linked content. (That's why usability experts tell you not to use underline for other purposes, lest you create the wrong expectation.)
- Buttons look clickable. (How often have you wasted time looking for what to click on because the button design didn't signal clickability?)
- Elements that look like buttons should *be* buttons. (So you don't click on something that signals button that turns out to be a header.)

Good signifiers are one important way that a design for learning can keep users focused on learning rather than on operating the interface. Signifiers can also be used to gently recommend certain options. For more on affordances and signifiers, see Norman's books *The Design of Everyday Things* and *Emotional Design: Why We Love (or Hate) Everyday Things*.

DESIRABLE DIFFICULTY AND ERRORS

Poor interface design can get in the way of learning by slowing it down, imposing hurdles, and using up precious cognitive load. However, things like slowness, hurdles, and challenge are essential for many kinds of learning. Educators employ tactics like *deliberate slowness, appropriate challenge, desirable difficulty,* and in some cases, even *productive failure* to improve learning every day. The difference is that, in these cases, the challenge is relevant and supports learning.

Desirable difficulty is usually designed into the learning activity by a learning designer, and not by the interface designer. But in some cases the interface designer will get involved. For example, if an interaction design creates obstacles, that might be OK *if* those obstacles are placed deliberately to support the learning in some well-considered way, such as to support reflection. The result should not distract the user from the learning experience.

Similarly, failure is also an option. Dimitri van der Linden and Sabine Sonnentag separate errors into three categories: positive consequence, negative consequence, and neutral consequence. Errors with a positive consequence are actions that do not give the desired result, but provide the learner with information to help her achieve an overall goal. Some educational researchers suggest providing insurmountable challenges to students because there is much to be learned from failing the first time around. However, this productive failure is a feature of the instructional design, rather than the interface design. With regard to error, the learning interface designer should

- Ensure that any obstacles are there to support the learning activity and are not simply the result of poor interface design.
- Create forgiving designs.
- Provide rich feedback.

We'll discuss the latter two in more detail in Chapter 9, "Learning Is Mobile."

EXPERTISE REVERSAL EFFECT

A major caveat to many of the strategies listed in this book is that guidelines sometimes break down when it comes to experts. This is known in the research world as the *expertise reversal effect*. In essence, strategies for interface and learning design are usually geared to novices.

If you're teaching biology or business to nonexperts, it's especially important not to overwhelm them with choices, and to provide them with guidance and be forgiving. However, if you're teaching advanced concepts in biology to a doctor or management strategy to a CEO, these design strategies have less impact. Research has shown that, unlike novices, experts are more flexible and can learn just as well from text alone as they can from a combination of text and visuals. Likewise, experts don't need information to be chunked and they can handle more control over their instruction.

In general, experts won't be hurt by design guidelines that apply to nonexperts. In a few cases, however, the rules for novices will actually decrease learning outcomes for experts by slowing them down (for example, breaking down information too much). Therefore, if you're designing for an audience of experts, it's worth reading more about their requirements. Check out Ruth Clark and Richard Mayer's book *e-Learning and the Science of Instruction: Proven Guidelines for Consumers and Designers of Multimedia Learning* as well as the research on the expertise reversal effect.

EXTRANEOUS COGNITIVE LOAD

Steve Krug's now legendary "Don't make me think" mantra helps link learnability with interface design for learning. Why shouldn't an interface grab the user's attention? Because if the user is thinking about how to use the website, she's distracted from the task at hand. For many websites, that task is finding information, making purchasing decisions, connecting with people, or meeting some other goal. In eLearning, the overarching goals are learning outcomes.

To put it absurdly simply, the more of the brain the user has to allocate to the interface, the less is available for learning (**FIGURE 4.1**). You want the user to devote as much attention as possible to learning. This might not always be feasible (the user may engage in multitasking or seek performance support on the job, for example). While you can't design your learner's context and environmental distractions, you can design your interface to stay out of the way. To rephrase Krug's usability mantra for our purposes: "Don't make me think about the interface, because I need to be thinking about the learning."

In educational psychology, the amount of information a human brain is attempting to process at once is referred to as cognitive load. Unsurprisingly, there's a limit. Of course, cognitive effort directed at learning is a good thing. However, attention that must be paid to things unrelated to the learning activity (like operating the interface) can be considered *extraneous*. It's the learning interface designer's responsibility to reduce extraneous cognitive load.

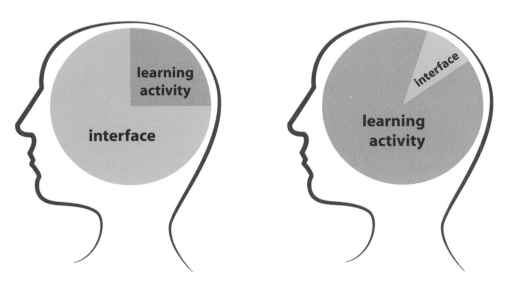

FIGURE 4.1 In simple terms, the more of the brain the user has to allocate to the interface, the less is available for learning. You want the user to devote as much attention as possible to learning.

A good example of extraneous load is found in what information architects refer to as "mystery meat navigation." You know those websites you come across that, in a misguided attempt to be clever and original, use some abstracted form of navigation with labels that appear only on rollover; or terms so vague or jargony that you click the interface blindly because, as with hot dogs, you just don't know what you're gonna get. The telltale sign of mystery meat is often the instructions: "Click on one of the circles at right to find out more." Should that kind of instruction be necessary?

If convention and familiarity have been tossed aside and you can't easily understand the navigation, the brain must turn to unraveling the mystery of the interface itself. You came to the site for a reason, but now you're thrown off task because you first have to figure out how to proceed.

INTRINSIC COMPLEXITY

Just as difficulty can be desirable when it aids learning, complexity can be essential. Remember that avoiding interface complexity is about reducing extraneous cognitive load. In the same way, it's important to separate the notion of *extraneous complexity,* the "bad" (avoidable) complexity associated with the interface or instructional methods, from *intrinsic complexity,* the complexity that's part of what is being learned.

Some learning interfaces will be necessarily complex because, for example, they involve high-fidelity simulation, like aircraft simulators, or because a large number of features and functions must be made available for authentic practice. In both cases, the interface complexity is essential to the learning experience. We'll look at strategies for managing intrinsic complexity in Chapter 8, "Multimedia and Games."

LEARNABILITY

We can't talk about learning and software without a mention of learnability. For one thing, it's important to clarify the difference between learnability and learning interface design, lest they become confused. According to the *Standard Glossary of Terms Used in Software Testing,* learnability is "the capability of a software product to enable the user to learn its application." In other words, learnability is strictly about easily mastering the software without instruction, not about learning the content presented.

Prezi and the learnability challenge

Upon its release, Prezi was a whole new paradigm in presentation software. Taking people out of the familiar is very risky business. Learnability was likely to be Prezi's biggest obstacle to uptake. It's no surprise then that the company was extremely careful in its handling of this aspect of the user experience. When I first signed up for Prezi, I didn't get an instruction manual thrown at me, but neither was I left stranded in a new-user wasteland ready to retreat.

Prezi embedded a set of simple tasks into the experience of opening my first blank document. For example, rather than showing me an interface feature or just asking me to "scroll down to practice using the controls," I was told to "scroll down in order to *find out something.*" It's a subtle difference, but it makes the little tutorial more like a game by adding a sense of purpose and triggering curiosity.

The company also aced the "show progress" heuristic by including a simple, highly visible, progress bar at the top that told me where I was, how much I had left to do, and, critically, that I could exit at any time. Knowing that I could exit any time I wanted to made me less likely to exit the tutorial. I was also given a way to skip things without exiting completely—a very forgiving touch. In the end, I figured that I'd learn faster by doing the little tutorial and I did, thereby helping me tackle a whole new paradigm in presentation software without getting flustered.

The Prezi tutorial is a great example of so many things. You get just the right amount of information, right when you need it, and then you're left alone to do your work.

Learnability shares much territory with usability, in that it also benefits from familiar conventions, consistency, intuitive design, and usability heuristics. Learnability is especially important for software and systems in which the user must overcome a learning curve before she can make full use of them.

In contrast, interface design for learning looks at how interfaces can support learning in general, whether it's learning how to use software, how climate change affects the earth, or how babies are made. It's about designing interfaces for digital learning that support the cognitive and affective (emotional) aspects of learning.

The heading typeface is friendly, the text is minimal, and there's plenty of white space, all of which makes the experience feel like it's going to be "easy" and "low cost to my time and effort." As the icing on the cake, I was presented with a beautiful, relaxing nature scene to lift my mood and make me more open to learning (we'll talk more about this in Chapter 7, "Learning Is Emotional"). The attention paid to this critical learning moment has no doubt been pivotal to the company's success.

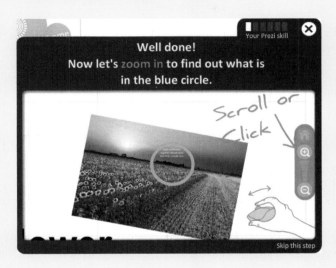

MENTAL MODELS

There are various contradictory ways of defining *mental model,* so I'll honor Occam's razor and go with the simplest, from usability pioneer Jakob Nielsen at Alertbox: "A mental model is what the user believes about the system at hand." It's the complex abstraction of the user's understanding about how a digital environment is shaped, how it works, what it will do, and what you can do with it.

Mental models don't necessarily have anything to do with reality, and that's what can cause so much user strife. *Why isn't this working? Why won't it let me do this? Why isn't this information here?* All of these are examples of user frustrations that result from an inaccurate mental model. The user believes that the system *should* work in such a way, *should* allow her to take a certain action, or that information *should* appear in this location. But it doesn't.

When there's a mismatch between what a user thinks the system should do (mental model) and the system reality, you have a few options:

1. Redesign the system to conform to the user's understanding.

2. Redesign the interface to better communicate the nature of the system in order to correct the user's mental model.

3. When all else fails, as with a very innovative interface (see Prezi sidebar), educate users.

For an example of mental model mismatches, read the Nielsen Norman Group article at www.nngroup.com/articles/mental-models.

PARADOX OF CHOICE

Choice and control are funny things. As human beings we're easily sold on the idea that more choice is better than less choice. In his book *Living with Complexity,* Don Norman talks about our penchant for feature-rich appliances and our inclination to spend more for functions that never get used. Pointing to washing machines, he notes that technology is advanced enough to build a one-button washing machine that would do everything automatically, but that no one would buy it. Instead, we pay more for the one that requires us to select from water temperatures, levels, spin cycles, timers, and specialty options, and then we just use the default settings.

But surely it's common sense that the more options we have, the more freedom we have, and therefore, the happier we'll be? How little we know ourselves. In *The Paradox of Choice,* Barry Schwartz explains that eliminating consumer choices can greatly reduce anxiety for shoppers and reveals a global disconnect between happiness and freedom. The reality is that, despite our taste for selection, there are limits on what our brains can handle. We're generally in a hurry and easily put off by too many choices, especially where the difference is minimal and the choices are of little importance.

In the world of technology, we often diagnose the infirmity resulting from too much choice as "featuritis." The result is a program that fails to function under the weight of too many options and controls. Learning interface designers, take note: In learning experiences, featuritis will not only impact usability and learnability, but also impair learning outcomes. For this reason, learning experience professionals will continually be negotiating the balance between helpful choice and overwhelming choice.

On the flip side, carefully designed choices can improve learning by giving beginners the guidance they need and experts the freedom they can handle. This is sometimes referred to as choice architecture. In later chapters, we'll look at design strategies for managing choice such as grouping options and employing defaults.

QUIET DESIGN

Most software design guidelines state that software applications and most Web sites should not call attention to themselves; they should fade into the background and allow users to focus on their own goals.

—JEFF JOHNSON, *Designing with the Mind in Mind*

There's a lot of talk about using visuals to grab attention, but fancy media won't make up for poorly designed content and activities. One of the biggest ways interface design can contribute to better learning is by getting out of the way.

Clichéd as it is, "less is more" heavily applies in the learning interface context. Educational interface design researcher Sharon Oviatt has used the term *quiet design*. A quiet design doesn't seek attention for its own sake. It doesn't interrupt with pop-ups, sales pitches, tangents, or obstacles. It fades into the background, emerging only when needed and only as much as needed, allowing the learner to be absorbed completely in the learning experience. Chunking and segmenting, using white space, adhering to consistency and conventions, and abiding by a minimalist color palette are all examples of ways in which interfaces can be kept discreet.

Of course, there will be exceptions. Children are far less put off by the liberal use of color. Bright colors are expected in toys and schoolrooms. But it's interesting to note that even here, the risk of distraction remains present. A study of kindergarten classroom design by Karrie Godwin and Anna Fisher found that kids paid attention better and learned more in a minimally decorated classroom than they did in a highly decorated one. But surely there's something sad about removing all the color and artwork that make the kindergarten class what it is? Indeed, every design decision is an exercise in balancing needs and constraints. While minimalism may yield better learning, it may be that those gains are negligible and that the psychological development of the children, from self-esteem to community building, must also be taken into account.

Online you may find other ways of balancing. Kids are attracted to colorful and decorative design, but how much is too much? There aren't many research or public testing results to turn to for answers to this question. However, I suspect it will depend largely on how it's handled. The beauty of the online environment is that it's far more flexible and adaptable than a physical setting. While you can't pin up and remove decorations from a classroom repeatedly throughout the day, online this same action is trivial. Online you can add color or graphics in one screen and pull them back when the learning activity comes around on the next. It's like pulling focus in a film. In this way, appealing imagery can be used to introduce a space, as ambiance or for variety in between tasks, and be removed or ghosted during the learning task.

SCAFFOLDING

In the classroom, a scaffold is a set of activities designed by the teacher to assist the learner to move through increasingly difficult tasks to master a new skill … activities are designed to help move students from point A to point B, to progress from what they know to what they need to know … to bring them through the zone of proximal development to achieve their potential.

—LINDA HARASIM, *Learning Theory and Online Technologies*

As with the construction variety, educational scaffolding is a kind of support structure provided to a student to help her reach a higher level than she would without it. The idea with scaffolding is that it can be progressively removed until the learner is able to complete the task independently. As Sara DeWitt of PBS KIDS said it in an interview with *Wired*: "Online games give us the opportunity for leveling and scaffolding, so that kids can advance to more challenging material in a way that is customized to them."

In an eLearning environment, scaffolding can take many forms. It's often an element of the instructional design, for instance, a document template with a preexisting structure, or a list of curated resources. Scaffolding can also be embedded into an interface. The LetterSchool app provides examples of both types of scaffolding (see Theory in Action sidebar).

Learning from LetterSchool

LetterSchool, an app by Dutch game maker Boreaal, is one of the many apps on the market created to leverage the advantages of touchscreens to teach preschoolers to make letter shapes. Kids use a finger to trace and write the letters of the alphabet.

Kids can choose any letter of the alphabet, at which point they're encouraged to move through a sequence to

1. Hear the letter name along with its sound and see it in a word.
2. Watch the letter being drawn.
3. Trigger the start of each line to be drawn to create the letter.
4. Trace the whole letter.
5. Write a letter by themselves.

This set of staged options provides instructional scaffolding that allows each kid to begin at her own level and move through stages with less help as she goes. What is especially notable is the app's excellent design for gracefully fading interface-based scaffolding (think of it as a kind of seamless contextual help or performance support). If the learner begins to struggle to correctly draw a letter, subtle visual cues, like arrows and tracer lines, appear. If she continues to struggle, these cues gradually increase. When she no longer needs the extra help, this visual support disappears completely. The app leverages the interactivity of the platform to detect struggling and adapt the interface accordingly.

The makers have described a list of other well-considered educational design decisions at letterschool.com.

Go further

- For a pocket glossary of commonly used eLearning terms and concepts, download Connie Malamed's app Instructional Design Guru.
- For a delightful and practical guide to eLearning instructional design principles, grab a copy of Julie Dirksen's *Design for How People Learn*.
- For a blend of interface and instructional design principles, check out Ruth Clark and Richard Mayer's *e-Learning and the Science of Instruction*.

SOURCES

Donahoo, Daniel. 2012. "PBS Quest to Build a Better Kids' App." *Wired,* July 27. http://www.wired.com/geekdad/2012/07/profile-pbs-kids-apps/.

Godwin, Karrie E., and Anna V. Fisher. 2011. "Allocation of Attention in Classroom Environments: Consequences for Learning." In *Proceedings of the 33rd Annual Conference of the Cognitive Science Society,* edited by Laura Carlson, Christoph Hoelscher, and Thomas F. Shipley, 2806–11. Austin: Cognitive Science Society.

Harasim, Linda. 2011. *Learning Theory and Online Technologies.* New York: Routledge.

Johnson, Jeff. 2010. *Designing with the Mind in Mind: Simple Guide to Understanding User Interface Design Rules.* Amsterdam/Boston: Morgan Kaufmann Publishers/Elsevier.

Oviatt, Sharon, Alex Arthur, and Julia Cohen. 2006. "Quiet Interfaces that Help Students Think." In *UIST '06 Proceedings of the 19th Annual ACM Symposium on User Interface Software and Technology.* New York: ACM Press.

Van der Linden, Dimitri, Sabine Sonnentag, Michael Frese, and Cathy van Dyck. 2001. "Exploration Strategies, Performance, and Error Consequences when Learning a Complex Computer Task." *Behaviour & Information Technology* 20(3): 37–41. doi: 10.1080/0144929011004799.

5

Learning Is Visual

*Why aesthetics matter for learning, and how
to design effective visualizations and
educational graphics*

‹‹ The Backstory

Why aesthetics matter

We get most of our information about the world through our eyes. The visual isn't just a veneer; it's the single most important source of information for most people.

Because the visual is so important, every element added to a design should have a reason to be there. Edward Tufte, the father of data visualization, describes this approach to minimalism in terms of maximizing your "data-ink," or the amount of ink on your page dedicated to representing data. Antoine de Saint-Exupéry put it more elegantly when he said, "It seems that perfection is reached not when there is nothing left to add, but when there is nothing left to take away."

But minimalist doesn't mean bland, as I hope the examples in this chapter will make clear. Visual elements can be gorgeous, seductive, and above all, valuable to the learning experience, without being loaded up with noise. Consider the design of the Evernote introduction (**FIGURE 5.1**). It's not exactly a course in rocket science, but it *is* Evernote's critical moment to teach new users how the tool works.

FIGURE 5.1 This Evernote mini-module avoids extraneous detail in a design that is attractive and playful.

Evernote's decision to use hand-drawn-style graphics, instead of slick images, demonstrates considered attention to the user experience. The effect is twofold: On the one hand it communicates that Evernote is also for analog stuff (napkin scribbles, Polaroids, and so on) and on the other hand, the friendly nostalgia is relaxing (a welcome emotion from a productivity tool). While a new user could easily get discouraged at the thought of yet *another* digital productivity tool, the pleasant muted illustrations elicit connotations of storybooks, doodling, and antidotes to digital stress.

And yet, the design remains simple, the focus is where it needs to be, and each element has a purpose. Even the sunbeams behind the box can be justified as they imply the infinite space promised by the tool. The arrows have just enough detail to communicate their affordances and not more, as does the minimal progress bar. The designers could have presented a text list, but they knew that an image had far more to offer at a glance.

THE AESTHETICS-USABILITY EFFECT

Aside from supporting clarity, communication, comprehension, and emotion, aesthetics hold another trick up their sleeve for learning: They can make an interface more usable. You read that right: Research has shown that where two interfaces are functionally the same, the one that's considered more attractive by users will be easier to use.

In his book *Emotional Design*, Don Norman explains that this has to do with how emotions affect our ability to solve problems. Finding something attractive is pleasant. When we're in a more positive mood, we're more forgiving of interface obstacles, and we're better able to solve problems creatively.

Therefore, it's not so much that an appealing design makes an interface more effective, but that it makes humans more effective. Thus, the human and the computer function better as a whole. This relationship between interface attractiveness and improved usability is known as the *aesthetics-usability effect*.

AESTHETICS AND CREDIBILITY

Whether turning to a book, a teacher, a friend, or a website, no one will invest time and effort in learning something new unless he trusts the source. Research has shown that users make snap judgments about a site's credibility based almost entirely on look and feel. David Robins and Jason Holmes show that the better the visual design of a site, the more credible users will believe the content to be. Rolf Reber and Norbert Schwarz showed that statements that are easier to read are more likely to be considered true. In short, even if your credentials are rock solid, your reputation with learners will suffer from poor visual design.

The power of visualization

What is to be sought in designs for the display of information is the clear portrayal of complexity ... the task of the designer is to give access to the subtle and the difficult—that is, the revelation of the complex.

—EDWARD TUFTE, *The Visual Display of Quantitative Information*

Beyond look and feel, many designers are tasked with creating educational graphics that represent data, structure, and concepts, and which allow phenomena, patterns, and relationships to be revealed.

Note that terms like *visuals, graphics,* and *visualizations* are used in various ways in various books. In this chapter, I use the terms *graphics* and *visuals* interchangeably to refer to any visual content object used to support learning, while *visualization* refers more specifically to representations of data and statistics.

Graphics are an invaluable part of human language and can support reasoning, creativity, engagement, innovation, decision making, and problem solving. They can combine words and images in a way that leverages the advantages of both, and they represent spatial relationships far more effectively than text. They're also stellar for showing changes over time, processes, and cause and effect. We'll look at strategies for these various use cases later in this chapter, but for the warm-up, first a mystery and a magic show.

VISUALS UNLOCK SECRETS

On a dark night during the Crimean War, a nurse tended to a dying soldier. But he wasn't dying from battle wounds; he was dying in a hospital from cholera due to poor sanitation, and it would take a well-designed graphic and a remarkable woman to make that clear.

If the name "Florence Nightingale" calls to mind a famously dedicated nurse, you wouldn't be wrong, but what fewer people know is that she was also a pioneer of applied statistics. Her diligent approach to data gathering and her brilliant innovations in data visualization saved countless lives and changed history.

She created famous graphs that she called her "coxcombs." By using these unique visuals, she was able to show, at a glance, that far more soldiers were dying of preventable diseases than were dying from war (**FIGURE 5.2**).

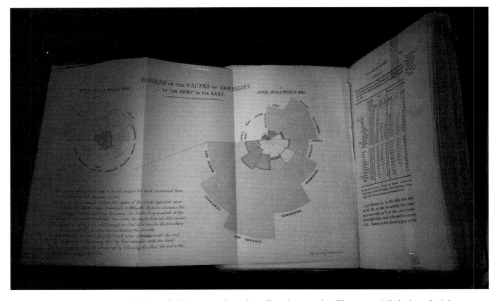

FIGURE 5.2 Florence Nightingale's innovative visualization at the Florence Nightingale Museum in London.

You can find a beautiful, interactive adaptation of Nightingale's graph at www. understandinguncertainty.org/coxcombs. There's also a selection of interactive coxcombs, complete with ActionScript code at www.indiemaps.com.

People who get turned on by data, like researchers and statisticians, know passionately that collections of numbers hold the answers to countless mysteries. But just as binary needs to be translated into a graphical user interface for people to understand it, so do statistics, research findings, and invisible processes need to be translated into a visual language to be understood. They get translated by computer systems, by experts, or by a combination of both, and once converted into visualizations, their beauty and secrets surface.

VISUALS MAKE US SMARTER

How have we increased memory, thought, and reasoning? By the invention of external aids: It is things that make us smart.

—DONALD NORMAN, *Things That Make Us Smart*

One way to think about an educational graphic is as a cognitive tool. Like a hammer enhances what an arm can do in terms of strength, graphics like diagrams, graphs, and maps extend what a brain can do in terms of reasoning.

Learning science researcher David Jonassen describes technologies as mindtools for learning: "Mindtools scaffold different forms of reasoning about content. That is, they require students to think about what they know in different, meaningful ways." Once you can see graphics in terms of how they extend human capacity, you can move beyond shallower notions of decoration and think strategically about how to best support cognition through design.

Of course graphics are already used liberally in eLearning, but it turns out we only get it right about half the time. A study by Sung-Hee Jin and Elizabeth Boling discovered that learners' ideas about the meaning of instructional images

Count me in: Personal informatics and learning analytics

One of the most abundant sources of data visualization today is personal informatics (www.personalinformatics.org). With technologies like the Fitbit, the Nike+ running app, and sites like Health Month, you can track your every move, from how many carbs you burned to how many times you got hung over, had sex, or felt happy throughout the day (no joke: www.drinkingdiary.com, www.bedposted.com, and www.trackyourhappiness.org).

All this data can be collected, analyzed, and flung back at you in the form of graphs and charts. Ideally, seeing the numbers of your life can support reflective thinking, self-awareness, decision making, and positive life changes.

These same principles are being applied to learning and dubbed *learning analytics* or *educational data mining*. Thanks to learning technology, educational organizations are swimming in data about study patterns, online learning interactions, performance, social interaction, and more. When all of that data is analyzed, it can lead to discoveries about how to improve student performance, support teachers, customize learning content, and support organizational decision making. The New Media Consortium's 2013 Horizon Report identified learning analytics as a technology likely to see widespread adoption within three years.

With the mounting popularity of personal, learning, and other analytics, data visualizations are an increasingly demanded feature of technologies—all the more reason to get them right.

aligned with designer intentions only half the time. Surely we can do something to improve that record.

So how can you reliably create educational graphics that work? By designing graphics based on how the human mind perceives them and works most effectively with them.

Designing for perception and visual thinking

It turns out that most of us are fairly deluded about how the whole vision thing works. We assume that we look around and see our rich world in impressive detail, like some HD panoramic camera.

But in reality, we absorb only very minute and fuzzy bits of the visual field and our brains (clever little gizmos that they are) fill in the rest for us—kind of like the context-aware fill in Photoshop. And also like the context-aware fill, our brains can get too creative or get it all wrong, hence the shocking unreliability of eyewitness testimonies.

We actually see things as a hi-res dot surrounded by a low-res approximation. But at least we see in 3-D, right? Not so much.

3-D AND DEPTH PERCEPTION

Our depth perception is nowhere near as complete as we think it is. Visualization researcher Colin Ware puts it at about 2.05 D. That's because what we actually see when we open our eyes is an interpretation of the world on two very similar 2-D planes (one from each eye). Our brains fill in the rest based on what we already know about objects and environments. To get more depth information about an object, we have to physically change positions so we can integrate information from a new angle.

The fact that our stereoscopic depth perception is so minimal is why the 20 percent of the population without full depth perception can get on just fine. I would know, since I can only see out of one of my eyes. Yet, I don't bump into things and I even sometimes win at mini golf. That's because much of the depth information we do receive isn't dependent on two eyes. People like me get by on the many monocular cues that everyone uses liberally. These elements of *pictorial depth,* used by artists and set designers, like vanishing points, occlusion, and shadow, help us navigate the third dimension.

Two-dimensional depth cues are excellent tools for the learning interface designer. In the strategies section of this chapter, we'll look at how you can use depth cues to communicate hierarchy and clarify meaning.

DESIGNING FOR THE VISUAL BRAIN

Our brains, guided by the task at hand, determine what we see in detail. They're very good at rapidly zeroing in on just the parts we need in order to pick up a phone, type a sentence, throw a ball, or read these words. This involves a sophisticated dance of imperceptible eye movements, feature detection, and memory.

But what does this mean for educational design? It means that by knowing how our brains hunt and focus, you can better guide learner brains in the right direction. For example, knowing that our brains are designed to look for edges, movement, and specific colors, you can direct focus through content by strategically employing these features.

For the full backstory, check out Colin Ware's *Visual Thinking for Design* or Connie Malamed's *Visual Language for Designers: Principles for Creating Graphics that People Understand*. The following section provides the basics you'll need to understand the strategies later in the chapter.

THE MAGIC SHOW OF COLORS

Color is a mighty tool for learning interface designers. It's been shown to help learners understand and remember, to increase engagement, and to enhance the effectiveness of visuals. But color is also a tricky beast. It carries meaning that differs across cultures, it's not uniformly perceived, and it depresses learning when overused. Therefore, it's important to wield this tool wisely.

Coming back to our delusions about how we see things, color provides us with some whoppers. For example, it's not as though brown will suddenly turn orange—except sometimes. It turns out that like space-time, colors are relative. Whether the same color is described as brown or orange, green or gray—even black or white—depends on the context. This truth is so difficult to accept that it has to be seen to be believed.

Researcher R. Beau Lotto's amazing color cube is an undeniable demonstration of how color perception is nothing like consistent (**FIGURE 5.3**). The central

FIGURE 5.3 R. Beau Lotto's color cube. The center tiles on the top and side appear brown and orange but are actually the same color. (Image by R. Beau Lotto at www.lottolab.org).

brown tile at the top is actually *exactly* the same color as the central orange tile on the side. If you don't believe it, you can view it on the creator's website with a mask and watch the colors transform before your very eyes.

This chapter has a number of strategies for using color effectively for educational graphics, taking into account the unique eccentricities of our visual system.

POP-OUT FEATURES—A DESIGNER'S ARSENAL

There are certain visual features that our brains target unconsciously as they zero in on essential detail. These include color, orientation, size, motion, edges, and depth.

Research shows that we recognize these pop-out features in less than one-tenth of a second—pretty impressive. So by using these features judiciously you can reduce the workload for learner brains and make sure the elements that stand out are actually the ones that should.

The reason these pop-out features are so salient is because each is acquired via its own separate channel (dedicated biological equipment), which means all of these features can be perceived simultaneously without a traffic jam. Herein lies a powerful opportunity: You can make more than one thing salient in a graphic simply by using a different channel for each, for example, making both stations and routes easy to see on a train map. The brain can then easily focus on just one or the other.

Interestingly, you could also use this theory to achieve the opposite effect. Hidden picture books like *Where's Waldo?* (also known as *Where's Wally?*) are an excellent example of how to make something almost impossible to find visually. Waldo cleverly employs multiple pop-out features: his edges are clearly delineated in black line and his clothing colors are straight from the pop-out palette. The trouble is, the other 2,000 objects on the page use the same features. When pop-out features are overused, the brain is overwhelmed and its standard strategies become less effective. Therein lies the enjoyment of a Waldo picture or the frustration of a poorly designed infographic. The elements in **TABLE 5.1** are recognized by the brain in under a second.

TABLE 5.1 Key elements of visual perception

UNCONSCIOUS ELEMENTS

Individual features we recognize unconsciously

Color
Movement
Position
Size
Edges
Depth

Patterns (combinations of features) we recognize unconsciously

Shapes and closure	Closed shapes and enclosing boundaries
Grouping	Implied by proximity, similarity, symmetry, bounding, and connectedness
Contrast	Juxtaposed elements that differ in color, direction, position, size, and/or shape
Luminance	The level of perceived brightness (important for distinguishing detail)
Texture	Surface property made up of repeated elements of contrast and orientation
Scenes (gist)	Scenes identified in less than a second with peripheral vision
Faces	Rapid perception and focus on faces, especially eyes

CONSCIOUS ELEMENTS

These direct our brains' interpretations of what and how we see

Memory	Memory includes our schemas and previous experience. It can be guided with priming.
Expectations	We're likely to see what we expect to see.
The task at hand	Our brains guide attention based on what's needed for the task at hand and can be blind to much else (see "What Gorilla?" sidebar).

WHEN KNOWING PREVENTS SEEING

One of the most beguiling aspects of perception is that people easily see what they have learned, yet they can completely overlook what they have not … . This is highly relevant to issues of learning; educators often provide explanations of phenomena that students have not learned to perceive, and therefore, students do not realize they are missing something … and it takes special strategies, contrasting cases, to help students see what is important.

—DANIEL SCHWARTZ AND JULIE HEISER, "Spatial Representations and Imagery in Learning," *The Cambridge Handbook of the Learning Sciences*

What Gorilla?

If you haven't already heard about the astonishing gorilla on the basketball court experiment, then you're in for a treat. You can watch it on YouTube: youtube.com/watch?v=vJG698U2Mvo.

This famous experiment is a colorful example of how effective our visual brains are at focusing, and how badly wrong we are when we assume we see everything before us. The 1999 study by Daniel Simons and Christopher Chabris asked participants to watch a video of two teams of basketball players and to count how many times the players in white passed the ball. Participants were great at focusing on that ball; so good in fact, that about half of them completely missed the large, black gorilla that walked through the game. This ability to completely ignore things we aren't attending to is referred to as inattentional blindness. You can read more about it in the book *The Invisible Gorilla*.

Users of computer software and Web sites often click buttons or links without looking carefully at them. Their perception of the display is based more on what their past experience leads them to expect than on what is actually on the screen.

—JEFF JOHNSON, *Designing with the Mind in Mind*

When you first look at a tide pool you'll probably report some rocks and a bit of seaweed. But stay a bit longer, look with curiosity and intent, and a whole world of ocean life will appear. They were always there, but it took a refocusing of your perception for them to become visible to your eyes. A marine biologist would have seen them straight away.

Learners, like the nonexpert at the beach or the art museum, often need some extra guidance to see what's plainly visible to the expert—all the more so when the thing to be seen defies expectation. This is where some of the strategies in this chapter, like using visual cues and directing attention, can come in handy.

» The Strategies
for designing visuals for learning

The strategies in this section are broken down into four subcategories:

1. Strategies to reduce overload
2. Strategies to guide attention
3. Strategies to support perception
4. Strategies to promote visual learning

Strategies to reduce overload

A core principle underlying effective visual design for learning is to minimize extraneous cognitive load. In other words, anything included in your graphics that doesn't support the learning is a potential distracter. The strategies in this section have been shown to reduce cognitive load for learners.

» STICK TO RELEVANT GRAPHICS

At the heart of most of the strategies in this book lies Richard Mayer's Multimedia Principle, which states that words and images are better than words alone for supporting learning. The big caveat is that the images you combine with words have to be *relevant* in order for the principle to apply. Mayer calls this the Coherence Principle, which states that adding interesting but irrelevant graphics can harm learning.

In other words, although glamming up a lesson with seductive stock photos is a tempting way to enhance appeal, these interesting but irrelevant images can actually decrease learning outcomes. But how do you define *relevant*?

Relevant graphics are those that help the learner process and interpret the learning content or help him engage in learning activity. So, before you add images to a lesson, consider the following:

- What is the purpose of this image? Will it distract learners from the task or make it difficult for him to focus on other elements on the page?
- If the image is generic, could an explanatory image (such as a helpful diagram) support the learning instead?
- Does the design guide visual focus to what matters most?

These questions go some of the way in helping keep images relevant. Mayer and Ruth Clark provide further guidance by defining educational graphic types. The following list is adapted from their book, *e-Learning and the Science of Instruction*:

- **Relational graphics** show how things interrelate, such as comparative graphs or interactive systems models.
- **Graphic organizers** provide an early overview by structuring the concepts in a lesson.
- **Transitional graphics** show change over time.
- **Graphics showing things that would otherwise be invisible,** such as atomic structure or the global movement of money.
- **Graphics that help place learning in context,** such as a case study image, a themed graphical user interface, or a virtual world.

In short, apply graphics with care; lean toward graphics that actively support learning, such as those listed above; and use strategies to guide visual focus to what matters.

Caveats and considerations

Images can be very powerful for evoking emotion. As we'll discuss in Chapter 7, "Learning Is Emotional," emotion can increase retention, focus, and learning. In some situations you may decide to add an image that supports attitude change, even if it isn't explanatory.

For example, an image of a head injury might be distracting in a lesson on procedures, but effective for a lesson on risk management. Of course, extraneous emotional content can be highly distracting. The relevance of graphics will depend on the learning goals.

A second caveat is the *expertise reversal effect* (explained in Chapter 4, "Basic Principles A–Z"). Experts can cope far more effectively with extra information, so paring down graphics is most important when designing for novices.

>> SIMPLIFY EXPLANATORY VISUALS

Research shows that people learn processes and principles better from visuals that are in a simplified form. Reducing visual elements will help learners recognize and understand graphics faster and let them focus on the important details.

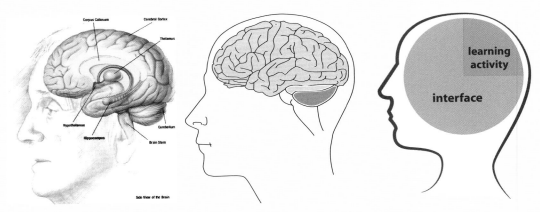

FIGURE 5.4 Three graphics of the brain at various levels of simplification.

For example, simple line drawings that illustrate a process are generally better than a series of photos showing the real thing. Likewise, an animation without background detail is often more effective than a video that is, by nature, high in extraneous detail.

In Chapter 4, I used a simple image of a pie chart brain to illustrate competition for attention between a user interface and a learning activity. Although I could have used a photorealistic image of the brain, the extraneous detail would be a distraction. In fact, I took a line drawing of a brain and then simplified it further, removing all but the key message (**FIGURE 5.4**).

Remarkably, people are just as good at recognizing objects in line drawings as they are at recognizing objects in photos, *and* information conveyed in line drawings is actually more memorable. This is because, when we scan an image, most of our visual activity occurs on the edges. So, an outline alone is enough to convey meaning.

For a master class in simplified form, look no farther than down your street or hallway for the ubiquitous pictogram. More than perhaps any other type of design, pictograms have to be as quickly and universally recognizable as possible. As such, they are utterly essentialized forms in which edges and connections are clear and color is used to make the forms stand out (**FIGURE 5.5**). For a treat, compare the various pictograms designed for each Olympic Games since 1964 at www.olympic-museum.de.

Strategies for simplifying your visuals

- Use line drawings.
- Use silhouettes.
- Use icons.
- Clearly show parts and connections.
- Remove extra detail.
- Clear the background.
- Make text legible, concise, and consistent.
- Employ thoughtful reduction (see next strategy).

FIGURE 5.5 Pictograms such as these National Park Service symbols are highly simplified forms designed using pop-out features to stand out from their surroundings and communicate quickly.

Caveats and considerations

There are, of course, contexts that call for highly detailed and realistic visuals, such as the kind of advanced practice learned in aircraft simulators. If you're aiming to prepare an intermediate or expert learner to operate in a real-life situation in which he'll have to navigate rich detail, then simplifying the environment probably won't give him the right kind of practice. Many interfaces are genuinely complex, and gradually, novices can be worked up from simplified simulations to richer ones.

>> USE THOUGHTFUL REDUCTION TO DESIGN DATA VISUALIZATIONS

It's not just diagrams that can benefit from simplification. Minimalism is also recommended for data graphics like graphs and charts. But how do you go about minimalizing visualization?

In his book *The Laws of Simplicity,* John Maeda suggests, "The simplest way to achieve simplicity is through thoughtful reduction. When in doubt, just remove. But be careful of what you remove." He goes on to explain that once you've reduced, you can hide remaining things with clever design. An increasing number of modern interfaces, like HootSuite and Google Drive, hide dozens of functionalities behind simple icons in toolbars that hide and reappear as needed.

Inline contextual actions used liberally by Google and others are options that appear *only* when the user hovers over a related item. For example, the user might see options to tag, share, or edit an item only when he hovers over it. It's as though the software is reading his intention through his mouse movements, keeping the screen delightfully clear of clutter yet rich in functionality when he needs it.

Along these lines, Edward Tufte demonstrates a process of starting with a bar graph and progressively removing visual elements that do not communicate data until he reaches a dramatically minimalist alternative (**FIGURE 5.6**).

But even minimalism can be taken too far. Visualization expert Stephen Few challenges dramatic minimalism and shows that it can actually reduce readability and make the message less clear. (See his article "Sometimes We Must Raise Our Voices" in the *Visual Business Intelligence Newsletter,*

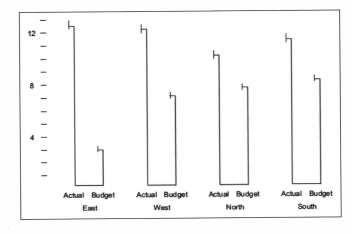

FIGURE 5.6 Dramatically minimalist bar graph recreated from Edward Tufte's original by Stephen Few for the *Visual Business Intelligence Newsletter*. (Reprinted with permission by Stephen Few).

http://www.perceptualedge.com/articles/visual_business_intelligence/ sometimes_we_must_raise_our_voices.pdf.)

>> GROUP IMAGES AND TEXT TOGETHER

For every kind of image, from photos and diagrams to data graphics and screen designs, it's advisable to keep words close to the images they pertain to. In a diagram, this means including labels within the image rather than separating them off into a caption. For data graphics, this may mean adding explanations directly into the graph space, labeling outliers, or integrating a legend into the design (**FIGURE 5.7**).

The important point is that by not separating text and related imagery, learners don't have to move back and forth trying to make connections. Research has shown that this simple guideline improves learning outcomes measurably.

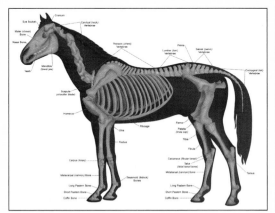
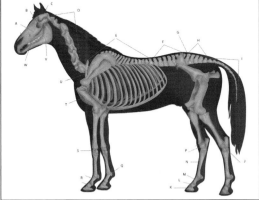

FIGURE 5.7 You can support learning by placing diagram labels near the part of the image they refer to, instead of separating text off into a caption or paragraph. (Adapted from an image by WikipedianProlific via Wikimedia).

Thoughtful reduction in practice

The graphs below from the Pearson Education site are good examples of visually appealing, yet restrained visual design:

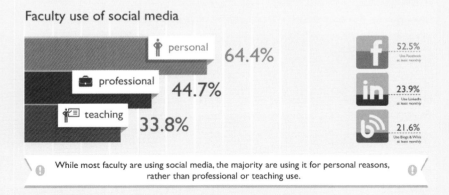

This graph created by Pearson Education demonstrates many thoughtful reduction techniques.

The graphs have a highly saturated but limited color palette and the icons are familiar to the intended audience, even after their color has been removed to avoid distraction. Depth cues are used selectively for labeling. Overall, there is little extraneous detail, like extra chart lines.

Of course, for the sake of experimentation, we could reduce even further. The labels could be a text layer against the bars and the diagonal texture lines could be removed. The comment only reinforces what the chart alone communicates, so it could be removed as well. The text beside the icons is nearly impossible to read, which means that the icon data could be interpreted in any number of incorrect ways, so this could be clarified. And finally, there's a small inconsistency with icon use; while the first two represent specific products, the third is actually intended to represent a product category in general. And while we're at it, why not round off the numbers. A further reduced version might look something like this:

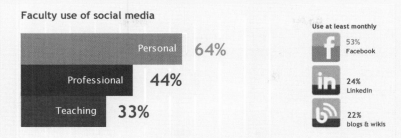

This graph could be reduced further by removing additional detail. Whether or not this further reduction is better would depend on the context.

Of course, Edward Tufte would probably have us strip the data completely. In fact, he would probably have us use a table since there are only six numbers to display. If you pare down further but retain color to communicate quantity (using a tonal scale), you get something like this:

64% Personal	(53% use Facebook at least monthly)
45% Professional	(24% use LinkedIn at least monthly)
33% Teaching	(22% use a blog or wiki at least monthly)

I'm not suggesting that the variations are better than the originals. In a learning scenario, the third solution may be the best way to go, but it's important to note that these graphs were not designed for eLearning. They're part of a report on the Pearson public site, which means they're for marketing. Of course, branding, image, and style pressures exist even for learning projects, and it's the learning interface designer's challenge to attend to each in ways that don't sacrifice the learning.

Strategies for readable text

- Use a font size of *at least* 10 points (bigger is better) and ensure that text is resizable.
- Avoid overly decorative fonts and outline fonts for body text.
- Use all caps sparingly.
- Use a typeface designed for screen reading.
- Use a maximum line length of 100 characters.
- Use structural cues and hierarchy, such as headings and bullets.
- Avoid presenting text centered or right-aligned.
- Avoid presenting text at an angle, for example, rotated or skewed.

›› DESIGN TEXT FOR COMFORTABLE READING

Bad readability, besides putting your learner in a foul mood, gets in the way of learning. Reading is about recognizing letter patterns, and learners do that best when the text is large enough to see and conforms to standards. This is why text in all caps and decorative fonts is harder to read.

In terms of size, larger fonts are more readable. Usability experts Jakob Nielsen and Hoa Loranger recommend a minimum font size of 10 points. And be sure to apply accessibility guidelines so that learners can increase the text size if they choose to.

Be careful using decorative fonts to make something look friendlier or easier. This can work well in small doses where the text is large, but for body text it will backfire because it's harder to read. Research shows that if task instructions are set in a decorative font, learners will believe the task is harder than it is.

Consider using one of the growing number of typefaces designed specifically for screen reading like Verdana, Tahoma, Georgia, or Azuro.

There's also evidence that learners read fastest when text is kept to 100 characters per line, but that, perversely, we prefer a shorter line, between 45–72 characters. So you can make the call based on efficiency or preference.

Caveats and considerations

Recommendations for readability become less important as the size of the text gets larger, as with headings. Many of the color, texture, and font effects that render text unreadable at standard paragraph text sizes don't apply to large headings.

>> USE LAYERS AND HOTSPOTS TO MANAGE LEVELS OF DETAIL

Hiding detail via hotspots is a great way to make a lot of information available in one graphic without overwhelming the learner. This technique is an affordance unique to digital media and an effective way to:

- Provide access to rich information while maintaining a minimalist presentation.
- Help learners integrate new knowledge gradually.
- Present detailed information in context.
- Allow experts access to more detail without overwhelming novices.

You can embed information into pop-ups or as overlays that are activated by clicks or rollovers (**FIGURE 5.8**). These let users drill down to further detail when they're ready. While a rollover requires the least effort, you can't hover on a touchscreen device like an iPad, so the interaction you use will depend on your target devices.

Layering has been used even with static educational graphics as a way of integrating large amounts of complex information and revealing it gradually. For example, some anatomy books have various body systems printed on transparent paper, such that the systems of muscles, bones, or blood vessels can be viewed individually or layered on top of one another as an integrated whole.

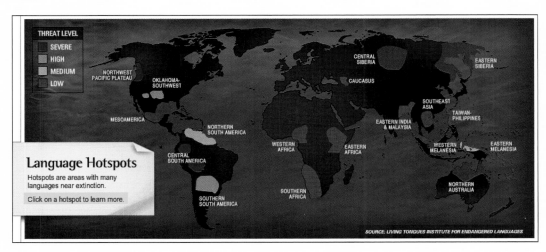

FIGURE 5.8 This interactive map example from the National Geographic website embeds drill-down information into clickable hotspots.

Quick and dirty interactive maps

You can create clickable maps with common slide presentation software like Power-Point or Prezi. In PowerPoint, you can use action buttons to add links to various parts of an image.

In Prezi, you can hide detail with zooming. One of Prezi's strengths is that it allows the presentation of a big picture view together with an elegant way to drill down to various levels of detail. Prezi files are also easy to make available on the web. Since Prezi is still new to many, you'll probably need to tell your learners how to navigate it.

>> USE NEGATIVE AFFORDANCES TO RULE OUT OPTIONS FOR LEARNERS

One way to reduce cognitive load is to reduce choices. This is particularly sensible when those choices aren't actually available. If it's not clear to a learner what he *can't* do, he'll waste time in trial and error.

Affordances are what *can* be done with an object while negative affordances are what *can't*. One well-established design pattern for indicating that a feature is inactive is to display it dimmed or grayed out. Leaving the option in place but dimming it indicates to the user that it's available only under certain conditions. Ideally, a tooltip or similar device will explain exactly what those conditions are.

Similarly, showing items in a locked state when they're not available *yet* is a common pattern in games, including educational ones. Levels, rewards, and upgrades are frequently locked and dimmed until they're activated by progress or achievements.

Strategies to guide attention

Stanford researchers Daniel Schwartz and Kevin Hartman point out that "the history of visual media comprises the invention of techniques and formal features that guide people's thoughts to particular outcomes." Following are strategies for using visual design decisions to do just that: guide the learner's attention.

Features for designing visual hierarchy

Color. Colors are frequently used to distinguish variables. The most easily distinguished colors are black, white, red, blue, yellow, and green. While colors do not imply a hierarchy themselves (there's nothing to say red comes before blue), variations in tone do, where greater saturation is associated with greater quantity as the four circles demonstrate.

Size. A hierarchy can be implied by a stepped increase or decrease in size.

Shape. Different shapes are commonly used to distinguish elements.

Texture. Texture can be used to distinguish among variables; for example, one group of items is pinstriped, while another is solid. Beware of visual interference (see "Avoid color and texture faux pas" later in this chapter.)

Directionality. In general, things placed at the top of a screen are considered more important than things below. For left-to-right readers at least, elements on the left are perceived to be more important than those on the right. Finally, motion can be implied in static images through motion lines, stroboscopic movement, arrows, and blur.

Depth. Depth can imply visual hierarchy because objects in the foreground are perceived as more important than those that are farther away. Depth can be implied two-dimensionally in a variety of ways. Larger objects placed "in front" of smaller objects imply a three-dimensional space, converging lines imply depth (the artist's vanishing point), and interestingly, cooler colors, like blue and green, appear farther away than warmer colors like red and orange.

>> SUPPORT LEARNING WITH VISUAL HIERARCHY

Hierarchies give us a cheat sheet. Newspapers, reports, and websites structure content with headlines, sidebars, bullet lists, and columns. Because of these formatting variations we can scan, spot, and focus on a specific detail in a matter of seconds. We couldn't achieve this if we were faced with a flat wall of words. Hierarchy can serve this same function in graphics.

Hierarchies also allow layers of meaning to coexist. Many educational graphics have multiple messages to convey, variables to make salient, or phenomena to reveal. These can be included in one graphic via different *viewing depths*. For example, a first glance at a graphic might convey its overall structure, mood, or intent, while deeper levels of analysis can convey patterns, anomalies, or relationships.

Depth and hierarchy

Interfaces have shown an increasing use of depth cues for hierarchy. Take Apple's Time Machine software, which displays images of computer backups in a line reaching farther away into the depths of outer space. This effect playfully references sci-fi culture, while using distance in space to communicate distance in time. Similarly, the Apple "coverflow" design displays album covers as a horizontal series of images in which the album in focus appears physically in front of the others in the group.

Apple's Time Machine interface uses depth cues to establish a visual hierarchy.

Designing for multiple messages is a bit of a circus act because you need to make important elements easy to see but avoid a competition for dominance.

The solution is to use various hierarchical levels and to assign distinctive features to each variable. In *Visual Thinking for Design*, Colin Ware points to the legendary London Underground map as an excellent example. This design icon contains three major levels: city → network of stations and lines → individual train lines:

- The first level (city) is easily perceived by clear edges that collectively convey the shape of the system and the citywide coverage of the map.

The Web Standards Sherpa site repurposes coverflow for its front page. Articles of lesser importance appear farther away in the distance.

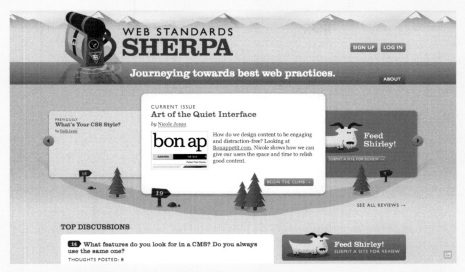

The Web Standards Sherpa site repurposes a "coverflow"-like design for its front page, where articles of lesser importance appear farther away in the distance.

- At a second level, stations and lines can be easily distinguished as labeled circles and thick lines. In this way, a user can focus on labeled circles to search station names or lines to study a pathway.

- At the third level are the individual train lines. Each line is assigned a distinctive color to distinguish it from the others. A user can easily trace the trajectory of just one line by focusing on its color and ignoring all else.

Harry Beck, the designer of this map, essentially took a large set of data (all of London's station names, train lines, locations, and connections), organized it into a multiscale visual hierarchy that privileged clarity over geographic accuracy, and created a cognitive tool so effective it has been replicated worldwide.

Attack with arrows

From diagrams and one-way streets to neon signs, our world is infiltrated by arrows. The simple reason is that the arrow offers excellent value. It's an incredibly simple symbol (one line and one triangle) that is dynamic, rich in meaning, and understood across cultures and literacy levels.

Arrows can indicate direction through time or space, motion, relationships, cause and effect, hierarchies, emphasis, and more—a handy repertoire for multimedia learning.

In addition to allowing various items to be distinguishable, good multiscale designs have various focal points with varying degrees of emphasis. This guides the eye along a path through the design. As Connie Malamed explains in her book on visual language, "Position, emphasis and movement provide a visual language for orienting and directing the viewer's vision along an intended path." With educational graphics, this path should be designed to guide learners through the content in a way that is didactically effective.

The Underground map example uses pop-out features like distinctive colors and differing shapes. The specific features you select to create a visual hierarchy will depend on your content and context. See "Features for designing visual hierarchy" sidebar for options.

Caveats and considerations

Things like motion and flashing light attract our visual processing to an extent almost beyond our control, hence the irritation caused by advertising banners and animated GIFs. So it's important to design carefully for unconscious signals, if only to avoid user wrath. High-frequency flashing can even induce seizures in some people. When it comes to learning, use signals like movement sparingly, if at all, such as to draw attention to rare or urgent messages.

>> SUPPORT LEARNER ATTENTION WITH CONSCIOUS SIGNALS

Beyond pre-attentive signals, which draw our eyes before we know it, are the conscious cues that draw on our reasoning. Research by Patricia Mautone and Richard Mayer shows that visual cues, like arrows and color-coding, improve information recall in multimedia learning.

Numbers and letters indicate hierarchy because we understand them as having an order. Metaphors, maps, and overview images can give direction and structure to the information in a graphic. For example, the image of a mountain peak, a ladder, a city map, a layer cake, or a tree implies structure in its own way. If your content already implies a shape thematically, consider using that shape to structure it (**FIGURE 5.9**).

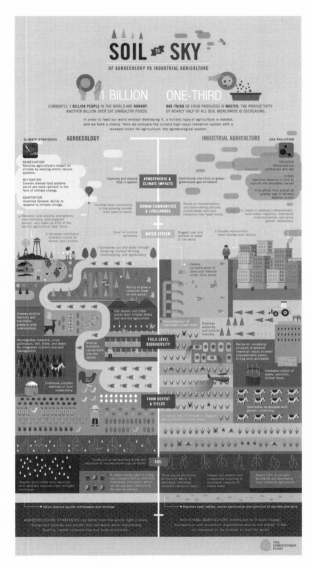

FIGURE 5.9 This infographic on agroecology structures content using a thematically appropriate descent through layers of air and soil (Courtesy of The Christensen Fund).

>> USE RULES OF RAPID RECOGNITION

Just as characteristics like edges and pop-out colors grab our visual attention in under a second, there is a unique category of *concepts* that do the same.

- **Scenes.** We understand the gist of a scene in a tenth of a second using mostly our peripheral vision. That is, we can instantaneously tell whether we're in a field, a grocery store, or a bedroom with just the blurry edges of our visual field.

- **Object category.** We excel at instantly identifying an object by category. While we may not be able to tell something is a guava or a golden retriever, we can tell it's a fruit or a dog in a split second.

- **Connection points.** We spot the points at which parts of an object connect in under a second, and these inform our rapid recognition of structure.

- **Structure.** We are remarkably adept at comprehending the overall structure of something, provided the connection points are clear.

Considerations and caveats

Sometimes you might not want an object to be rapidly identified. A learning activity may need to incorporate practice in identifying obfuscated forms. What if you were training learners to identify even difficult-to-distinguish objects in chaotic settings, such as clues in a crime scene or prohibited material in a baggage security scan. In this case, exposure to various standard and nonstandard views of the objects, with and without visible connections, may be required.

Strategies to support visual perception

The following strategies describe ways to use the physiology of perception to improve learning.

>> AVOID COLOR AND TEXTURE FAUX PAS

Mixing certain colors and textures can cause unexpected effects like moiré, vibration, and difficult discernment. This kind of visual interference tends to occur when elements in a design are not sufficiently distinct from each other, and more specifically, when features in the same processing channel are combined. For example, since our brains identify color as a function of red/green and blue/yellow differentials, red text on a green background requires use of the same

Strategies for supporting rapid recognition

When you're creating icons or abstract images (like pictograms) that need to be recognized as quickly as possible, try these strategies:

Use typical examples. For example, if you want to represent fruit, depict an apple rather than a quince (regional definitions of "typical" may vary, of course).

Use standard views and sizes. Stick with familiar views that show all connections. For example, don't depict an apple from above. Stephen Palmer, Eleanor Rosch, and Paul Chase found that there is a preferred perspective at which we both imagine and most quickly recognize objects; they call this the "canonical view." For example, people almost always draw a coffee cup from slightly above with the handle at the side. This canonical view is usually a three-quarter perspective in which the front, side, and top of the object are all visible.

A recent MIT study by Talia Konkle and Aude Oliva found that people have size preferences as well. Overall, we prefer objects to be sized in a way that is roughly proportional to their size in the real world. This object-to-frame size ratio preference is referred to as "canonical visual size." For example, people tend to draw that coffee cup smallish in relation to the paper size (as if the paper rectangle were a field of view). They would use up more space to draw a larger object like a refrigerator. Therefore, representing an object on screen smaller or larger than its canonical visual size could communicate that it is over-sized or undersized (like a toy). Depicting the cup as tiny within the frame could make it look like a toy cup, and depicting it very large could make it look like a ride at Disneyland.

Show connection points. Make sure that, whatever your views or angles are, connection points are visible.

pathway (traffic jam!) and is therefore difficult to see. Likewise, we spot texture largely as a difference in grain, so detailed lettering over a grainy texture is hard to discern (**FIGURE 5.10**).

If you're using pattern to communicate meaning, stay clear of moiré and vibration effects by avoiding cross-hatching, even-width stripes, checkerboard patterns, evenly spaced dots, and other densely repetitive patterns. Instead, try using variations in hue or tint screens such as grayscale, or circumventing the need for pattern-coding altogether by using directly placed labels.

Top-Down Processing In Cognitive Psychology

General	**See It To Believe It**
	Here are some optical illusions that illustrate the power of top-down processing.
Historical Experiments	Typography Illusions
	A Bird in the Bush
- Stroop	A Few Illusions in Perception that are Related to Top-Down Processing
- Object-Search	**Other Top-Down Processing Links on the Web**
	Top-Down Processes -- A PsyQuest
- Canonical Perspective	Top-Down Processing in Auditory Perception
	Some Top-Down Negations and the Opposing Theory of Bottom-Up Processing
Top-Down Illusions	Artificial Intelligence and What Best Models the Human Brain-- Top-Down or Bottom-Up?
Other Links	**References**
References	Biederman, I., Glass, A. L., & Stacy E. W. (1973). Searching for objects in real world scenes. Journal of Experimental Psychology, 97, 22-27.
	Palmer, S. E., Rosch, E., & Chase, P. (1981). Canonical perspective and the perception of objects. J. Long & A. Baddely (Eds.), Attention and performance IX (pp. 135-151). Hillsdale, NJ: L. Erlbaum Associates.
	Solso, Robert L. (1998). Cognitive psychology (5th ed.). Needham Heights, MA: Allyn and Bacon.
	Stroop, J. R. (1935). Studies of interference in serial verbal reactions. Journal of Experimental Psychology, 28, 643-662.

FIGURE 5.10 The useful information on this page is obscured by its presentation. The background pattern makes text harder to distinguish, the overuse of color may harm retention, and the use of bright colors for text may cause eye fatigue.

>> USE LUMINANCE FOR VISUAL DETAIL

Research shows that it's easier to discern detail in black and white. This is because light contrast (luminance) allows us to see details, much more so than color differences. So when you need to show detail, make sure the colors you use are high contrast. Although black and white are obvious choices, other high-contrast combos like dark blue on white or yellow on black are also effective.

Another interesting point about luminance is that, while we see gradual changes from one color to another simply as color change, we add meaning to gradual changes from light to dark: we see these shifts as contour (shape and shadow).

>> USE DEPTH SELECTIVELY

We're quite flexible with regard to depictions of depth. Since we don't really see in three dimensions, we're perfectly happy with images that combine two- and three-dimensional attributes. This knowledge can be used to apply depth selectively to learning graphics in order to show structure, imply hierarchy, or create emphasis.

In general, it's best to save full 3-D graphics for situations in which 3-D is uniquely suited to the learning goals, such as when understanding the three-dimensional structure of an object or environment is important.

In many cases, 3-D graphics add distracting detail without added benefit. Sometimes, however, they can be effective and even minimalist. Designers can use subtle, grayscale 3-D models to provide an alternative to full color that is clean, communicates well, and is visually appealing (**FIGURE 5.11**).

FIGURE 5.11 In this eLearning program set in a construction site, the 3-D image creates a sense of place without the distracting detail of color. The yellow labels stand out easily against the grayscale world. (Courtesy of Savv-e Pty. Ltd.).

Strategies for implying depth

Colin Ware advises that we're completely comfortable with unrealistically mixed depth cues: "The choice of the designer is not three-dimensional versus two-dimensional, but which of the depth cues to apply."

Use these strategies to imply depth:

- Occlusion (when one object blocks another object, it looks closer)
- Perspective
- Size
- Texture (the graininess of a texture increases as it gets farther away)
- Cast shadows
- Shading
- Height on the picture plane (things farther away in a landscape appear "above" things that are closer)
- Depth of focus (blurry versus sharp—this effect is strong in photos with a low depth of field)
- Reference to nearby known objects
- Degree of contrast (as in a fog, things farther away have less contrast)

>> SUPPORT LEARNING AND LEARNABILITY WITH COLOR-CODING

Research shows that assigning distinctive colors to different elements in a graphic can help learners understand and retain information. Color-coding also makes interfaces and infographics easier to use, as colors help us organize and search for information.

The two essentials for color-coding are distinctiveness and consistency. Of course, there's a limit to how many different colors designers can use before one color starts looking too much like another color. Colin Ware suggests the limit is between six and twelve for small symbols. The best results come from using red, green, yellow, and blue followed by those colors we have common names for like brown and purple.

Keep in mind that the background and surrounding colors can significantly change how a spot of color is perceived (see the R. Beau Lotto cube earlier in this chapter). In general, when you're creating a color-coded image, or whenever color correctness is important, stick to black and white, neutral tones, or subtle pastels for your background.

Caveats and considerations

Remember that due to the significant percentage of the population who are colorblind, it's unwise to use color alone to code information. So if you're using color-coding, consider a redundant-coding approach, such as applying distinctive shapes as well. Also remember to consider the various cultural meanings of colors.

Strategies to promote visual learning

The following strategies describe ways to design for visual learning to help learners reason, understand, construct, remember, transfer, and innovate new knowledge effectively.

>> TRANSLATE LARGE DATA SETS INTO ABSTRACT GRAPHICS

Abstract graphics is a catchall term for all graphs, charts, and diagrams that visualize a large data set. Rather than show the learner a picture of something specific, such as the universe, an abstract graphic would creatively present data, such as the number of galaxies with and without sun-like stars. Ideally, the messages buried within this data, such as the likelihood of life on other planets, can be seen more clearly.

As with the Florence Nightingale story earlier in this chapter, some truth will be realized only when numbers are transformed into visuals. Likewise, with massive data sets, implications may be identifiable only through visualization.

So what are your options with regard to abstract graphics? Graphs and charts are just some of the most common. Infographics (short for information graphics) are less formal and often combine formal graphs and charts with rich imagery to create a narrative. For a more complete menu of ways information can be presented visually, see **FIGURE 5.12**.

>> STAY CLEAR OF THE LIE FACTOR

It's easy to forget that data visualizations can be distorted to exaggerate, bias, or to make a particular point. One distortion strategy is to visualize a change

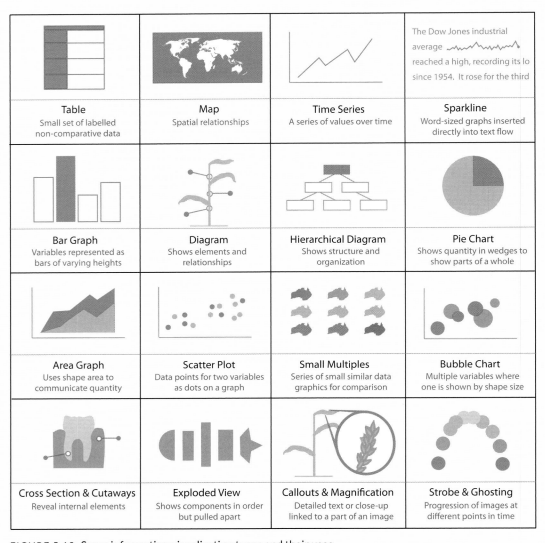

Table Small set of labelled non-comparative data	**Map** Spatial relationships	**Time Series** A series of values over time	**Sparkline** Word-sized graphs inserted directly into text flow
Bar Graph Variables represented as bars of varying heights	**Diagram** Shows elements and relationships	**Hierarchical Diagram** Shows structure and organization	**Pie Chart** Shows quantity in wedges to show parts of a whole
Area Graph Uses shape area to communicate quantity	**Scatter Plot** Data points for two variables as dots on a graph	**Small Multiples** Series of small similar data graphics for comparison	**Bubble Chart** Multiple variables where one is shown by shape size
Cross Section & Cutaways Reveal internal elements	**Exploded View** Shows components in order but pulled apart	**Callouts & Magnification** Detailed text or close-up linked to a part of an image	**Strobe & Ghosting** Progression of images at different points in time

The Dow Jones industrial average reached a high, recording its lo since 1954. It rose for the third

FIGURE 5.12 Some information visualization types and their uses.

as much larger than it really is. Another common con job involves showing an increase in expenditure over time without accounting for monetary inflation or variables like population growth. Edward Tufte translates this distortion into a mathematical formula he calls the "Lie Factor."

$$\text{Lie Factor} = \frac{\text{size of the effect shown in graphic}}{\text{Size of the effect in data}}$$

The strategy here is apparent enough. As you translate your data into visual form, be diligent with your proportions, and be careful not to distort the facts. For more information, see Tufte's classic book, *The Visual Display of Quantitative Information*.

Read the Wikipedia entry under "Misleading graph" to learn more about the wide variety of techniques that are frequently used to distort data (from improper scaling to the abuse of 3-D). Fox News Network regularly broadcasts distorted graphs and charts, if you want real-life examples (www.mediamatters. org/research/2012/10/01/a-history-of-dishonest-fox-charts for examples with explanations on the type of distortion employed).

>> USE SEGMENTING, SEQUENCING, AND LAYERING TO TAME COMPLEXITY

Instructional designers are well acquainted with the notion of segmenting, or chunking, the idea that learning content should be broken into manageable parts that the learner can process one at a time.

A sequence is a series of segments in chronological order. Research shows that sequences increase processing efficiency and understanding, and that segmenting improves learning outcomes.

Segmenting can be helpful in taming complexity without killing it. In his book *Living with Complexity,* Donald Norman challenges our obsession with simplicity. He warns against confusing complex with complicated and highlights that many things are naturally and necessarily complex.

Oversimplifying a data graphic can put the integrity of the information at risk. Connie Malamed suggests that designers *clarify* information rather than *simplify* it. Clarification can come from multiple views, layering of detail, and segmenting.

Chunks, working memory, and the magical number 4

The idea that the limit on our working memory is 7 ± 2 is almost cliché. This seems to explain the memorable nature of the seven-digit phone number. But research explains that the limit is on *chunks*, not *digits*. One chunk might actually contain three numbers, and indeed, phone numbers are more memorable when communicated in two chunks of three to four digits each.

More recent research has recast the actual memory limit at 4. What this means for educational graphics is that it's probably helpful to limit groups and choices to no more than four items.

Caveats and considerations

There is a risk to segmenting that comes from artificially separating parts in a process. If the learner is unable to understand the segments as a whole, segmenting can backfire. To help prevent this, provide support for understanding overall structure at the beginning and present big picture views.

›› AVOID INTERFERENCE

Visual interference occurs when elements in a design are insufficiently distinct. In general, features in the same processing channel will interfere with one another. For example, our brains look for textures more or less as a function of grain, and for color as a function of red/green and blue/yellow differentials. This is why red text on a green background is difficult to see and detailed lettering over a grainy texture is hard to discern.

But interference can also come from cognitive conflicts, based on our prior experience and knowledge of the world.

The *stroop effect* occurs when two cognitively opposing concepts are used together (like a green stop sign). The message here is to ensure that your visual design aligns with the message. *Incongruence* occurs when an object appears in an unusual context (like a grizzly bear driving a car.) By nature we're drawn to focus on the riddle in order to resolve the conflict.

Caveats and considerations

You can also deliberately use incongruence to defy expectation, stimulate curiosity, or challenge assumptions. A photo of an object mysteriously defying gravity might be used to kick off a lesson on magnetism. Because incongruence challenges our established mental schemas, it's often used by advertisers to get attention or stimulate curiosity.

›› USE MULTIPLE REPRESENTATIONS

Research shows that there are advantages to providing more than one educational graphic on the same topic. These are often called multiple representations, and they can be anything from graphs and equations to photos and video. According to researcher Shaaron Ainsworth, multiple representations have three key functions:

- Show complementary information.
- Narrow the interpretation of a graphic.
- Support deeper understanding.

The election graphics case study below is a good example of how multiple data visualizations allow the learner to construct deeper understanding.

In "Designing Effective Visualizations for Elementary School Science," Marcia Linn and Yael Kali list multiple representations as one of four key principles for interactive visualizations: "Multiple representations allow students to identify connections that are salient in one representation but not in another. Multiple representations become even more powerful when they are dynamically linked to each other and synchronized, so that changes in one representation cause appropriate changes in the other."

Caveats and considerations

Multiple representations go wrong when a learner can't understand one or more representations, or the relationship between them. This can occur when a learner lacks prerequisite information or because a representation is provided in an unfamiliar form. Shaaron Ainsworth cautions that learners also need to be able to understand the relationship between the representation presented and what they're learning.

Learners can also have trouble knowing which representation to look at when, and they can find it difficult to relate the information from one representation to another. Therefore, ensure that labeling conventions are consistent from one graph to another and consider design strategies like increasing proximity, superimposing related information, or embedding hotspots to support learners with making connections between them.

>> USE A SYSTEMATIC APPROACH

Effective design should start with a visual task analysis, determine the set
of visual queries to be supported by a design, and then use color, form, and
space to efficiently serve those queries.

—COLIN WARE, *Visual Thinking for Design*

Most abstract graphics are tools that support reasoning or problem solving.
When we look at a map, diagram, or infographic, we might be making a comparison, looking for answers, or searching for patterns, anomalies, clusters, relationships, or causality.

For a question like "Has population gone up in the past five years?," the symbols
representing population quantity might be placed against time. For a question
like "Is there a relationship between spending and profit over time?," two graphs
might be positioned side by side, or superimposed to support comparison. To
optimize the efficacy of your graphic, you need to know what cognitive tasks it
will need to support.

As with user interface design generally, designing educational graphics requires
a systematic approach of research, analysis, planning, and testing.

Ruth Clark and Chopeta Lyons have outlined a five-phase iterative visual
design model:

1. Define the goal.
2. Determine the context (audience, environment, medium, constraints).
3. Design the visual approach.
4. Identify communication function of visuals to match content types.
5. Apply principles of psychological instructional events to visual
   design decisions.

For full details, see their book *Graphics for Learning: Proven Guidelines for
Planning, Designing, and Evaluating Visuals in Training Materials.*

The New York Times election graphics

Journalism infographics offer some of the most inspiring examples of educational graphics available today. *The New York Times* US 2012 election graphics offered a master class in elegant and effective interactive visualizations that showed real attention to the user experience. (You can play with the graphics at http://elections.nytimes.com/2012/results/president.)

The diverse package of graphics communicated journalistic integrity in its considerable effort to present information in a helpful, undistorted, and transparent way. For example, they collated predictions from various sources into one table, making comparison easy. Rollovers revealed the real data behind visual symbols in maps and tables. And multiple representations built a fuller, more accurate picture of the data. For example, maps showing state, county, and popular votes were all available.

The designers also supported people's desire to use real information to predict the election outcome, and provided interactive maps of various possible scenarios. "What if Florida goes to Obama instead of Romney?" a user might have asked. This user could click and drag the Florida circle from Romney's group into Obama's to test out this scenario and the numbers would automatically update. The resulting interactive graphic was informative, clever, and fun to use.

Overall, *The New York Times* 2012 election graphics are great examples of several key principles of data graphics:

- **Appealing and clean minimalist design:** Muted borders, three distinctive colors, and use of tint rather than patterns for value and quantity.

- **Intuitive visual hierarchy:** A first glance provided enough insight to motivate further inquiry, while interactive hotspots and multiple representations allowed for more sophisticated analysis and a broader view.

- **Intrinsic motivation:** The graphics showed attention to audience needs and curiosity and supported their desire to manipulate and explore data.

- **Effective use of interactivity:** The interactive elements provided nested levels of detail, backed up visual claims, and allowed users to explore and construct knowledge with the data.

Go further

For a fuller story on visual perception, visual thinking, and how you can design for them, check out these resources:

- *Visual Language for Designers* (2011) by Connie Malamed, and her blog elearningcoach.com.
- *The Visual Display of Quantitative Information,* 2nd ed. (2008) by Edward Tufte.
- *Visual Thinking for Design* (2008) by Colin Ware.
- *ElearningExamples.com,* a blog of educational graphics, including infographics and visualizations with plenty of inspiration.
- The National Science Foundation publishes annual visualization award winners online at nsf.gov/news/special_reports/scivis.

SOURCES

Ainsworth, Shaaron. 1999. "The Functions of Multiple Representations." *Computers & Education* 33 (2–3): 131–52. doi:10.1016/S0360-1315(99)00029-9.

Ainsworth, Shaaron. 2008. "The Educational Value of Multiple-Representations When Learning Complex Scientific Concepts." In *Visualization: Theory and Practice in Science Education,* edited by John K. Gilbert, Miriam Reiner, and Mary Nakhleh, 191–208. New York: Springer.

Clark, Ruth C., and Chopeta Lyons. 2010. *Graphics for Learning: Proven Guidelines for Planning, Designing, and Evaluating Visuals in Training Materials.* San Francisco: Pfeiffer.

Clark, Ruth C., and Richard E. Mayer. 2008. *E-Learning and the Science of Instruction: Proven Guidelines for Consumers and Designers of Multimedia Learning,* 2nd ed. San Francisco: Pfeiffer.

Few, Stephen. 2009. "Sometimes We Must Raise Our Voices." *Visual Business Intelligence Newsletter,* January/February. http://www.perceptualedge.com/articles/visual_business_intelligence/sometimes_we_must_raise_our_voices.pdf.

Jin, Sung-Hee, and Elizabeth Boling. 2010. "Instructional Designer's Intentions and Learners' Perceptions of the Instructional Functions of Visuals in an e-Learning Context." *Journal of Visual Literacy* 29 (2): 143–66.

Johnson, Jeff. 2010. *Designing with the Mind in Mind: Simple Guide to Understanding User Interface Design Rules.* Amsterdam/Boston: Morgan Kaufmann Publishers/Elsevier.

Jonassen, David H., Chad Carr, and Hsiu-Ping Yueh. 1998. "Computers as Mindtools for Engaging Learners in Critical Thinking." *TechTrends* 43 (2): 24–32.

Kali, Yael, and Marcia C. Linn. 2008. "Designing Effective Visualizations for Elementary School Science." *Elementary School Journal* 109 (2): 181–98.

Konkle, Talia, and Aude Oliva. 2011. "Canonical Visual Size for Real-World Objects." *Journal of Experimental Psychology: Human Perception and Performance* 37 (1): 23–37. doi:10.1037/a0020413.

Lidwell, William. 2003. *Universal Principles of Design.* Gloucester, MA: Rockport.

Maeda, John. 2006. *The Laws of Simplicity*. Cambridge, MA: MIT Press.

Malamed, Connie. 2011. *Visual Language for Designers: Principles for Creating Graphics that People Understand*. Beverly, MA: Rockport.

Mautone, Patricia D., and Richard E. Mayer. 2001. "Signaling as a Cognitive Guide in Multimedia Learning." *Journal of Educational Psychology* 93 (2): 377–89. doi:10.1037/0022-0663.93.2.377.

Nielsen, Jakob, and Hoa Loranger. 2006. *Prioritizing Web Usability*. Berkeley, CA: New Riders.

Norman, Donald A. 1993. *Things that Make Us Smart: Defending Human Attributes in the Age of the Machine*. Reading, MA: Addison-Wesley.

Norman, Donald A. 2003. *Emotional Design: Why We Love (or Hate) Everyday Things*. New York: Basic Books.

Norman, Donald A. 2010. *Living with Complexity*. Cambridge, MA: MIT Press.

Reber, Rolf, and Norbert Schwarz. 1999. "Effects of Perceptual Fluency on Judgments of Truth." *Consciousness and Cognition* 8 (3): 338–42. doi:10.1006/ccog.1999.0386.

Robins, David, and Jason Holmes. 2008. "Aesthetics and Credibility in Web Site Design." *Information Processing and Management* 44 (1): 386–99. doi:10.1016/j.ipm.2007.02.003.

Schwartz, Daniel L., and Kevin Hartman. 2007. "It Is Not Television Anymore: Designing Digital Video for Learning and Assessment." In *Video Research in the Learning Sciences,* edited by Ricki Goldman, Roy Pea, Brigid Barron, and Sharon J. Derry, 335–48. Mahwah, NJ: Erlbaum.

Schwartz, Daniel L., and Julie Heiser. 2006. "Spatial Representations and Imagery in Learning." In *The Cambridge Handbook of the Learning Sciences,* edited by R. Keith Sawyer, 283–98. New York: Cambridge University Press.

Simons, Daniel J., and Christopher F. Chabris. 1999. "Gorillas in Our Midst: Sustained Inattentional Blindness for Dynamic Events." *Perception* 28 (9), 1059–74.

Tufte, Edward R. 2001. *The Visual Display of Quantitative Information,* 2nd ed. Cheshire, CT: Graphics Press.

Ware, Colin. 2008. *Visual Thinking for Design*. Amsterdam/Boston: Morgan Kaufmann Publishers/Elsevier.

Weinschenk, Susan. 2011. *100 Things Every Designer Needs to Know About People*. Berkeley, CA: New Riders.

6

Learning Is Social

How we can design interfaces that foster
social interaction, collaborative learning,
and communities of practice

❮❮ The Backstory

We learn better together

Training often gives people solutions to problems already solved.
Collaboration addresses challenges no one has overcome before … .
The 21st century mind is a collective mind where we access what we
know in our friends' and colleagues' brains. Together we can be smarter
and can address ever more challenging problems.

—TONY BINGHAM AND MARCIA CONNER, *The New Social Learning*

The idea that we learn from others isn't big news, and some educators maintain
it's the only way we learn. In Chapter 2, "How We Learn," we looked at social
constructivism and situated learning theories, both of which describe learning
as inseparable from its social context. Lev Vygotsky described knowledge as
something we co-construct as part of our interaction with one another.

In the twenty-first century, learning is no longer just social—it's
cial. Collaborative learning now manifests itself on a whole new s
classic one-on-ones to worldwide discussions involving millions.
ily engage with a diverse set of experts and fellow learners, naviga

waters smoothly with tools that let us chat, text, blog, microblog, comment, create, and publish online. Experts claim that in this new connected world, the community itself is the curriculum rather than simply the path to accessing it.

COLLABORATIVE AND NETWORKED LEARNING

Long before tools like Facebook and Twitter were commandeered for learning, educators in *computer-supported collaborative learning* (CSCL) were experimenting with the power of online collaboration. CSCL explores how computers can be used to help people learn in collaboration. It draws on the fact that people learn by asking questions, following lines of inquiry together, and observing one another. Examples of CSCL can vary in scale from a pair of students collaborating in front of a computer for half an hour, to a virtual community of thousands working together over years on a project.

Beyond providing channels for communication, CSCL systems provide pedagogical support such as scaffolding in order to structure, enrich, and motivate collaboration. We'll look at some examples of interface scaffolding later in the Strategies section of this chapter.

Another way to look at social learning is through the lens of *networked learning*. Networked learning considers the webs of connections among people and resources across a community and their use as nodes that support one another's learning.

Project Noah (www.projectnoah.org) represents a kind of networked learning environment with ecology as its theme. The site is home to a global community of nature enthusiasts of all ages who share knowledge about their local plants and wildlife. It's also strongly linked to ecological missions and "BioBlitzes," organized events in which a group of people set out to capture as much data as they can on specific species in a set amount of time.

The beauty of communities like Project Noah is that novices have as much to gain as experts. An enthusiastic teenager with a strong interest in exploring the natural world may find the encouragement she doesn't get from classmates. The community gives her a unique space where she can virtually apprentice with scientists, collectors, and explorers, all of whom share her passion. At the same time, such crowdsourcing gives experts unparalleled data collection potential. She might stumble on a new species, and, at minimum, she contributes a data point to a countrywide survey of flora and fauna.

The Project Noah app and website are beautifully designed, with some jaw-droppingly stunning nature images and an interface that's a delight to use (**FIGURE 6.1**). The look and feel bring warmth, clarity, curiosity, wholesomeness, and the glory of nature to the forefront. Clearly, learning environments like these can be practical and productive, as well as inspiring.

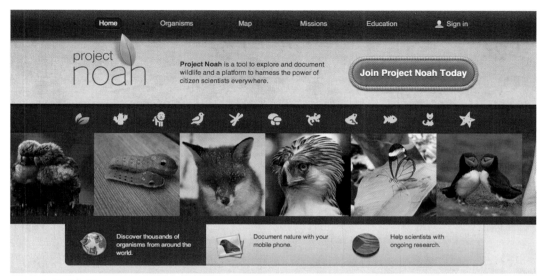

FIGURE 6.1 Project Noah's warm, tactile, and beautiful interfaces inspire engagement in nature spotting activities.

COMMUNITIES OF PRACTICE

Communities of practice, a term coined by Jean Lave and Etienne Wenger in the early 1990s, describes groups of professionals (or enthusiasts) who come together around an interest or profession in order to learn from one another. Examples include formally established groups, like the community of managers at Mind Tools (www.mindtools.com), or the doctors who connect via physicians' associations online. Other examples include communities that develop organically as collections of Twitter users unite around a shared topic or employees on an enterprise social network create a subgroup for themselves around their area of expertise.

The research and experience that has occurred under the aegis of various related fields, including networked learning, CSCL, and communities of practice, have much to teach designers about how to serve the varying needs of different digital communities. We'll look at some of the guidance available later in the Strategies section.

Participatory culture

One of the biggest ways in which interface design can support social learning is by facilitating participation. While participation in and of itself doesn't guarantee learning, studies have shown that it tends to increase group productivity and learner satisfaction, decrease dropout rates, and improve learning outcomes. Lucky for us, we've entered an era in which people are participating almost obsessively.

In the twenty-first century, we like to DIY, share, contribute, create, publish, comment, and mash up. It's these activities that feed communities of practice, peer learning, collaborative work, the maker movement, wikis, and crowdsourcing. Social participation is also central to gaming, as Eric Klopfer explains in his book *Augmented Learning: Research and Design of Mobile Educational Games*:

> In massively multiplayer online role-playing games (MMORPGs) ... each player develops particular specialties that makes them unique and valuable on a team .... Each problem (e.g., slaying a monster, protecting a castle, retrieving artifacts) is much too difficult and immense to be tackled alone. Instead they require players to form these guilds, many of which are long-lasting, and build relationships and team skills.

And yet not all communities get the participation necessary to thrive. So what fosters a thriving community of learners? Successful communities meet users' personal needs (the desire to meet people), let users engage around an interest (gaming), help them gain knowledge and skills (knitting), or allow them to contribute to the common good (Rotary Clubs). Often, it's a combination of these factors, as seen in open-source software communities like Wikipedia.

In the second part of this chapter, we'll look at some of the design strategies that can influence whether a community fades out, bursts into flames, or truly thrives.

PERSONAL LEARNING ENVIRONMENTS

Imagine if education and everything that it entails were customized to fit your schedule, your needs, your weaknesses, your strengths, and your style. Many believe we're experiencing a shift in education that's taking us further down just such a road. After all, we already curate our own learning experiences by pulling together resources from around the web, connecting via social networks, reflecting, questioning, and seeking knowledge.

We create a kind of constellation of people, information, and things, and we carry portals to this universe in our pockets. Special tools like Symbaloo EDU and Net-Vibe make the process of constructing a personal learning environment easier.

One of the interesting things this implies for designers is that users can integrate any technology into their personal learning constellation, be it a social network, a spreadsheet program, or a video game. Therefore, in the design process for *any* technology, it's worth considering scenarios in which users are learners. The idea that people might be learning with our technologies, even when these aren't learning technologies per se, makes the imperative to understand how to design for learning all the more significant.

>> The Strategies
for the design of social learning environments

The strategies in this section are broken down into three subcategories:

1. Strategies for improving social presence
2. Strategies for encouraging participation
3. Strategies for nurturing conviviality and community

Strategies for improving social presence

Research shows that we learn better when we perceive social presence. The key word here is *perceive*. Even just choosing to write from a first-person perspective and in conversational tone is enough to improve learning outcomes. We're hard-wired to pay more attention when it feels like someone is talking directly to us.

And yet, a key challenge for online learning is often the disconnected, faceless experience it produces. The first step to successful interaction with other people is sensing that they're actually there, even if they're not. Following are some interface strategies for increasing this sense of social presence.

>> DESIGN FOR RICH IDENTITIES

Communities are defined by the people in them, so letting individuals create identities online helps them express themselves, feel included, connect with others who are similar, and know where they have unique expertise. According to Tony Bingham and Marcia Conner, "A core capability of any online community is its member profiles. Viewing a person's profile should essentially provide the same feel as visiting his or her office—complete with pictures on the desk and certifications and awards on the walls."

Perceiving people's identities is also a key facet of trust. In order to be free to learn we have to trust others, in terms of their competence as well as socially (as in, they won't point and laugh when we ask questions).

If profiles can be linked to other systems that already store user information (name, e-mail, projects, and so on), then you can automatically populate those fields to

User perspective: Boundaries on sharing

Sometimes in the swell of excitement over social networking, and in a rush to look tech-savvy, institutions pounce on social media in the belief that their learners (those tech-savvy young-sters) will love them for it. I have a message for them: You are not your users.

I was sitting in a focus group with ten undergraduates who were generously sharing their views on how they'd prefer to connect with the university on the internet. To the surprise of many, when asked if the department should use Facebook, they all simultaneously shifted awkwardly in their seats. As images of drunken parties and passionate exploits raced through their heads (OK, I'm speculating there), they indicated that they wouldn't like the idea of their teachers "seeing the things that get put up on Facebook." They pre-ferred the official refuge of an LMS forum for their questions to be answered.

Interestingly, they were already using Facebook to learn from one another, but those groups were spontaneously created by new students each year as they sought to con-nect to their cohort of classmates.

Their concern about oversharing is understandable. After all, there have been stories of people being dumped, fired, sued, and even arrested for information they put on Facebook. Different communities, and different technology affordances, can serve very different purposes. Thus, it's important to consider how multiple memberships interact (and stay separate), and how learners can control what they share.

save your learner time and avoid empty profile syndrome. Elements of identity can also exist beyond a profile or description page. One approach is to allow learners to highlight their best work in a portfolio or by pinning it to their wall.

Another good reason to require some form of digital identity is to encourage participation. In their research, Selma Vonderwell and Sajit Zachariah found that learners feel more obligated to participate when they can see one another.

Encouraging the addition of personal information to profiles can increase a sense of conviviality and lead to serendipitous connections. However, just what is shared will depend on whether your learners are safe within a company's fire-wall or exposed to the universe, as well as on what's appropriate for the context and audience. Different groups of professionals will have different values and ideas about what should or shouldn't be shared in their context. In the midst of one profiles project, I watched a manager scoff openly because an employee had included the names of his pets in his public bio. To the manager, this personal touch smacked of unprofessionalism. Furthermore, sometimes what is considered appropriate depends on the technology being used (see sidebar). At any rate, learners should have control over what they make public about themselves.

>> INCLUDE USER IMAGES

Since the exchange of textual information—a medium with low social presence—is still the dominant mode of communication in virtual communities, it's important for community developers to support community members with relevant graphical, textual, and video interfaces, such as avatars, graphic images, and video chat.

—JOON KOH, et al., *Encouraging Participation in Virtual Communities*

In the virtual world, people can be present but invisible, and without the appropriate presence cues we lose some of the benefits of social learning. This is where photos or avatars can be helpful.

Ensure that users have the option to upload profile images and thumbnails on other screens, such as forum posts. It may sound basic, but the LMS configuration at my organization doesn't have such an option, and this makes it significantly more difficult for learners to remember names and get to know one another, even when they also meet face to face.

Michael Allen advises designers to make photos part of the interaction:

Inclusion of photos of people humanizes the learning space. If part of a process is performed by someone, submitted to someone, or created for someone's benefit, let's interact with faces. Ask learners to move teams together, drag a photo of a person into position to perform a task, and otherwise work with "people" rather than just letting photos of people adorn the screen (which is better than not having photos at all).

Newer learning systems based on social media models, such as Pearson's Open-Class or Edmodo, place photos and profiles more center stage. But for reasons of personal privacy and preference, users should always have control over whether or not their photos are published, and ideally, they should be able to select the images themselves. That way a learner can opt to upload a photo of her dog or favorite character if she wants to balance anonymity with a sense of identity.

>> SUPPORT SOCIAL AWARENESS WITH VISUALIZATION

Much goes unseen and unsaid in a virtual environment. Without the benefit of nods, smiles, and gestures, we have to do a lot of guesswork about what others are thinking and feeling. This is where interface design decisions can help.

You can bring out social concepts that might otherwise be missed online by representing them graphically. Emoticons can signal simple emotions, badges can show levels of expertise, and icons or lists can communicate copresence (who's online).

You can visualize group activity, such as varying levels of participation or popular conversation topics, using a word cloud. Font size in the cloud can be based on quantity, quality, or popularity of postings, as determined by ratings, shares, or responses.

You can also utilize a system that visualizes team dynamics. For example, Glosser (www.glosserproject.org) shows which learners were responsible for each part of a collaboratively written document on sentence rollover. This can help learners see if one writer dominates or another hasn't contributed at all.

But be mindful of the message that your cues are sending to learners. Visualizing quantity suggests that quantity is valued and could lead to a slew of poor-quality posts. Likewise, popularity cues could lead to groupthink. Ideally, you can work iteratively, adjusting the design to meet the unique dynamics of each community.

Another consideration is how the visuals are applied. Implicit tools are those that generate interface elements automatically based on user data. Explicit tools give learners the opportunity to label themselves, others, interactions, or artifacts in a particular way.

Of course, you may not want to slap automatic smiley faces all over a site for corporate execs. As always, the appropriate combination and style of cues like emoticons, icons, badges, and visualizations will depend on the audience, their familiarity with similar systems, and the style of the group.

>> SHOW THE NETWORK AND ITS CONNECTIONS

Group identity and social presence can both be supported by graphical representations of a community and its connections. Of course, this is easier said than done and difficulty in doing this increases with the size of the group. For example, you might create an online marauder's map (like the magic one in

FIGURE 6.2 Students in an MIT-based MOOC located themselves on the world map. Only a small segment of the participants are pictured, as the total overflowed onto ten map pages.

Harry Potter) that shows the presence and location for a small group of users, or more realistically, a geomapping widget that shows each community member as a pin on the world map.

Of course, things get trickier once your community hits the hundreds or thousands. But it's been done. The more than 10,000 students in a MOOC offered by the MIT Media Lab located themselves on a shared Google map, which made it significantly easier for them to connect regionally while supporting a coherent sense of a diverse community (**FIGURE 6.2**).

A group at IBM Research used data on 73 million relationships among 450,000 people to create a visual analytic tool that supports expertise location, team building, team coordination, and workplace relationships (http://www.watson. ibm.com/cambridge/tr_abstract/11-13.shtml for the whole story).

Naturally, this is as much (or more) a programming job as it is a design job, but don't underestimate the design challenge of creating a graphic representation of 73 million relationships (see Chapter 5, "Learning Is Visual").

Another example is TouchGraph, a Facebook app that creates a map of the user's network and organizes it by categories (**FIGURE 6.3**). Graphics like these can include thumbnail pictures or collective symbols of members in selected

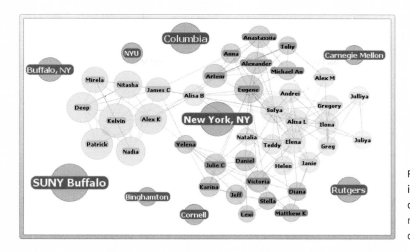

FIGURE 6.3 TouchGraph is a Facebook app that creates a map of the user's network and organizes it by categories.

categories (country, discipline, interest, and so on). They might initially present a summary, but allow zooming in or hotspots that reveal deeper information.

Letting users view others (and themselves in relation to others) in one map can reveal commonalities and diversity and support serendipitous interaction and trust. It can also give learners the sense of being all together in one place at one time for the same reason—something that's easy to miss in online learning but is so important to community.

>> CONSIDER VIRTUAL AGENTS FOR DELIVERING INSTRUCTIONAL CONTENT

As mentioned above, we're hardwired to pay more attention when we're interacting directly with people. This is probably why virtual coaches, tutors, characters, and avatars have been shown to help people learn. Keep in mind that, to support learning, agents should be used for instruction and not simply entertainment. Agents can be good for providing hints, explanations, and demonstrations, but should be used sparingly so as not to become irritating.

In one study by Courtney Darves and Sharon Oviatt, early elementary students spontaneously asked 100–300 questions in a one-hour solitary session as they talked to digital fish that taught them about marine biology.

Pedagogical agents can take many forms, from video hosts walking from screen to screen, to off-screen narration guiding the user through a lesson (refer to the intelligent tutor example in Chapter 3, "A View of the eLearning Landscape"). Interestingly, realistic characters are not more effective than cartoon characters and, in fact, an agent does not even need to be visible, as long as a voice can be heard.

If the agent's voice is audio (rather than text), it should be a human voice rather than a machine voice for best results. So don't blow the budget on a 3-D, animated avatar with a robot voice. A simple illustration with a human voice (visible or not) is enough for learning gains. You can take this further and ensure that the voice is extroverted for best results. Another study by Darves and Oviatt compared voice style in instructional tutors, finding that "children asked 16% more science questions when conversing with animated characters embodying an extrovert voice that resembled the speech of a master teacher (higher volume and pitch, wider pitch range), rather than an introvert voice."

As a final note, while an agent needn't have a realistic human appearance, it should have realistic human behaviors, such as human-like eye-gaze and gesturing. (Note how many characters in animations and games continue to blink even while idle.)

Strategies for encouraging participation

The strength of the online element is that the learning community can be widely distributed … . However … just setting up a social networking site does not mean that you have a community. In fact, the challenging issues are not the technical issues, they are the cultural issues of getting the community going.

—CHRIS DEDE, *Harvard Graduate School of Education*

>> MAKE USABILITY A PRIORITY

Inadequate system responsiveness, lack of reliability, and difficulty of use have been repeatedly blamed for poor participation within learning communities. This is sometimes a result of their experimental origins. Many educational technologies are developed at educational institutions as academic or research projects without design funding or multidisciplinary teams.

This brings me to a flashback sequence. The technology has been deployed and users are throwing themselves off balconies because it's so unpleasant to use.

I'm approached in the hall by a well-intentioned engineer, who looks at me doe-eyed and says, "They hate it. Can you work your magic?" He hands me the virtual equivalent of a motherboard, and I'm stuck trying to package it into a decent experience (with no budget left for changing the interaction design). Sigh—all in a day's work.

The bottom line is this: If you want users to collaborate, start with usability, don't just end with it.

›› SHAPE THE PATH TO ENTRY

Sometimes the hardest part of establishing community is getting people started. Interface design can play an important role in shaping the path to participation for new users. (We'll look at this in more detail in Chapter 9, "Learning Is Mobile.") We can also call on BJ Fogg's work on persuasive technologies and choice architecture here. Start by breaking the larger activity of getting started in a community into baby steps. Research has shown that people are much more likely to follow through with an action if they're helped through the first step.

Edmodo is a great example (**FIGURE 6.4**). When a teacher signs up, she receives a short welcome e-mail that contains a set of simple instructions anchored by a big blue button that says, "Introduce yourself."

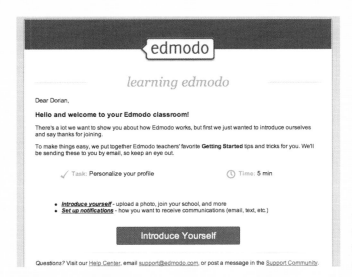

FIGURE 6.4 Edmodo nudges new teachers to get started by enticing them to complete a manageable and delightful task.

This is far more specific than just "Get started" and it appeals to two natural desires: to connect with others and to express one's identity. Edmodo chose a getting started task that sounds reasonably fun and made it only one click away.

But Edmodo has one other nudge up its sleeve. A colleague of mine who does professional development for various groups like doctors and teachers shared an insight into what makes these professionals unique. Typically, time-poor experts want to pick and choose content from an upskill course to suit their needs. As such, designers often create an open, nonlinear navigation menu to accommodate this. Sometimes they may use design cues to gently suggest an optional chronological order. This worked well for her team, until they got to teachers.

While general practitioners and surgeons completed only the modules that suited them, teachers worked diligently through each and every module in the order suggested, returning the feedback that there was far too much to do in the course. Teachers practice what they preach and respect assigned tasks. Clearly, Edmodo knew its audience when it stimulated initial participation by assigning a task, and pointing out that it would only take 5 minutes!

>> LEVERAGE SOCIAL INFLUENCE

People are influenced by others' opinions and behaviors, especially when they're uncertain themselves. Knowing this, you can design testimonials, ratings, and reviews to influence behavior. If you want to encourage users who are wavering to participate or contribute, present evidence that others are doing it and getting value from it.

For example, new users in a virtual community are more eager to share information if they find out their friends are already in the network and collaborating. Ratings and reviews are more influential when learners know more about the person behind them, so rich profiles linked to social validation features can make them more effective.

But the desire for social validation can also go wrong—when it funnels learners into a state of groupthink.

>> DESIGN TO PREVENT GROUPTHINK

We can make better decisions together, but we can also make poorer decisions together. Groupthink occurs when members of a group don't express new ideas, opposing arguments, or opinions because of the social pressures within the group.

Symptoms of groupthink include rationalization, peer pressure, complacency, moral high ground, stereotyping, censorship, and the illusion of unanimity.

The problem with groupthink is essentially a lack of alternatives or views being presented, which can hinder learning in classroom scenarios or have devastating consequences for high-stakes decision making. To help prevent groupthink, interface designers can include elements that encourage the antidotes:

- Give people a way to write down and share ideas ahead of time before a synchronous meeting.
- Include tools for brainstorming that reward quantity of ideas over quality.
- Include tools for friendly debate.
- Consider visualizing group participation to reveal overly dominant personalities or members on the periphery.
- Allow learners to rate how confident they are in their decisions before they show those decisions to others.
- Let users vote or comment anonymously.
- In more structured educational environments, include facilities for listing pros and cons or other ideas, or for taking on distinct roles such as devil's advocate.

You can find more excellent information, including a list of tools and techniques for avoiding groupthink, at www.mindtools.com/pages/article/newLDR_82.htm.

>> DESIGN TO SUPPORT SCAFFOLDING

In an educational context, social interaction often requires educational guidance to support interactions that are most productive for learning. This is especially true when learners are trying new ways of interacting or when the interaction required is more sophisticated than just a chat or comment-based discussion.

For example, knowledge-building tools like Compendium, Cohere, and Knowledge Forum provide environments for people to collaboratively create, organize, and interrogate ideas. Cohere scaffolds idea sharing with type labels (such as idea, tool, prediction, or argument) and by automatically visualizing relationships between different ideas (**FIGURE 6.5**). Knowledge Forum allows certain users (like teachers) to create their own scaffolds to guide collaboration.

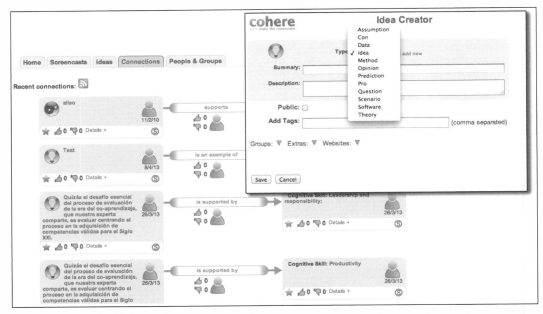

FIGURE 6.5 Cohere is a tool for sharing ideas and visualizing relationships between them.

Allowing instructors (or learners) to easily assign roles for particular events can also provide pedagogical support. Vonderwell found that "students who were assigned specific roles maintained online presence throughout the discussions and participated more frequently than the rest of their group members."

The writing support tool Glosser (www.glosserproject.org) scaffolds the review of written documents, either your own or someone else's. The "gloss" provided by the tool includes alternative views of the text that highlight structure, argument, and topics covered.

>> DESIGN FOR PERSISTENCE

One of the dramatic differences between interaction online and off is that everything online can be recorded, archived, reviewed, and analyzed after the fact. This can be a huge benefit to learners. For example, participants who have trouble keeping up with a live session can replay it later. Students can review sessions to study for exams, or as they're developing an essay or project.

Kylie Peppler and Maria Solomou suggest that archiving is also important for creativity and innovation in a virtual community. They explain that in order to maintain a constant path of innovation, past artifacts (virtual creations, recorded interactions, and ideas) must be kept so they can be built on.

Of course, just storing things is never enough. They must also be findable. Allowing learners to tag (creating a "folksonomy"), organize, and search effectively ensures that the persistence is added value.

>> BALANCE THE POLARITIES OF SOCIAL LEARNING

In their book *Digital Habitats*, Etienne Wenger, Nancy White, and John D. Smith describe three fundamental challenges faced by communities trying to learn together. They describe these challenges as polarities. For interface designers, the challenge is to ensure that the interface supports both sides of each polarity.

- **Togetherness–Separation.** Groups need to experience togetherness through what they share in common, but a group's diversity is also valuable to learners. An interface design can help promote a feeling of togetherness by making similarities, actions, identities, and online status visible. It can also help members express and benefit from uniqueness by making diverse contexts, expertise, experience, and self-expression visible.

- **Participation–Reification.** Communities need to engage in flexible dynamic interactions, but they also need to be able to take what matters from that interaction and reify it—create, modify, and store it as something concrete. An interface design can help learners cycle between interaction and artifact creation by integrating features for both, for example, by attaching chat spaces to artifacts or media-creation tools to discussions.

- **Individual–Group**. Interfaces can help learners individualize their experience by letting them filter information to their needs. Zite, FlipBook, and Pinterest do this in various ways, by allowing users to subscribe selectively, using personal information to guide content delivery, letting the user curate what she finds or rate content in order to train the system to filter for her. These kinds of tools also help manage the growing reality of multi-membership. These days, learners are part of many communities simultaneously, so consider how you might leverage, or at least account for, these multi-memberships. For example, many services offer to post automatically to other accounts or to integrate information already stored elsewhere. This individualization helps learners connect to the group more effectively by consolidating that which binds them to others.

>> DESIGN FOR ALL MEMBER TYPES

Whether or not people use your tool isn't only about usability, it's also about suitability. How well does it meet their needs? It may be easy to use but have nothing to do with their goals, which makes user research critical. Knowing what types of members are usually found in communities is a good place to start. Here are some of the most common member types found in online learning communities (think about these when you're developing personas):

- **New member.** A new member is curious. She needs to feel welcome and safe. She must be encouraged to explore. An interface might help her automatically see others with similar interests, existing themes, or discussions that she might be interested in, or discover how she is unique in the group.

- **Passive member.** A passive member observes, but doesn't contribute much. In a MOOC, a passive learner might log in once or twice to watch the seminar videos or browse discussion. (Note: I deliberately avoid the term lurker. These aren't shady characters hiding in dark corners. They are learning by observing, which may be precisely what meets their needs.)

- **Active member.** An active member participates in discussion, creates, shares artifacts, and regularly checks in with the group. An interface will make these activities easy and enjoyable, helping her to visualize her contributions to the group. In a formal class, instructors will aim for all learners to be active.

- **Leader.** A leader is an active member who proactively seeks to build the community. An interface might help her create subgroups, recruit participants, answer questions, or moderate discussions.

- **Elder.** An elder is veteran member of the community. She knows it inside and out because she's been around for a while. An interface might support her in helping or mentoring others by creating videos, answering questions, or welcoming new members.

Social media for learning

Daniel Burn, an EdTech development manager and researcher of social media for learning, offers interface designers some key things to consider when designing social media in an educational context:

Support impetus, remove barriers. "Usage is related to impetus and barriers: The impetus is the 'How much do I need to use this?' and teachers often solve this by making the social learning interactions compulsory. The barriers are related to how hard the system is to get at, and how hard it is to use."

Send the right message. "You have to be careful how you frame your social media tools—students will ask 'Why should I use this, rather than Facebook?' and 'Why should I behave differently in here as compared to Facebook?' It needs to be very clear that this is a different kind of space, where different behavior is expected. Design cues are crucial in creating this."

Integrate social media into the larger educational context. "Social media often works in a kind of vacuum—Facebook, for example, operates mostly purely as interactions between people. An important question is: How does your social media system connect into the curriculum, the learning outcomes, and materials related to the course?"

Consider the symphony of communications. "Think carefully about the different forms of conversation that can happen in the social space, and how they interact. A forum is reasonably simple, in that there are posts and replies; but social media can have multiple communication mechanisms: status posts, posts that attach to other people, posts that attach to learning/curriculum objects, likes, ratings, view histories, back channels, and so on.

"Not all social media have all these tools, but most have more than one. When designing, think about how these interact: Does one conversation mode undermine others? Does one make others redundant and less likely to be used? Are some considered more or less pedagogically valuable, and if so, does the system shepherd users toward the more desirable communication modes?"

Strategies for nurturing conviviality and community

Community can be a value in itself; a joining together that offers the benefits of belonging, commitment, mutuality, and trust. These are environments where people are free to learn.

—TONY BINGHAM AND MARCIA CONNER, *The New Social Learning*

>> DESIGN FOR SPECIFIC COMMUNITY NEEDS

If you're involved in the design of a social learning environment, your brief could cover a feature, a tool, or a platform; you might even be assembling and configuring existing tools into a kind of community habitat. Here are some of the questions to add to your analysis phase, based on the level at which you're designing (adapted from *Digital Habitats*):

- **Feature.** Does the design support the specific ways in which a community conducts its activities? Does a feature add or reduce complexity? Can a feature be turned on or off? Does a feature inherently appeal to beginners or to more experienced users? What members' skill levels make a feature valuable?

- **Tool.** What range of activities does the community engage in? Which of these activities need to be well-supported by tools? Are there features that help make content portable across tools? Can members import content from other tools into the community?

- **Platform.** How well does the platform combine the tools that a community needs? Does the navigation help in using each component tool? Can tools be turned on or off at will? Does it support multiple communities at once? If so, what are the limits and how easy would it be to launch a new community? Can users easily form subcommunities?

- **Habitat.** How compatible is a given platform or tool with others that the community or its members use? Can members use just one sign-on to access various tools? How does the look and feel vary across the different tools? Do all the different tools appear to be located together, even if they're hosted across a series of servers and services? How does the navigation work between tools? Can the user tell where she is when using any given tool and find her way back home to other tools?

Creating a digital habitat

At the Centre for Research on Computer-Supported Learning and Cognition (we call it CoCo for short), where I work with a dedicated team (some call us CoConuts), we were funded to build a studio for educational design. The new studio would be a combination of physical and virtual space in which designers of all types could work collaboratively while their interactions were recorded for research purposes.

After multiple team trips to Ikea and watching my colleagues teeter on ladders installing hi-tech doodads in the ceiling, the first iteration of the physical space was complete. It was now time to attend to the virtual half.

First off we held an ideation workshop in the space to gather requirements from the team (who would also be users of the virtual space). After we brainstormed, debated, giggled, and prototyped, I took the resulting collection of insights and promised to return with some prototypes for testing.

Prototyping a digital habitat for educational designers. (Image courtesy of Beat A. Schwendimann).

Days later, staring at the prototypes, it dawned on me that, as exciting as it would be to develop a bespoke integrated digital space, the best solution was far simpler: to aggregate cloud-based tools that already existed.

more 》》

>> There were two very good reasons for this. On the one hand, we were faced with a daunting lack of a programmer (who'd never arrived from overseas) and on the other hand, most of the free tools that would serve our habitat were *already* used by everyone on the team. So when I showed up to the meeting, prototypes in tow, I whipped them out to show what an ideal space might look like. Then I showed them how we could magically create something similar with freely available cloud-based tools.

The cloud solution had many advantages. It was free. It required no development time, hosting, or maintenance. And it came with regular automatic updates. It also let us remain linked with a larger community, which meant we weren't being siloed into a walled-up system. Using free, cloud-based tools allowed for permeability without removing our ability to keep things private.

But the services solution had disadvantages too. Relying on fragmented tools could undermine the sense of coherent place that helps nurture a community. Thus, the interface design would have to provide that glue.

Feature creep and obstacles to learnability. Another two nasties I was eager to head off at the pass were feature creep and obstacles to learnability. I've seen so many solutions fail because, let's face it, we're all really busy. If a technology doesn't meet our needs precisely, if it's too hard to use, or if the learning curve is too high, we'll put it off until "later" and the tool will grow cobwebs.

Then there's feature creep. The tech-passionate will want to add cool tools and experiment with new innovations all the time. Most people, however, aren't in it for the technology and too many options threaten learnability. So here again, this would be a temptation to keep at bay. As such, we decided on a minimalist process in which we would start with just three tools and add others based on our needs as they arose. Moreover, any addition would be trialed before we officially integrated it into the digital habitat.

Integration. A lack of interoperability between tools would generally have been another disadvantage of combining separate services, but it was serendipity that we found we could meet our needs with Google's set, which naturally, integrate well together.

Currently, we're combining Google Drive (for storage and collaborative work) and Google Hangouts (for virtual meetings and to visually project our remote friends onto the walls during meetings in the studio). We bridge our work to the outside world with standard tools for blogging and microblogging. It's nothing fancy, but then sometimes the best design decisions aren't. Check back on Twitter to see how it's going (@STLSydney).

>> USE INTERFACE CUES TO ENCOURAGE CONTRIBUTION

One of the major issues around reaping the benefits of social learning has to do with motivation. How do you get people to contribute? What are the conditions for fostering community online?

A study by Hyang-Sook Kim and S. Shyam Sundar that tested interface cues in discussion forums showed that displaying cues for number of posts, views, replies, and ratings of usefulness (and, by inference, similar cues like shares, likes, and reposts) encouraged participation of two types: evaluation of content and contribution of content. They also found that popularity cues (likes, ratings) were more influential than authority cues (expert badge). They offer the following advice to interface designers:

- Consider including at least two cues: the number of posts by a user (which communicates authority in the community) and ratings of helpfulness (which encourages a "bandwagon effect" or "everyone else thinks it's good, so it must be"). Both positively affect member attitudes toward the site and its content.

- Cues conveying the number of times posts are shared are powerful in reinforcing community bonds, thereby enhancing users' contributions to message boards and energizing them to contribute more (**FIGURE 6.6**).

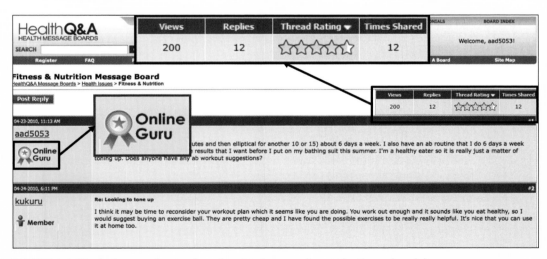

FIGURE 6.6 Displaying cues for number of posts, views, replies, and ratings of usefulness can encourage participation. This online message board has interface cues conveying authority (or expertise) and the level of community interest in the message thread. (Courtesy of Hyang-Sook Kim and S. Shyam Sundar).

>> DESIGN TO PREVENT TROLLING

Anonymity increases trolling and conflict behavior since users feel safe from social repercussions. Including some form of identity, even a representative one such as an avatar, will reduce these unwanted behaviors. (This is all the more reason to design for rich learner profiles within learning communities.) Likewise, the presence of a moderator in a group reduces the number of negative interactions.

>> DESIGN FOR MATCHMAKING

The value of a network lies in its connections. People who have more connections do better at work, are better at learning, and make better decisions. For this reason, most social media present users with automatic suggestions of people with whom they might connect or subgroups they might want to join. Matchmaking occurs around artifacts as well as people at places like Goodreads (whose slogan is "Meet your next favorite book") or at Amazon.com, where viewing one product leads you to "similar items" in three different ways: automatic suggestions, user-created lists, and social influence ("People who bought this also bought…").

At the multinational consulting firm Deloitte, organizational data is combined with user-contributed information about projects, job roles, and interests in order to link people who are otherwise scattered all over the world. Tony Bingham and Marcia Conner tell the story: "New hires can easily find five people who went to the same college they did, three who worked for the same company, and two who grew up in their small town. Whenever someone with a similar history joins the organization, he or she can get an alert with the ability to make these kinds of connections." It's a great way to warm up a crowd.

Go further

The following resources are full of wisdom about design interfaces that foster social interaction, collaborative learning, and communities of practice:

- *The New Social Learning* by Tony Bingham and Marcia Conner offer inspirational examples, including how social media and participatory culture transformed the CIA. Far from being a fluffy trade book, it's loaded with highly informed corporate case studies and practical advice, and it's highly entertaining to boot.

- *Digital Habitats* by Etienne Wenger, Nancy White, and John D. Smith is a practical and insightful guide to understanding and supporting learning communities with technology.

- *Designing Social Interfaces* by Christian Crumlish and Erin Malone is an excellent reference on effective patterns for designing interfaces for social interaction.

- Etienne Wenger and his *Digital Habitats* coauthors created a wiki to describe and list the various tools for supporting communities (www.technologyforcommunities.com/tools).

SOURCES

Allen, Michael W. 2011. *Michael Allen's Online Learning Library: Successful e-Learning Interface: Making Learning Technology Polite, Effective, and Fun.* San Francisco: Pfeiffer.

Bingham, Tony, and Marcia L. Conner. 2010. *The New Social Learning: A Guide to Transforming Organizations through Social Media.* San Francisco: Berrett-Koehler.

Crow, Tracy. 2010. "Learning, No Matter Where You Are: Q&A with Chris Dede." *Journal of Staff Development* 31(1): 10–12.

Darves, Courtney, and Sharon Oviatt. 2005. "Talking to Digital Fish." In *From Brows to Trust: Evaluating Embodied Conversational Agents,* edited by Zsófia Ruttkay and Catherine Pelachaud, 271–92. Springer Netherlands.

Kim, Hyang-Sook, and S. Shyam Sundar. 2011. "Using Interface Cues in Online Health Community Boards to Change Impressions and Encourage User Contribution." In *Proceedings of the SIGCHI Conference on Human Factors in Computing Systems,* 599–608. New York: ACM Press.

Klopfer, Eric. 2008. *Augmented Learning: Research and Design of Mobile Educational Games.* Cambridge, MA: MIT Press.

Koh, Joon, Young-Gul Kim, Brian Butler, and Gee-Woo Bock. 2007. "Encouraging Participation in Virtual Communities." *Communications of the ACM* 50 (2): 68–73.

Peppler, Kylie, and Maria Solomou. 2011. "Building Creativity: Collaborative Learning and Creativity in Social Media Environments." *On the Horizon* 19 (1), 13–23.

Vonderwell, Selma, and Sajit Zachariah. 2005. "Factors That Influence Participation in Online Learning." *Journal of Research on Technology in Education* 38 (2): 213–30.

Wenger, Etienne, Nancy White, and John D. Smith. 2009. *Digital Habitats: Stewarding Technology for Communities.* Portland, OR: CPsquare.

7

Learning Is Emotional

Why emotion is critical to learning and how design can influence it

≪ The Backstory

Emotion in design for learning

Let's bust a myth here and now: Learning is not strictly a cognitive process. To see through this centuries-old misconception, we need to dip into the colorful wilderness of emotions and decision making.

In *Looking for Spinoza, Joy, Sorrow, and the Feeling Brain*, neuroscientist Antonio Damasio describes patients who, due to brain injury, have retained normal cognitive function, but have lost emotional function. Remarkably, despite being cognitively intelligent, these patients were unable to make basic life decisions like what to eat for dinner.

Studies like these show that emotions are actually critical to decision making. Likewise, whether we're happy, sad, bored, frightened, or frustrated, our emotions will affect our ability to learn, problem solve, and be creative. But how exactly do emotions impact learning and what can designers do about it?

Engagement and motivation

> While we are not advocating gratuitously sweet interfaces, designers must realize that helping to focus and engage learners is part of their responsibility.
>
> —SHERRY HSI AND ELLIOT SOLOWAY, *Learner-Centered Design*

The first (perhaps most obvious) emotional dimension of learning is engagement. Instructors and designers want their learners' attention and they want to keep it; on the one hand because they'll learn better and on the other hand because they'll enjoy the experience more. Strategies for directing visual attention, providing relevance, stimulating curiosity, and providing the right level of challenge all play a part. But motivation is also central to engagement.

BORN MOTIVATED

No one has to bribe babies to get them to practice walking until they've mastered the art. The motivation to learn is wired into human nature for evolutionary reasons. But clearly we don't always feel motivated to learn everything all the time. Motivation is a mammoth topic in academia, business, and popular culture. How can learners be motivated to dig deeper, employees to work harder, or children to clean up their rooms?

B. F. Skinner would recommend punishment and rewards (see Chapter 2, "How We Learn," for more on operant conditioning). But contemporary psychologists and educators like Edward Deci, Alfie Kohn, and Daniel H. Pink have written whole books dedicated to revealing how problematic this approach can be. Deci's wise advice is this: "Ask not how we can motivate people. Ask how we can create the conditions for people to motivate themselves." This brings us to the two sides of the motivation coin: extrinsic and intrinsic motivation.

EXTRINSIC AND INTRINSIC MOTIVATION

> The most basic distinction is between intrinsic motivation, which refers to doing something because it is inherently interesting or enjoyable, and extrinsic motivation, which refers to doing something because it leads to a separable outcome.
>
> —EDWARD DECI AND RICHARD RYAN, *Intrinsic and Extrinsic Motivations*

Deci and Ryan explain that intrinsic and extrinsic motivation should not be pitted against each other. According to what they call *self-determination theory,* the key drivers of motivation are autonomy, competence, and connectedness. Similarly, in his best-selling book *Drive,* Pink describes the core drivers as autonomy, mastery, and purpose.

Autonomy, common to both theories, stands out as a key to separating helpful types of motivation from unhelpful ones. For example, intrinsic motivation is by nature autonomous and is generally considered the ideal form of motivation for learning. It is associated with positive learning outcomes, a feeling of competence, persistence, and creativity.

In reality, learners can't always be intrinsically driven to do what they need to do. That's where extrinsic motivation comes in.

THE POWER OF EXTRINSIC MOTIVATION

According to Deci and Ryan, some forms of extrinsic motivation, like the intrinsic variety, are also highly autonomous, and therefore valuable to life and learning. For example, a student who's memorizing a list of pharmaceutical ingredients because she really wants to graduate and become a doctor isn't doing it because the memorization itself is fun (that would be intrinsic motivation), but because it's linked to her self-determined career goals (she's acting with autonomy).

A volunteer who devotes time to packing birthing kits for midwives in developing countries isn't doing it because assembling boxes is a blast, but because he's motivated by a compassionate desire to help others. The motivation is extrinsic to the task, but highly self-determined and as such, very rewarding. Pink would describe these examples as being driven by purpose.

On social media, influences such as reciprocity, gratitude, and status, as well as positive self-image, ambition, and career goals, are common self-determined extrinsic motivators.

Autonomy is so influential to motivation that even mundane tasks like sorting items can be made more interesting if people are simply allowed to do it in their own way.

Many studies have shown that autonomous extrinsic motivation is associated with greater engagement, better performance, lower dropout rates, higher-quality learning, and even greater psychological well-being.

THE LIMITS OF EXTRINSIC MOTIVATION

So what are the extrinsic motivators that get all the bad press? In short, they're the ones that remove the learner's sense of autonomy. Nuns with rulers, threats of detention, intense competitive pressure, or contingent rewards (like money or virtual currencies if used as a primary motivator) are all unrelated to learning goals and can leave the learner driven by external forces. These have been shown to have limited or even destructive effects on motivation.

Kohn suggests that the use of some extrinsic motivators can even sabotage intrinsic motivation. In *Punished by Rewards*, he presents research that shows the long-term downside of a rewards-based motivational culture. He explains that rewards motivate people to get rewards; this in turn, trains them to *need* rewards in order to be motivated, degrading intrinsic motivation over time.

Likewise, studies comparing children who are asked to draw for fun with those who are asked to draw for a reward have shown that the children who are given rewards actually draw *less*. Although they are equally motivated to draw at the beginning (because it's fun!), once an extrinsic reward is introduced, their evaluation of the activity literally changes from "fun" to something worth doing only for pay. Paying someone to do something makes it work; it suggests that it's a burden. In cases like these, the extrinsic reward is not only ineffective, it's actually destructive.

In a learning game, if the learning goal is to add numbers, but the game goal is to collect tokens, the learner will focus on winning tokens. Learners are more likely to try to cheat the system when they're in it only for extrinsic rewards. On the other hand, a game that provides feedback that reflects the learner's growing mastery of real-world skills related to adding numbers, such as managing and spending money, intrinsically motivates those skills.

Pink warns against contingent or "if-then" rewards: If you perform, *then* you get paid, or *if* you do your homework, *then* you get cake. He shows how contingent rewards lead to very short-term motivation, a higher likelihood of unethical or risky behavior (cheating), and poorer performance. Therefore, he recommends that extrinsic rewards be given only after the fact as a *bonus*, not as a carrot.

For example, many skill and practice games for kids require them to select correct numbers or letters from a list to earn rewards. I watched my 4-year-old develop a powerful strategy for one of these: Instead of trying to think about what letter would complete the word, she would just try them all as fast as she could, which guaranteed her another banana for the monkey. We might say she was "gaming the system," but really she'd just found the most efficient path to reaching the goal of the game (feed the monkey). The learning goal was something entirely different.

In this case, the bananas were a contingent reward. If she got the correct letter, she earned a banana. The reward was tightly linked to the action in a predictable way (one banana for each correct guess).

In contrast, in the popular Reading Eggs program, kids of the same age are rewarded with golden eggs, but the approach is much more effective. In the preschool portion of Reading Eggs, the number of eggs given for an activity is unclear, and rewards come only at the end of a series of activities—thus, they're not tightly linked to task performance itself. In this way, the eggs are more of a bonus and also become a method for showing progress toward mastery in a way that kids can understand. By collecting eggs and moving along a game board path, even very young children can see that they're making progress, increasing their competence, and gaining mastery. The eggs are also like praise that provides positive reinforcement as feedback on progress. (See the sidebar for more details.)

UNLEASHING INTRINSIC MOTIVATION

There are two types of intrinsic motivation that designers of learning interfaces can focus on:

- Motivation intrinsic to a task
- Motivation intrinsic to being human

The motivation to pack birthing kits is driven by a higher purpose and a desire to connect with others. When a learning task itself is not motivating, ask yourself how you can tap into those motivators that are naturally wired into the human system: autonomy, mastery, competence, connectedness, and purpose.

Learning to read with Reading Eggs

Reading Eggs, one of the most widely used online programs for school-age children, employs various approaches to design for motivation.

Intrinsic motivation. Reading Eggs includes many references to the kinds of characters and narratives that make reading inherently fun for kids. A virtual library gives learners access to dozens of eBooks in the most popular kid genres like fantasy, sci-fi, and nonfiction. Virtual trading cards that kids can collect and swap link back to these themes as well.

Extrinsic rewards as progress feedback (preschool learners). Reading Eggs combines virtual rewards in a way that reflects kids' developing mastery of the content. In the preschool category, children receive golden eggs upon completion of a multi-activity lesson, which reflects their progress in a concrete way. ("Look, Dad, I have 220 eggs!") To make this work well, it is important that:

- There's no set number of eggs that learners must attain. Requiring a certain number would put too much focus on egg collecting.
- Eggs are given at the end of a multitask lesson and not tightly contingent on specific tasks. They're more of a bonus than a carrot, as Pink describes.
- Kids don't know how many eggs they'll get for a lesson, making them less likely to focus on counting and strategizing about them.
- Eggs are visually treated as secondary. They're added to a small collection spot on the side of the screen rather than put forward as goals in and of themselves.

These design decisions mean that learners are unlikely to make egg collecting their driving goal. Instead, the eggs reflect their advancement through the program—their competence as readers, and their growing mastery of literacy concepts. This allows even very young children to see graspable evidence of otherwise abstract progress. "Look, you can better recognize one more vowel sound now!" may be a bit esoteric for a 4-year-old. A simple visual symbol like a golden egg transforms that progress into something he can be proud of.

Bonus visual rewards. Surprise songs and animations are sprinkled unpredictably throughout lessons. These delighters provide moments of positive reinforcement and general glee.

By collecting eggs and moving along the game board path, even very young children can see their progress, increasing their sense of competence and helping them gain mastery.

Extrinsic rewards as feedback on mastery (school-age learners). Virtual rewards get far more sophisticated in Reading Eggspress, the program for school-age learners. While the preschool program consists of a series of linear lessons, Reading Eggspress provides more choices to suit a variety of interests.

Some activities are designed as mini-games in which children can compete against others or receive virtual trading cards and golden eggs as rewards for participating. (The trading cards also encourage "side-effect" learning on topics like geography, biology, and mythology.) Eggs act as currency for buying objects so children can customize their avatars or their virtual apartments. Sounding dangerously extrinsic? Perhaps, but here again, some small design decisions make a big difference.

First of all, the number of eggs awarded is tied to the difficulty of the book. Also, children can't just skim a book to get eggs. Eggs are rewarded only after learners pass a challenging comprehension test.

more ❯❯

>> Certainly it would be interesting to see objective data about the success of various parts of the program with different learner groups. While I've not been able to nail down publicly available research data, there's no shortage of teacher evaluations and parental reviews, which are overwhelmingly positive. I believe the design details are critical to balancing the benefits of rewards while staying clear of the pitfalls. Future work in this area will no doubt help designers to identify what works best.

The Reading Eggspress world includes activities in many literacy areas as well as multiple systems of reward and positive reinforcement. This multifaceted immersion is probably part of the reason that kids continue to explore rather than focus on collecting one particular reward type.

The Reading Eggspress library is home to hundreds of eBooks in all of the most popular kids' genres from fantasy and adventure to animals, art, and comedy. This selection supports intrinsic motivation (curiosity and storytelling). As a bonus, the library has its own fish tank, forest pixie, and black hole, each in its appropriate section.

Virtual trading cards provide side-effect learning about topics in history, biology, and literature.

My second-grader celebrates when he uses his eggs to buy a dragon for his apartment, and more importantly, he loves reading the books in the program and puts considerable effort into re-reading them in order to pass the comprehension quizzes. He once exclaimed halfway through a real-world paperback, "Too bad I don't get reading eggs for real books, otherwise I would have heaps!" He was reading a real book for the love of it, and the eggs were a way to measure his own effort and competence (it was a hard book, so worth "heaps" of eggs). This symbolic measure for him was not bound to the virtual world.

Social presence. Reading Eggspress is full of social cues. Characters walk around the stadium and move through the caves with the learners. Children can choose to compete with others online at any time. This is reinforced in the real world when children go to class and share their progress with friends. Learners never feel that they're engaged in a solitary activity.

Rewards for effort. At the Eggspress stadium, children can choose to compete and even if they don't win, their efforts are celebrated: "Congratulations! You came second!" says the results screen, and the learner is presented with stats (feedback on progress), including any words he got wrong, and the opportunity to practice these for better results in future.

Motivation intrinsic to a learning activity is too often neglected in the design of digital learning experiences, but I believe that UX designers are just the right people to tackle it. Why? Because it takes empathy, ideation, and a knack for storytelling. Rather than relying on extrinsic motivators like points, competition, and speed rounds, think about what is inherently motivating about the topic. In the case of reading and writing, there are many answers: storytelling, identification with a character, and self-expression, to name just a few. Kids get wildly excited by Harry Potter, they identify with superheroes, and they use social media to tell the stories of their own lives.

How can you tap into this kind of motivation, which is so much more powerful than badges and scores to help teach lifelong literacy skills? You could place spelling words into stories instead of random lists. You could ask students to write a letter to Hogwarts, rather than just filling out a template. You could design collaborative global story activities so that all children, even lower-ability writers, could be part of something special, thus increasing their sense of competence. You could invite famous writers to contribute.

The point is, while the onus of activity design generally rests with teachers and instructional designers, when you have an opportunity to contribute, challenge your team to go beyond extrinsic motivation, think creatively, ask experts in the topic what they love about it, and tap into the heart of what makes the learning exciting by nature.

The path to motivation is nuanced and must be tread with care. As you'll see in the Strategies section, you can use multimedia to tap into intrinsic motivation when possible, and connect learners with related extrinsic goals and values that support autonomy, mastery, connectedness, and purpose.

REWARD PROCESS, NOT TALENT

Researchers have shown that children who believe that success is due to the effort they put in will succeed more as adults than will children who believe that their competence is due to their innate talent or intelligence. The issue is whether they believe that competence is fixed or something that can be built up. Neuroscience has proven that the brain is highly flexible and has the capacity to change at any age. People whose beliefs align with this reality benefit significantly.

Stanford psychology professor Carol Dweck explains:

Parents must stop praising their children's intelligence. My research has shown that, far from boosting children's self-esteem, it makes them more fragile and can undermine their motivation and learning. Praising children's intelligence puts them in a fixed mindset, makes them afraid of making mistakes, and makes them lose their confidence when something is hard for them. Instead, parents should praise the process—their children's effort, strategy, perseverance, or improvement. Then the children will be willing to take on challenges and will know how to stick with things—even the hard ones.

The brain can continue to develop new skills even in old age. Therefore, as designers of learning experiences for people of all ages, we should ask whether our feedback is leveraging Dweck's advice. Are we inadvertently supporting a "fixed mindset," attributing achievement to innate talent or aligning performance with self-worth? Or do we acknowledge effort, value strategy, and celebrate progress?

Emotion and problem solving

According to Donald Norman, "Positive emotions are critical to learning, curiosity, and creative thought." By using design to support positive emotions in learners, we're creating an environment that better supports their learning. One way to do that is through aesthetics, and in fact this very principle plays a part in usability.

In Chapter 5, "Learning Is Visual," we looked at the aesthetics-usability effect, the gist of which is that attractive things make people feel good, which in turn makes them think more creatively. This is why appealing interfaces are easier to use.

So what's the opposite? Are people less creative when they're feeling anxious or stressed? Yes. In an episode of the TV show *Monk*, the brilliant but highly phobic detective is stuck in an elevator. Rather than using his exceptional problem-solving skills, he stands there pressing the same button over and over again, repeating the words "lobby, lobby, lobby, lobby … ." A woman with him says she doesn't think that's going to work. He responds by saying, "I know" and continuing to press the button. Too much stress can narrow learners' focus so much as to severely limit their thinking (tunnel vision).

A certain amount of stress can be good, as it can focus attention to help learners achieve a goal. For example, in *Emotional Design,* Norman describes the design of a security system in a power plant. When something goes wrong, signals like red lights or alarm sounds are employed because getting and focusing attention quickly is essential.

However, too much stress can focus people's attention so much that they miss even obvious solutions. They're less likely to be open to creative problem solving when they're anxious. We've all been there with our computers, repeatedly pressing the same button and thinking, "Why isn't it working?!"

Similar things happen when people are sad. As with fear and anxiety, when people are sad they want what is familiar, so they opt for low-risk options and take paths they've taken before. They're far more willing to try something new when they're happy.

Researchers in emotion have shown that the mood change prompted by something as simple as a funny versus a sobering video clip is enough to impact behavior. The potential for multimedia to influence mood, and therefore learning, becomes strikingly clear.

These are just some of the reasons designers are acknowledging the role of emotion in digital experiences. In fact, you may have noticed that websites, and software, are developing personalities. We'll look at that more closely in the Strategies section.

Positive emotion and learning

Positive affect arouses curiosity, engages creativity, and makes the brain into an effective learning organism.

—DONALD NORMAN, *Emotional Design*

If positive mood supports problem solving, creativity, curiosity, and learning, how can we create interfaces and multimedia components that start people off in a positive mood? Great usability, quality look and feel, and playful, well-designed interaction can all play a part. Interface can't make up for a poorly designed educational activity, but it can set the stage for an amazing experience.

Affective computing and learning

After years of focus on cognitive processes, researchers are beginning to study emotional processes in learning. Those in the field of affective computing are devising ways to detect emotion in learners and then use this information to create more effective virtual tutors or to better target feedback.

Emotion itself can be thought of as another form of feedback. Like social cues, emotional cues help us understand one another, respond to situations, and solve problems. If computers were better at reading and giving us this kind of feedback, our experience with them would likely be more effective. While computer emotional feedback probably won't look the same as human emotional feedback (hopefully, I mean, we anthropomorphize our objects enough as it is), keep an eye out for more emotionally responsive educational technologies in the near future.

Emotion and memory

Emotion has a powerful influence on memory. Research has shown that information is more likely to be retained if it's emotionally charged. Sometimes an emotional message can reinforce why the material is important. For example, anti-smoking advertisements that star real smokers dying of lung cancer are highly memorable.

Sometimes emotional content can be effective at connecting learners to the human realities behind faceless facts and statistics. Personal stories with closely cropped images of faces can convey meaning, evoke empathy, and improve learning around issues like mental illness, poverty, or harassment in the workplace. As such, designers of infographics often combine statistics with imagery that helps viewers make the emotional connection between the numbers and the phenomena involved.

>> The Strategies
for designing for emotion in learning environments

The strategies in this section are broken down into three subcategories:

- Strategies for inspiring creativity
- Strategies for supporting engagement and flow
- Strategies for sparking motivation

Strategies for inspiring creativity

Inspiring delight, calling on nature, and showing personality are just some of the ways that designers can set a positive mood for learners, which not only improves their experience, but also boosts their ability to be creative.

>> SET A POSITIVE MOOD FOR CREATIVE THINKING

If a learning experience requires open-minded thinking, take extra care not to create stress for your learners. Avoid cues that call them to urgent attention like ticking timers, blinking red lights, people watching, signs of criticism, or threats of failure.

Instead, favor clean, open designs that signal possibility, as well as obvious ways to erase, undo, edit, or experiment safely. Aesthetic cues that trigger positive emotion are those that signal safety, warmth, and food. Incorporate images and experiences that are warm, sweet, bright, soothing, symmetrical, rounded, smooth, or soft. Use images of smiles, faces in baby-face proportion, and food.

In her book *100 Things Every Designer Needs to Know about People*, Susan Weinschenk suggests that if you want to design to support creativity, you must first identify the kind of creativity you want to support. She reports on research done by Arne Dietrich that outlines four types of creativity:

- **Deliberate cognitive creativity** calls for a solid knowledge base in an area and plenty of time to work on the problem at hand. Interfaces can provide access to knowledge, people, and other resources to support this kind of thinking.
- **Deliberate emotional creativity** fuels self-discovery and requires quiet time. A useful tool might automatically quiet distractions like notifications and e-mails.

- **Spontaneous cognitive creativity** allows for truly outside-the-box thinking and requires the learner to remove the problem temporarily from conscious awareness. Just as scientists sometimes make discoveries in their dreams, learners sometimes need to forget about things to allow the mind to make new connections. A tool that provides variety and downtime could help unconscious processing occur.

- **Spontaneous emotional creativity** is the stuff of great artists. Weinschenk points out that it's probably not possible to design for this kind of creativity, but artists do have a penchant for open lofts, so perhaps there's something to be learned by the cathedral effect (see below).

>> SHOW PERSONALITY

As we saw in Chapter 6, "Learning Is Social," engagement is increased by a sense of social presence. When real people are involved in a collaboration, they can be a source of motivation for the learner. However, even when there's nobody around, social presence cues embedded in an interface can reveal the people behind the software (in the same way that writing in first person reveals the author behind the book) and this can be enough to increase learner focus and engagement. That's one of the reasons an interface that conveys a sense of personality can make a learning experience more pleasurable and engaging.

Many websites today have picked up on the benefits of expressing a personality. Take, for example, the following interactions.

- **The friendly interface:** Coursera's dynamic registration screen replies with "Nice to meet you" as you type in your name.

- **The polite interface:** "Pardon the interruption," said Google when it popped up a dialogue box related to my action.

- **The humorous interface:** Flickr, one of the first web services to have a distinctly humorous personality, improves the upload experience with the ghosted words, "Hold on there, tiger."

These sites inject a bit of delight into an otherwise frustrating or tedious experience. In turn, this makes users more forgiving of their software. This kind of feedback is certainly an improvement on the old school alternative: "Operation failed. Error type 3."

In his book *Designing for Emotion*, Aarron Walter suggests creating user personas for the interface itself. He provides a template at www.aarronwalter.com/design-personas.

>> LEVERAGE THE BIOPHILIA EFFECT

Ever get the feeling that an ocean view from the office would have a magical effect on your well-being? Well, you're not wrong. Research shows that views of nature can reduce stress and increase focus and attention. Studies have actually linked the views people have from their bedroom windows to better performance on attention tests. A leafy view (as opposed to a city view) was linked to better performance. This phenomenon is called the biophilia effect and can be explained by the fact that, although we enclose ourselves in concrete jungles and digital spaces, we're still carbon-based life-forms.

Among nature photos we have a particular penchant for savanna-like environments such as pastures and open countryside. Can it be just a coincidence then that Prezi chose a field image for its training intro? (Refer to the Prezi sidebar in Chapter 4, "Basic Principles A–Z.")

Similarly, I think it's largely the biophilia effect that keeps me returning to YogaToday.com. While most exercise videos are shot in a studio, every episode of Yoga Today is filmed in the great outdoors against a stunning backdrop of the Rocky Mountains or open grasslands. Of course, reducing stress and increasing focus and concentration is exactly what you want for yoga, so it's a perfect application of the biophilia effect to the emotional design of the site's instruction (**FIGURE 7.1**).

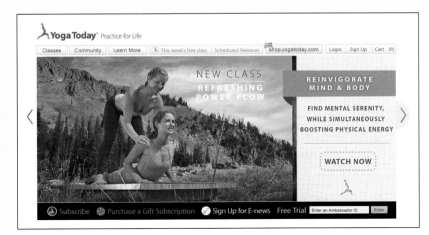

FIGURE 7.1 Classes at Yoga Today are filmed against stunning natural backdrops, which supports a relaxed and focused learning experience.

>> LEVERAGE THE CATHEDRAL EFFECT

Here's another interesting one: Ceiling height can either undermine or support problem-solving performance. This is known as the *cathedral effect*. As explained by William Lidwell, Kritina Holden, and Jill Butler in their book *Universal Principles of Design:*

- High ceilings promote abstract and creative thinking.
- Low ceilings promote concrete and detail-oriented thinking.

I couldn't help but be reminded of the artist's loft versus the programmer's cave. Artists have long favored spacious lofts as ideal settings for abstract, open-ended creative thinking. In contrast, programmers gravitate toward dark, enclosed spaces that help them focus on the minutiae that can make or break their work.

Before you get defensive, of course artists also manage detail and good programmers are also very creative, but it's interesting to note that these different types of professionals have tended to naturally select environments that align with the cathedral effect.

Although the cathedral effect refers to physical spaces, screen designs can also be spacious and open to possibility, or feature-rich and optimized for detailed work.

Take, for example, the prototyping software Mockups created by Balsamiq. Mockups supports the design of undetailed wireframes for testing. It's *not* for designing aesthetics and it's decidedly not for detail. In fact, the interface is deliberately simple, free of distractions, and spacious, and all the shapes and lines look sketchy to mimic low-fidelity paper prototypes (**FIGURE 7.2**).

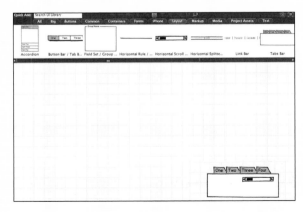

FIGURE 7.2 Mockups, created by Balsamiq, is simple, spacious, distraction-free, and deliberately sketchy to support open-ended, creative thinking.

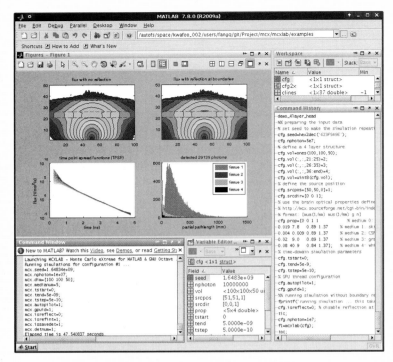

FIGURE 7.3 Matlab puts diverse sources of detailed information and functionality close at hand to create a complex cockpit of focus. (Image by Qianqian Fang, MCX.sourceforge.net.)

Compare that to Matlab (**FIGURE 7.3**). Matlab is software used by programmers, engineers, and mathematicians. In this case users have all the detailed information and functionality they need in a complex cockpit of focus. In a way these interface designs communicate to their users what kind of thinking the program is intended to support.

The question for interface designers is this: Which type of thinking do you need to support in your program, and when and how will your interface design support it?

>> INCLUDE DELIGHTERS

It might sound like a cheap ploy, but research shows that giving treats to your collaborators before a meeting helps make them more creative. As with funny video clips and nature views, it doesn't necessarily take much to tip people's moods in a happier direction.

In his book *Seductive Interaction Design*, Stephen Anderson describes some of the benefits of designing delightful moments of surprise:

From a neuroscience perspective, being surprised releases a cascade of dopamine, a reward chemical. We actually get a brief high from this momentary surprise. Surprise can be a very minor change that adds flavor and variety to an otherwise routine experience … . The term *delighters* comes from the hospitality industry and is used to refer to little things added to an experience that create delight and joy.

The positive emotion that comes from surprises is contingent on their randomness. Examples of delighters on the web include the way Google's logo changes on certain days, unlocking of rewards in video games, or Easter eggs slipped into websites.

MailChimp, which manages e-mail campaigns, delights users with a monkey paw high five when they send or schedule a campaign (**FIGURE 7.4**). The site also provides changing exit goodies. For example, at the time of this writing, when users log out, they are given a link to the next episode in a series of bespoke web comics featuring product mascots Freddie the Monkey and Mannie the Mandrill.

Delighters in the form of creative interaction feedback or surprise rewards can put smiles on learners' faces. Smiles prime learners for creativity, making this a strategy worth keeping in mind. But keep these Easter eggs subtle and few. They shouldn't interrupt the flow of an activity, become overly predictable, or distract from the learning itself.

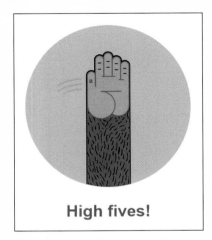

High fives!

FIGURE 7.4 Users of MailChimp get a high five from Freddie the Monkey when they schedule a campaign. This form of visual feedback surprises and delights with humor in a way that's appropriate to the site's target audience.

Strategies for supporting engagement and flow

In the modern world of endless multitasking and distraction, grabbing and keeping a learner's focus is no easy task. The strategies below are sure to help.

>> BEWARE OF PRIMAL ATTENTION GRABBERS

According to Susan Weinschenk, the things that grab people's attention most persuasively are movement, human faces, food, sex, danger, loud noises, and stories. Now, please don't run off and add racy photos to your learning app to get more attention. Things that grab attention in this primal way are more likely to be distracting than to support learning. People are hardwired to stay focused on the face, food, mating opportunities, or danger. If that image is intrinsically related to the learning (you're creating a "learn to cook" app or a visual guide to the *Kama Sutra*), then these attention grabbers make sense, but otherwise, they'll probably just steal attention and add to cognitive load.

Stories, however, are a special category, as they can be tailored for relevance. And while content isn't generally in the purview of interface designers, insofar as pictures tell stories, designers can use them, too. We'll talk more about using stories and narrative later in this chapter.

>> USE SEGMENTING AND VARIETY TO SUSTAIN ATTENTION

Usability experts and psychologists alike remind us of the limited attention span of people on the web. Users are primed to click, move, scan, and act when they're online, so moments in which they have to sit around passively, such as to watch a video, download a file, or read text, are likely to make them antsy.

As mentioned in Chapter 8, "Multimedia and Games," if you're going to include a talking-head video in an online course, customize it for the web and provide access to it in topic-based segments of about 10 minutes or less each. Lynda (www.lynda.com) does an excellent job of chunking courses into mini-tutorials. This not only makes it easier to manage learner attention, it lets learners choose topics relevant to them and review more easily.

Also consider adding an activity, downtime, or new information between segments of passive information to keep learners involved.

My ten years of data as a professor show that giving students a seemingly insurmountable challenge is the best motivator to learn.

—JOHN MAEDA, *The Laws of Simplicity*

If a task is too easy, it gets boring fast. Engagement requires an appropriate level of challenge, so sometimes the trick is to make it a bit harder. In general, activity difficulty rests in the hands of the instructor. However, there are times when adding interface-based challenge can do the trick. Many educational apps for kids use interaction design to add a layer of challenge to skill-practice activities.

Take, for example, the Numbers League app, which embeds arithmetic into a classic superhero narrative. The graphics are slick and the designers have employed humor to add a light touch to the superhero genre. This could have been another gimmicky example of superficial gamification, but instead they include some important design choices that make the app an effective tool for learning.

The learner must assemble superheroes from various head, torso, and leg combinations. Each body segment has its own number, thus different superhero combinations add up to different numbers (**FIGURE 7.5**). One hero may be made up

FIGURE 7.5
Numbers League by Bent Castle Software not only employs slick, high-quality graphics with a delightful touch of humor, but also supports the development of math strategies with its interaction design.

of a 3, a 2, and a 4. The learner has to find the combination that will match the bad guy's number in order to trap him. The great thing about this is that it's not just practice—kids are developing strategy. Dealing with numbers in chunks, like learning to break 5 into 2 and 3, or 10 into 6 and 4, is a skill that supports mental arithmetic and math concepts.

The learner also has autonomy: He gets to choose from a set of bad guys and decide the order in which to trap them. Thus, at any given time, he's strategizing about which bad guy to target with which combination of numbers.

Coming back to the idea of making things harder, you might think adding an extra layer of challenge to an arithmetic app would be counterproductive to helping kids practice math, which is already hard. Instead, the quirky context and strategy involved gives the game the right amount of challenge to make it fun and provides feedback on progress.

Another interesting example comes from the world of serious games. Unmanned is an IndieCade Grand Jury prizewinner that uses branching scenarios to create an eerie and provocative inquiry into the paradoxes and ethical questions surrounding drone warfare.

The heart of the game is mostly dialogue, and because simply clicking through dialogue isn't enough to make a game, Unmanned presents this storytelling in parallel with context-relevant mini-games. The mini-game layer combines with the story layer in a way that adds challenge.

>> MAKE IT EASIER

We've all been there: When a task gets too hard, we get frustrated, discouraged and finally, bored. In other words, we lose the sense of competence and autonomy that are critical to motivation. You can make interactions easier by breaking them into segments, creating scaffolding, making hints available, providing access to resources and examples, and introducing new elements more gradually.

The LetterSchool app described in Chapter 4 generates subtle visual cues, including arrows and guidelines, that appear only when the learner struggles to draw a letter. As soon as the child no longer needs the extra help, these cues disappear entirely. This elegantly makes the activity a bit easier just when it's about to get too hard.

>> APPLY CONSTRAINTS

Adding constraints to a task can obviously increase challenge, but it can also make it easier by lowering the cost of participating. For example, the success of microblogging lies in its constraint (140 characters in the case of Twitter).

It's often the vast openness of a challenge that can be overwhelming for learners. Only a small percentage of people will take on the huge blank page of a blog post. Constraints can give people a place to start and make a daunting task feel manageable.

Many games and learning activities are centered on constraints, like the marshmallow challenge, which tasks teams with constructing a stable structure using only marshmallows, spaghetti, tape, and string in a set amount of time (www.marshmallowchallenge.com). Creativity arises from the team's ability to work effectively within these constraints.

The Twitter example is useful because it's a very simple interface design decision (a character limit placed on an input field) that's had massive consequences. Another upside to this constraint is that people think a lot harder about how they say things when they're limited. Therefore, constraints can increase quality outcomes. Stephen Anderson points to Rypple (recently renamed www.work.com), which uses a 400-hundred-character limit to encourage experts to provide feedback in a community of practice. You can apply the same approach to learning environments to improve the quality of reviews, comments, assignment summaries, and so on.

>> MIX UP THE LEVEL OF CHALLENGE

Increasing and decreasing difficulty can both be employed to help sustain motivation in a learning activity. Michael Allen suggests mixing it up during a session, rather than increasing challenge over time:

Don't continually make challenges harder. Mix in some easier ones for practice and review, including some really easy ones just to remind learners how much progress they've made. Mixing challenge levels increases fun and interest.

Game designers know this well. In *Gamification by Design,* Gabe Zichermann and Christopher Cunningham explain that level difficulty is neither linear nor exponential. Although the overall complexity is always on the rise, the difficulty graph for games dips at intervals. Those moments of easier challenge boost the user's confidence.

No matter how dry you think your information is, using stories will make it understandable, interesting, and memorable.

—SUSAN WEINSCHENK, *100 Things Every Designer Should Know about People*

The love of stories is woven into the fabric of humanity—it's been shaped by thousands of years of storytelling. Stories include characters we identify with and struggles that engage our emotions. They evoke powerful emotional states like surprise, anticipation, empathy, sorrow, and joy. We get involved because we care about the characters, we can relate to the situation, and we want to know what happens. We also, by nature, seek resolution where there is dissonance.

There is much to be learned from theater, film, and other visual forms of story-telling. I originally trained as a director, and have found that the composition and storymaking involved has many overlaps with design.

Peter Goodyear and Lucila Carvalho describe the design of learning environ-ments and resources as "set design." Michael Allen likens eLearning to theater, recommending that it should "begin a story with someone or something at risk" and "put the learner in a position to help."

Allen also suggests letting learners play different parts:

By giving learners various roles to play, they can come to understand alter-native perspectives and more deeply understand dynamics or processes. For example, if you're teaching customer service, let the learners play the role of an unhappy customer. They'll actually gain a deeper sense of why learning effective skills is important.

Indeed, taking part in a story can be a powerful way to develop empathy. In *The New Social Learning,* Tony Bingham and Marcia Conner describe a virtual learning experience in which learners take on avatars of different skin colors to experience diversity in new ways. Peter Yellowlees and James Cook created a virtual reality psychiatry clinic in Second Life, which allowed participants to ex-perience hallucinations common to people with psychosis. Over 600 people who voluntarily toured the clinic reported that it improved their understanding of mental illness and that they would recommend it to a friend (showing that the experience was both effective and rewarding.)

Positive computing: Design for positive emotion and well-being

It's now uncontroversial to say that digital technologies are changing our brains. In *Positive Computing*, a book I coauthored with Rafael Calvo, we look at ways to design technologies to better support factors of well-being and human potential, such as flow, empathy, reflective thinking, mindfulness, and self-esteem. We envision social networks that are designed to foster social intelligence, word processors that sustain flow, and collaborative learning environments that prevent cyberbullying by actively encouraging empathy and self-awareness.

Furthermore, research has shown that increases in well-being lead to increases in academic performance, so progress in the emerging field of positive computing will inevitably complement and inform the design of learning environments. For more information on the field, visit www.positivecomputing.org.

Toontastic is an app that puts story creation in the hands of young learners. Upon starting the app, learners are introduced to the prototypical story arc: setup, conflict, challenge, climax, and resolution. But this isn't just information thrown at them—it's knowledge they can get their hands into, put into use, and deconstruct. The arc itself is presented as a rearrangeable menu.

Furthermore, the Toontastic design doesn't force learners into convention. Learners have an impressive amount of control over story structure and design. For example, a learner could create a story made up only of conflict scenes. In so doing, he might just learn something about why that isn't very compelling (some action movie writers would disagree).

Comic strips, some infographics, and even assembly graphics are other forms of visual narratives. If you're interested in assembly instructions, Colin Ware provides cognitive principles in his book *Visual Thinking for Design.* Cartoons are lovely because they achieve such efficiency, expressing a full range of human emotions in simplified line drawings. This efficiency relies on the human tendency to see patterns, imply form, and personify anything.

So think like a filmmaker, a cartoonist, a novelist, or even an archaeologist— they weave stories out of historical evidence. Use the tricks of other trades to direct attention and sustain engagement.

Strategies for sparking motivation

Interface design helps get learners excited, curious, and motivated to learn. Below are strategies for fostering both intrinsic and effective extrinsic motivation.

>> TAP INTO INTRINSIC MOTIVATION

While many choices relating to motivation will be determined by instructional design, interface design decisions also have a powerful role to play in supporting intrinsic motivation. Graphical metaphor, atmosphere, and emotional imagery can all play a part in igniting a sense of purpose and excitement intrinsic to the content.

Take, for example, two different treatments of a writing program. Designing the environment to look like a racetrack may tick off gamification requirements but tell the learner that speed is the most important thing, which will prime him to think in terms of efficiency and winning. The motivation to compete is not intrinsic to writing. Take the same writing program and design it more along the lines of Hogwarts or Middle Earth and you're putting imagination and creativity center stage while helping learners connect with the love of story and character.

If a fantasy example seems to belie the laws of clarity and simplicity discussed in Chapter 5, remember that graphics can be richer on introductory pages and scaled back for lesson pages. Not only that, font and color choice can link to intrinsic motivation (**FIGURE 7.6**).

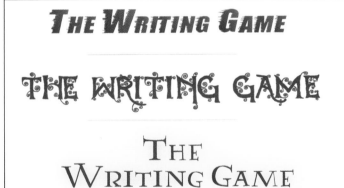

FIGURE 7.6 Font and color choice can affect motivation. Styling a writing game like a race primes learners to value speed, while styling it like a fantasy or adventure story could call on an inherent love of story and character. (The fonts used here are Breezed Caps, Dearest Dorothy, and Lumos, available at fontspace.com.)

>> EMBED LEARNING INTO MEANINGFUL ACTIVITY

Learners will be more motivated to engage in an activity if they can achieve real things as they do it. If users are learning how to use spreadsheets, can they complete a real, job-related task as they do it? In a social learning environment, can learners bring real dilemmas they face at work to the table for collaborative problem solving? Can children create something to express themselves and share with their parents and friends in the process of learning about story structure, a historical time period, an art movement, or a scientific principle?

>> USE MULTIMEDIA TO PROVIDE CONTEXT, SHOW RELEVANCE, AND FUEL CURIOSITY

Daniel Schwartz and Kevin Hartman describe multiple ways in which you can use video to pique learner curiosity, show topic relevance, and contextualize information in ways that make it meaningful—all of which are methods for raising intrinsic motivation. Like video and animation, games can also be used to contextualize learning. (See Chapter 8 for more detail on video and games.)

Teachers naturally play to learners' curiosity ("What do you think will happen if I mix these two chemicals?"), as do magazine headline writers (sometimes shamelessly, with the overuse of words like "shock" and "scandal").

Curiosity is a kind of captivating intellectual tension. It's described as the feeling we have when there's a gap in our knowledge and we want to resolve it. The likelier it is we can access the missing information, the more motivated (curious) we become.

Stephen Anderson suggests that the introduction of controlled uncertainty to a web experience can make interactions more fun and effective. "If I know eight of ten items, I'm more curious about the remaining two than if I only know two of ten … . If you want to make someone curious, make them aware of something they don't know," he explains.

You can use visuals and multimedia to create a mystery, show missing information, create cognitive dissonance, and let the learner interact with information, experiment with solutions, and resolve a mystery.

>> SUPPORT AUTONOMY BY OFFERING CHOICES

As discussed in the first part of this chapter, autonomy is central to motivation and flow states. If learners believe that scores like grades are given at random, and not authentically matched to their performance, they lose interest. Likewise, if the only control a learner has over a learning environment is clicking the Next button, the experience gets old fast.

Ask yourself these questions: Are you giving learners options for how they engage in, proceed through, or solve problems within a learning experience? Could you provide more choices with regard to sequence, customization of elements, topic, approach, or access to resources?

When you're faced with a repetitive task or underwhelming content, take Anderson's advice: "Consider playful ways for users to organize and label information themselves." This approach draws on learners' natural desire to find patterns and make order out of chaos.

Caveats and considerations

As discussed in Chapter 4, it's important to balance choices and avoid overwhelming learners. Strategies for managing many options are discussed in the next few chapters.

>> SUPPORT SELF-EXPRESSION

The modern web is rife with examples of people voluntarily spending time on self-expression and customization. Customizing a profile or avatar is not only fun, it can increase the user's investment in the site. Self-expression is something we enjoy by nature, and it helps humanize relationships on the web.

Here are just a few opportunities for self-expression you can provide for learners:

- Customize the content and aesthetics of homepages and profile pages.
- Customize work interfaces by selecting which tools are included.
- Subscribe, follow, and share content.
- Customize the appearance of avatars in virtual worlds.
- Input personal information on interests, skills, and lifestyle.

>> SHOW AND REWARD PROGRESS

Motivation and engagement can die fast when learners can't tell what they've accomplished or what's ahead of them. Of course, showing progress is a basic tenet of modern web design. The need to see evidence of progress is founded on the desire to have achievements recognized, to get feedback as we approach a goal, and to see that we've mastered new knowledge and skills.

You can also break down evidence of progress on a long-term goal, such as completing a course or getting a degree, into smaller achievements and status upgrades.

Showing progress can also relate to the inherent desire to complete sets. Many sites use the power of progress and set completion to encourage users to add detail to their profiles, including LinkedIn. Users add work experience to LinkedIn largely because they feel instinctively pushed to complete the task and the incomplete progress bar up the top of the page reminds them that they haven't.

As Susan Weinschenk recommends, "Look for ways to help people set goals and track them." She points to Livemocha, a language learning site in which various forms of progress and mastery are built in. "You can see at a glance where you are in the course, where you are in the lesson, and how much progress you have made overall," she explains (**FIGURE 7.7**).

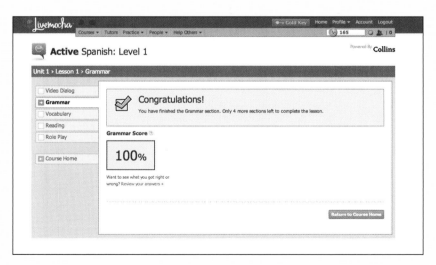

FIGURE 7.7 On Livemocha, a language learning site, users can see at a glance where they are in a lesson and how much progress they've made overall.

How you show progress can make a big difference. After all, you don't want learners to be driven by the impatient desire to "get this thing over with." Consider showing how far the learner has come (what he's learned, what abilities he's attained, how he's improved) rather than simply, how much is left to do. Also, as exemplified in the Reading Eggs case study above, use visual rewards to represent progress. These rewards should value effort and improvement, rather than just wins or innate talent.

>> SUPPORT SOCIAL LEARNING

People will be motivated to use a product just because it allows them to connect with others.

—JEFF JOHNSON, *Designing with the Mind in Mind*

Together with autonomy and competence, connectedness is the third pillar of motivation theory. Remarkably, social interaction is also associated with higher-quality learning and greater psychological well-being. So don't forget to consider the strategies for supporting social interaction and collaborative learning discussed in Chapter 6.

Go further

- In *Emotional Design: Why We Love (or Hate) Everyday Things,* Donald Norman lets emotion out of the bag and into the usability picture.

- *Seductive Interaction Design: Creating Playful, Fun, and Effective User Experiences* by Stephen Anderson covers many aspects of design for motivation and engagement.

- *The New York Times* bestseller *Drive* by Daniel H. Pink and *Why We Do What We Do* by Edward Deci both look more deeply at intrinsic and extrinsic motivation. I also recommend the excellent TED Talks by each of them.

- *Flow: The Psychology of Optimal Experience* by Mihaly Csikszentmihalyi has been a powerful influence on both psychology and design.

- *Positive Computing: Technology for Well-Being and Human Potential* by Rafael Calvo and Dorian Peters (yes, me) includes chapters dedicated to design for positive emotions as well as motivation and engagement, and covers some of the links between well-being and learning technology.

SOURCES

Allen, Michael W. 2011. *Successful e-Learning Interface: Making Learning Technology Polite, Effective, and Fun.* Michael Allen's E-Learning Library. San Francisco: Pfeiffer.

Anderson, Stephen P. 2011. *Seductive Interaction Design: Creating Playful, Fun, and Effective User Experiences.* Berkeley, CA: New Riders.

Bingham, Tony, and Marcia Conner. 2010. *The New Social Learning: A Guide to Transforming Organizations through Social Media.* San Francisco: Berrett-Koehler.

Damasio, Antonio. 2003. *Looking for Spinoza: Joy, Sorrow, and the Feeling Brain.* Orlando: Harcourt.

Goodyear, Peter, and Lucila Carvalho. 2013. "The Analysis of Complex Learning Environments." In *Rethinking Pedagogy for a Digital Age: Designing for 21st Century Learning,* 2nd ed., edited by Helen Beetham and Rhona Sharpe, 49–63. New York: Routledge.

Highlights for Parents. 2008. "Interview with Dr. Carol Dweck—Developing a Growth Mindset."

Hsi, Sherry and Elliot Soloway. 1998. "Learner-Centered Design: Addressing, Finally, the Unique Needs of Learners." In *CHI 98 Conference Summary on Human Factors in Computing Systems.* ACM. http://portal.acm.org/citation.cfm?id=286697.

Kohn, Alfie. 1999. *Punished by Rewards: The Trouble with Gold Stars, Incentive Plans, A's, Praise, and Other Bribes.* Boston: Houghton Mifflin.

Norman, Donald A. 2003. *Emotional Design: Why We Love (or Hate) Everyday Things.* New York: Basic Books.

Ryan, Richard M., and Edward L. Deci. 2000. "Intrinsic and Extrinsic Motivations: Classic Definitions and New Directions." *Contemporary Educational Psychology* 25 (1): 54–67. doi:10.1006/ceps.1999.1020.

Schwartz, Daniel L., and Kevin Hartman. 2007. "It Is Not Television Anymore: Designing Digital Video for Learning and Assessment." In *Video Research in the Learning Sciences,* edited by Ricki Goldman, Roy Pea, Brigid Barron, and Sharon J. Derry, 335–48. Mahwah, NJ: Erlbaum.

Ware, Colin. 2008. *Visual Thinking for Design.* Amsterdam/Boston: Morgan Kaufmann Publishers/Elsevier.

Weinschenk, Susan. 2011. *100 Things Every Designer Needs to Know About People.* Berkeley, CA: New Riders.

Yellowlees, Peter M., and James N. Cook. 2006. "Education about Hallucinations Using an Internet Virtual Reality System: A Qualitative Survey." *Academic Psychiatry* 30 (6): 534–39.

Zichermann, Gabe, and Christopher Cunningham. 2011. *Gamification by Design: Implementing Game Mechanics in Web and Mobile Apps.* Sebastopol, CA: O'Reilly Media.

8

Multimedia and Games

How to design with animation, video, audio,
and games for better learning outcomes

<< The Backstory

Dynamic, interactive, and participatory media

Once upon a time media was something other people made and you consumed, often by yourself, and largely while sitting still. Today, that model has transformed into a fast-paced network of collaborative media making. Mizuko Ito and her colleagues put it more academically: "Rather than conceptualize everyday media engagement as 'consumption' by 'audiences,' the term *networked publics* foregrounds the active participation of a distributed social network in the production and circulation of culture and knowledge."

Essentially, our "networked publics" are highly interconnected webs of people creating video, audio, texts, images, game experiences, and stories together by sharing, commenting, blogging, liking, mashing up, modifying, and crowdsourcing. We're now cooking, sharing, and eating media for breakfast, lunch, and dinner. And we've taken to learning the same way.

The story of how we learn with multiple media, formally and informally, is unfolding by the minute. In this section, we'll look at the relevant findings on how media is best used for learning, what research can tell us about which media to use when, and general strategies for improving learning experiences with combinations of media.

Multimedia = better learning

As mentioned in Chapter 2, "How We Learn," psychologist Richard Mayer has proven that people learn better from a combination of text and visuals than they do from text alone. He's called this the multimedia principle. While this probably doesn't come as a shock, it's important to know that visuals have been conclusively shown to lead to better learning experiences.

Visuals can mean not only illustrations, photos, infographics, and diagrams, but also interactive elements, video, animation, and simulations. Likewise, *text* can refer to written words as well as audio or narration. Together these make up content and environments like 3-D worlds, chat rooms, discussion forums, wikis, blogs, and apps for activities like bookmarking, collaborative writing, curation, video making, podcasting, and gaming. The list grows daily.

Harvard researcher Chris Dede reminds us that the need for interactivity and personalization is not new to learning:

Interactivity and individualization are central to learning, whether the experience is face-to-face or online. In a face-to-face setting, you don't want to be just sitting in lectures, you want to have lively discussions where your voice is frequently heard, and online, you don't just want to be reading PDFs or watching videos, you want to be part of a lively, interpretive community that's sorting out these different types of things .... Just as we need a range of pedagogies to match different styles of learning, we need a range of media to match different styles of learning.

That being said, it's now essential to note that combinations must be designed correctly to yield the learning advantages. As we saw with static graphics in Chapter 5, "Learning Is Visual," some images do not improve learning when added to text. In this chapter, we'll look at what to do, and what not to do, in the case of dynamic graphics.

Video

If you get a sudden urge to learn how to poach an egg or make an origami Jedi, what's the first thing you do? In all likelihood, you search for a video demo.

OBSERVATION AND THE BRAIN

Video is special. It has a unique, visceral appeal with its dance of light, sound, and color. But it's also special because it allows us to see things happening in a realistic way. Whether it's a live news broadcast or a medical procedure, we become witnesses to something in rich detail. This verisimilitude means stories we watch on video (or film) can have a profound effect on us emotionally. A swell of music, a startling image, a close-up—filmmakers use all these powerful tools to guide attention to the details that tell a particular story.

And that's not all: Video is also special cognitively. Since the days of our knuckle-dragging ancestors, *watching* has been a fabulous way to learn. Studies have shown that watching, and even just *thinking* about, physical things activates the same parts of the brain that are activated when we actually *do* those things. These are mirror neurons at work and they seem to explain things like learning by imitation.

Teenagers seem to know this instinctively. Usability research by Jakob Nielsen and Hoa Loranger found that

Teens especially liked websites that had videos to give them a better perspective on complex concepts. Channel One had demos they appreciated because it made it easier to visualize the steps and avoid having to read the instructions.

Video and the web are a powerful combination because together they allow for easy annotation, cutting, labeling, editing and commenting, and according to experts, it's when video is contextualized and manipulated that it creates the best learning experience.

Stanford researchers Daniel Schwartz and Kevin Hartman explain, "Video does not have to be stand-alone like a TV program. Video is a more forgiving and powerful learning medium when it is embedded within a larger context of use. Footage rarely makes a self-contained video story, but when embedded within a multimedia environment, it can be used in many creative ways to encourage learning interactions."

LEARNING WITH VIDEO: FROM PROCEDURE AND PERFORMANCE TO MOTIVATION AND ATTITUDE

Video can be used to demonstrate expert performance (coaching, surgery, counseling, teaching) or to let a learner review her own performance. It can also be used as a way for senior employees to mentor newcomers, for classmates to get to know each other, or to provide context for a lesson.

Video can also be used to change attitudes. We use the term "role model" because we know that people (famously teenagers) will imitate styles, behaviors, and attitudes of teachers, celebrities, or fictional heroes. Knowing this, to raise the profile of math and science careers, the US government teamed up with television. Not long after, shows like *Numb3rs* and *The Big Bang Theory* appeared. Similarly, the US department of defense funded the Engage project at Carnegie Mellon (www.etc.cmu.edu/engage), which "seeks to develop interactive game-based technologies for pre-K through grade three students to inspire them to become future innovators by educating them in STEM skills." Media can shape people's attitudes toward a subject.

It's also worth remembering that video assets don't have to be professional quality to be useful. Thanks to the ubiquity of cameras on mobile phones, instant amateur uploads can sometimes be as instructive. For example, one utility company has a system that lets its workers on the ground upload videos of their repair situations on location when they want to seek advice from others on the job. These videos aren't slick, edited productions, and they don't need to be. What's important is that they capture real-life issues on the job in real time. Schwartz and Hartman classified some different ways that video can be used for learning into a valuable diagram (**FIGURE 8.1**).

Animation

Like video, animation is engaging at a visceral level, it's associated with entertainment, and in today's digital world, it can be participatory. One advantage of animation over video is that it can be minimalist. When animating a procedure, for example, you can leave out the realistic but potentially distracting detail that video typically contains, allowing the learner to focus her working memory on what's relevant.

Key
① Classes of outcomes
② Learning target
③ Assessments
④ Genres

FIGURE 8.1 Daniel Schwartz and Kevin Hartman's diagram shows some of the ways video can be used effectively as part of a learning experience. (Image courtesy of Daniel L. Schwarz and Kevin Hartman.)

I often marvel at good cartoons because they can achieve such an artful efficiency due largely to our tendency to anthropomorphize anything. (Put a pair of glasses on a nearby object and watch it come alive.) There's a scene in Disney's *Aladdin* in which a magic carpet comes to life. In just a few minutes, this object with neither eyes nor face nor limbs expresses curiosity, excitement, and pathos. A full range of human emotion can be conveyed in the simplest of line drawings. The artist's talent is in knowing which lines are important. As designers we sometimes fixate on making animations more realistic, even though people are often more emotionally drawn to simplified and stylized characters (**FIGURE 8.2**).

Giving learners tools to create their own animations can be an interesting way to provide them practice with communicating their understanding, or to reveal the errors in their mental models.

Moving beyond *when* to use animation (or video), we arrive at the question of *how* to use it most effectively for learning. We'll look at some of the impact factors, like the use of cues and learner control, in the Strategies section.

FIGURE 8.2 Who needs full-on 3-D animation when 2-D can be this much fun? Bob is a slightly animated character from an eLearning course by Hitachi Systems. (From the course About Social Media Guidelines by Hitachi Data Systems; demo at www.articulate.com/community/showcase.php.)

Games, simulations, and virtual worlds

The New Media Consortium's Horizon Report has identified game-based learning as a significant emerging technology for education three years in a row. There's nothing terribly new about using games in education (duck, duck, goose?). In fact, play is among our first strategies for learning. And yet games are sure to prompt some eye rolling when mentioned anytime after kindergarten. That's why believers in meaningful games had to rebrand them "serious games" to get them the attention they deserved.

There are many books on the use of serious games, models, simulations, and gamification for eLearning. (I encourage you to read some of those listed at the end of this chapter.) It would be impossible to cover such a significant and rapidly growing topic in just one section of a chapter, but I'll pull out some issues that relate specifically to interface design decisions that impact learning.

The trend in gamification led to an assumption on the part of some that adding badges, rewards, and scoreboards to just about anything makes it a game. While it's tempting to think that adding game rewards and goals will increase a learner's motivation and thus help her learn better, you have to ask the question, what's this motivation about? Does the game increase her motivation to learn what she's learning? Or is she now motivated only to collect points? (Refer to the discussion of motivation in detail in Chapter 7, "Learning Is Emotional.")

Effective learning games retain contextual cues, align game goals with learning goals, and drive interest with intrinsic, as well as autonomous extrinsic motivation.

Models, simulations, and complex systems

How can there be global warming if it's so cold? Every time I go out without an umbrella it rains—am I causing the rain? As humans, we're partial to fairly simplistic, linear, centrally controlled, and predictable explanations of things. This is based on our practical experience with the world and it's sensible up to a point. The trouble is, a lot of really important things don't work that way.

Ecosystems, biological systems, economic markets, and social behavior are just a few examples of the complex systems in the world that are frequently nonlinear, self-organizing, random, and unpredictable. So it follows that in order to tackle complex problems like climate change or population growth in the twenty-first century, we'll need a way to improve our ability to understand these complex systems in more sophisticated ways. Many learning scientists are pointing to models to do just that.

No, not the runway variety (although a study on how attractive people impact learning could be compelling). Actually, it's *systems models* and *simulations,* sometimes in the form of games, which hold such promise for helping us learn the complex. Computer models have been used for education for well over a decade and with learners of all ages.

Models, whether physical (a scale model of a house) or conceptual (a statistical model), are simplified representations of systems that explain their underlying structure, rules, and behavior. These models can be visualized and experienced far more easily now with computer technology.

The terms *model* and *simulation* are often used interchangeably, but researcher Beat Schwendimann suggests that while a model is a simplified representation of a system, a simulation is the process of using a model to study that system. Look at it this way: A model is a representation, while a simulation provides an experience.

Model it

You can play around with manipulating models or make your own with the freely available NetLogo software. NetLogo is an environment for creating and engaging with models that's used by researchers and students alike (http://ccl.northwestern.edu/netlogo).

Simulations for education range from fully virtual games like vLeader, which has models of leadership at its core, to mixed-reality experiences involving device-supported role-playing, to the comparatively simpler, but astonishing, Solar Walk app, which lets users wander around in a model of the solar system for direct experience of its mind-boggling scale.

In an interview with Oxford University researcher Ken Kahn, author of the Modelling4All project, he explained to me how educational models are used to create computer games: "There are two basic possibilities. One is that you become one of the elements in the simulation (so you're one of the fish in the school), or, you could be the kind of 'god figure' where you're controlling the whole thing (like the mayor or public health official). So combining modeling with game making works out very well."

The most familiar example of the god figure approach is, of course, the Sims series of games. In SimCity, users play the very powerful mayor, changing parameters, unleashing random events, and building new elements to create civic prosperity (or some user-defined variation thereof). Many educators have used entertainment simulation games like SimCity to engage students in learning about the complexities of the represented system (in this case, urban planning).

Sims creator Will Wright calls his games modern Montessori toys that let kids explore and discover principles on their own. In a TED talk, he comments on the incredible power that creation can have on motivation: "What we noticed with the Sims is players love to make stuff and when they made stuff themselves they had a tremendous amount of empathy for it."

While most educational games for grades K–12 are "skill-and-practice" games for curriculum areas like math and spelling, they can also be adventures that integrate concepts into real-world scenarios, like the physics game Ludwig (www.playludwig.com). Games can also be used for serious social and political learning as with Frontiers, a multiplayer game that lets teams experience life as refugees as they attempt to escape persecution in Africa and seek asylum in Europe. (See the sidebar for more on games about empathy and social change.)

Finally, research has shown that social interaction is the biggest motivator for people to play games. Experts and players alike often point to the team-based problem solving, leadership skills, and cooperation required for success in multiplayer games like World of Warcraft as potential areas of educational value. Channel these advantages into well-crafted learning experiences and you have a potentially epic combination.

VIRTUAL WORLDS

Models, simulations, and games are often played out in 3-D virtual learning environments (VLEs) otherwise known as virtual worlds. For example, a learning experience might be orchestrated in a system like Second Life. It might take place in a bespoke world created with a tool like Unity. Or it could manifest as a goal-directed quest within a clearly game-like experience.

A virtual world isn't a game in itself, but as soon as learners have a quest, they become players in that world. The quest may be collecting scientific data in order to form a hypothesis, as in the Harvard-based VLE Quest Atlantis, or collecting archaeological artifacts and analyzing primary resources to solve a historical mystery.

It can be useful to think about learning experiences involving models, simulations, or games on a scale of interactivity (**FIGURE 8.3**). At the far left of the scale, learners sit passively watching a game demo or observing what happens over time as a model runs. In the middle, players interact with the system and with others. At the far right, they generate their own models, games, or other content.

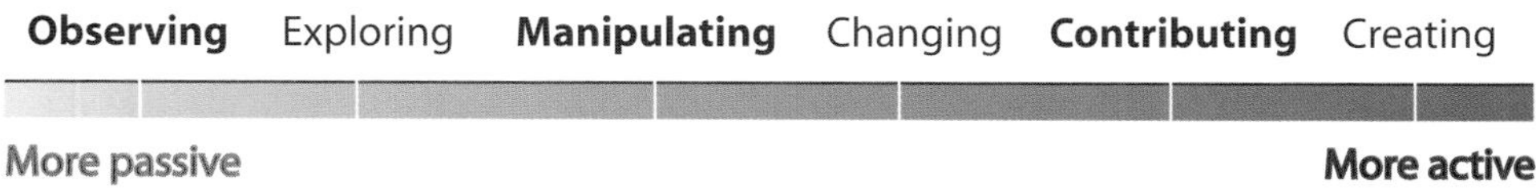

Observing Exploring **Manipulating** Changing **Contributing** Creating

More passive   More active

FIGURE 8.3 Learners can engage with multimedia in ways that are very passive, very interactive, or something in between, as shown in this interactivity scale.

MINI-GAMES AND APPS

Sometimes mini-games are included in larger serious games for practice or variety. They usually come in the form of apps for children or adults. Many are mobile versions of simulations and games, such as those described above.

These mini-games and apps may provide practice in things like multiplication, French pronunciation, music notation, atomic bonding—you name it, there's an app for that. This is an exciting space to work in because the reach is potentially massive, some of the most inspiring visual design for eLearning can be found in this area, and there's still a lot to learn about how to make these genuinely supportive of learning.

Perhaps the three biggest pitfalls of design for learning apps are as follows:

1. **Relying too heavily on contingent extrinsic motivation.** Extrinsic motivation can be powerful, but it can also render an app useless if used incorrectly (refer to Chapter 7).

2. **Forgetting to design for transfer.** I've seen beautiful apps fail to have educational value because they recast the content in ways so fantastical and distanced from reality that anything learned becomes untransferable to the real world. Ensure that the game retains real-world context and cues so that learning in the app can be applied where it's really needed.

3. **Not evaluating the app for educational outcomes.** It may pass all the usability and satisfaction tests, and users may even report that they learned something, but to really find out whether they did, you need to incorporate measures of learning gains. What learning objectives does the app support? Can users meet those objectives after using the app?

The best part of the job is having an excuse to play games ("No, really, I'm working!"). Most games are free or cost just a few bucks, so there should be little stopping you from trying them out. iTunes has an education category that applies to all ages.

For computer games, you can download Steam (www.steampowered.com) for an easy way to try demos and get games on sale. While Steam is an environment for entertainment gaming (not educational games), you'll find entertainment games on physics (like Puddle), economics (Democracy), and history (Age of Empires), as well as virtual worlds that experiment with nonlinear storytelling (Dear Esther). So get to work and go play.

Gaming for a better world

While games often center on saving the world, they're seldom viewed as a serious asset to society. But what if games really could help save the world, or at least help make it a better place? Games for Change (G4C) has embarked on just such a quest. G4C is a community, organization, and festival whose mission is to catalyze social impact through digital games.

For example, Half the Sky is a Facebook game designed to raise awareness of and practical support for the health and freedom of women and girls worldwide. The promise of this game is that it not only presents very important issues, but it does so in a way that builds comradery, empathy, and empowerment (www.halftheskymovement.org).

The revolutionary game Foldit lets players solve puzzles for science. People all over the world are folding proteins into ever-more efficient shapes, contributing knowledge essential to curing diseases like AIDS and cancer.

One of the most widely known proponents of using games for real change is Jane McGonigal, veteran game designer and author of *Reality Is Broken: Why Games Make Us Better and How They Can Change the World*. By way of example, she was part of a team that created World Without Oil, an alternate-reality game that challenged players to survive without oil, and "Evoke—a ten-week crash course on how to change the world" (www.urgentevoke.com). Among her most recent work is the app SuperBetter, a mobile tool designed to support personal well-being, injury recovery, and mental and physical resilience.

Accessibility

Accessibility issues can be particularly hairy (but especially important) for interactive and multimedia learning. Video and animation may not be visible to learners who are vision impaired or audible to those who are hearing impaired. Multimedia may not play properly on older systems. Programs like Flash aren't available on all devices and are often blocked by corporate firewalls. Beautiful virtual worlds have been created for classroom use, but may fail to run on classroom computers. As discussed in Chapter 3, "A View of the eLearning Landscape," the biggest reason to ensure that your designs comply with accessibility guidelines is so you can actually reach all your users.

>> The Strategies
for designing multimedia and games for learning

The strategies in this section are broken down into three subcategories:

- Strategies for effective use of audio
- Strategies for effective use of video and animation
- Strategies for the design of educational models, games, and simulations

Strategies for audio

Although the use of sound is sometimes neglected as a design element, it can impact learning in positive or negative ways. The strategies below will help you ensure that your use of audio helps rather than hinders your learners.

>> AVOID BACKGROUND SOUND

Research shows that adding background sound, however topically relevant, increases extraneous cognitive load and, therefore, can harm learning. Background sounds include music or ambient sounds, for example, machine gun fire in a lesson on World War II.

Of course, this rule applies most for screens in which learners need to focus on concepts or knowledge. Sound can be helpful to support attitude change and to contextualize subjects. (For example, you could use that machine gun fire subtly in a short intro video designed to contextualize a topic, but keep it away from the core content or activity screens.) Likewise, the Frontiers game employs the unsettling hum of a helicopter coming in and out. In the context of a game that might be said to support attitude change and empathy, realistic ambient sound that creates a sense of unease supports the game's goals and the experience.

The captivating little apps in the Powers of Minus Ten series include sound in a way that adds definition to the experience. This use of sound is likely to be most effective with young users for whom the value of the app is largely in experiencing microscopic worlds for the first time. For young learners, the music creates a sense of excitement and helps differentiate each level of scale.

However, the sound would make it more difficult to focus on the explanatory text. Therefore, for a biology student who needs to glean more detail from the program, the sound could be a distraction. Ultimately, the decision about whether or not to include sound, how to include it, and whether it should be constant, fade out, or be controllable, should be determined by the audience, the learning goal, and testing with real users.

>> USE ACOUSTIC CUES

Sounds *can* support learning when they're used consistently to draw attention to important events. According to Nielsen and Loranger, "Sound as feedback can be very effective to confirm selections or alert to errors." The press of a button, the swoosh of an e-mail, the click of a virtual camera shutter—sounds are frequently used as part of a responsive interface. In learning experiences, if I can hear the rock drag against the ground when I move it, or the water splash when I drop a virtual fishing line into it, I know my action has worked, and the act is much more satisfying. These kinds of sounds lend physicality and texture to a virtual interface, contributing to engagement as well as usability.

Caveats and considerations

Users are unlikely to be happy with sudden, loud sounds or repetitive sounds. Some software handles this by creating multiple kinds of sound feedback so that correctly answered quiz questions, for example, elicit various responses, rather than the same reply (correct!) or sound (buzz!) over and over.

Also, remember that research on users and their physical environment is essential. Nielsen and Loranger have found that chirps and chimes appeal to kids, but not to teens and adults; sound can be disruptive (or really embarrassing) in shared environments like offices; and that multitasking teens get exasperated when sound competes with the music and other media they're listening to.

>> WATCH FOR TANGENTS

As with background sound, irrelevant text, be it print or audio, has been shown to decrease learning outcomes. Mayer gives an example of a lesson on the physics of lightning. When a fascinating story about a man who got hit by lightning was added to the lesson, students learned less. Mid-lesson tangents like this, though interesting, can impair learning.

As always, the goal of the learning experience will determine what's "irrelevant." Good storytellers and speakers know that personal anecdotes and surprising stories can delight an audience. Possibly the only thing I remember from one college biochemistry class was the professor's story of how the pharmaceutical company Bayer, trying to find a cure for morphine addiction, invented heroin (if you're curious, read "Heroin: A Hundred-Year Habit" at www.historytoday.com). This story probably wasn't on the test, but it cut straight through to an intrinsically motivating fascination in me about the strange interplay of the human body and organic chemistry.

Here's the moral of the story: If you're aiming to engage learners with an interesting story, look for one that also demonstrates a principle or point included in the learning objectives. The heroin story demonstrated how a simple chemical process that yielded medication in one instance could produce a dangerous drug in another. In essence, it helped me to see how very small differences at the chemical level could make for massive differences at the organism level (not to mention the societal level).

If your learning goal is to help learners understand a scientific process, then an irrelevant but interesting story will probably get in the way (and this is what the research shows). However, if the goal of the experience is attitude change or to incite intrinsic interest in the topic, then a relevant, captivating story may be the right way to go. Sequence, of course, matters. Interrupting the flow of an explanation is unlikely to ever be a good idea. However, launching a lesson with a colorful narrative before you get to the explanation may be more effective.

>> EMBRACE NARRATION

As veteran storytellers, humans are hardwired to listen to other people talk. In fact, according to psychologist Susan Weinschenk, listening to someone talk creates a brain syncing that helps the listener understand what's being said. The story also imparts a meaning to the words that a person reading the same words might not herself infer. Spoken audio, such as a charismatic lecture, video interview, or narration, can have a special effect.

Narration is also useful because, while written words add to load on visual perception, narration goes through the hearing channel. Thus, an animation is more effective for learning if explanatory text is provided as synced audio narration, rather than as written text competing with other visuals on the screen.

Strategies for video and animation

Learning often comes naturally from dynamic visuals. But it's also easy to be seduced by them when they're not helpful. The following strategies will help you know when to use video and animation for learning.

>> STICK TO RELEVANT VIDEO

As mentioned earlier, research warns against adding sidebar stories for the sake of interest because this can hurt learning. The same is true for interesting but irrelevant video. Schwartz and Hartman's diagram (refer to Figure 8.1) is an excellent guide to various types of relevant video. One of the best times to use video is when it provides something only that medium can provide.

FrancoToile, a resource for French-language learners created in Canada, leverages what web video has to offer to expose learners to the sounds, dialects, and slang of native French speakers from across the globe (**FIGURE 8.4**). Text alone could never demonstrate the subtle differences in pronunciation and usage in the way that watching and listening to someone speak can. Moreover, watching a variety of real people using the language conveys the diversity of French speakers in different countries.

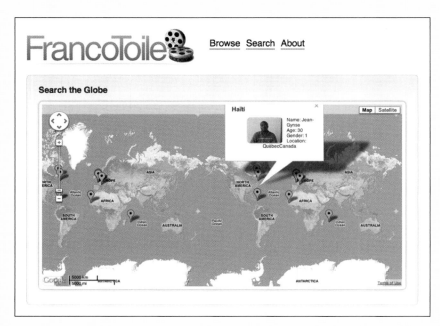

FIGURE 8.4 FrancoToile leverages what video has to offer to expose learners to the various sounds, dialects, and slang of native French speakers around the globe.

>> SEGMENT VIDEO AND CUSTOMIZE IT FOR THE WEB

When TV was first invented, producers filmed only stage plays. Don't make the same mistake with web video. Sticking a camera at the back of a lecture theater is seldom the best way to create educational video for the web. Nielsen and Loranger recommend breaking long clips into small, compelling segments and limiting them to 5 minutes in length. Of course, their research was done on general websites and learners will likely tolerate longer video within formal learning environments. So how long is too long?

Scott Klemmer's Stanford HCI course on Coursera (www.coursera.org/course/hci) is a good model for online lecture videos. Rather than just filming a live lecture, the course includes scripted and edited custom lectures that are cut into stand-alone topic segments of 10 to 20 minutes each. This makes the videos easier to digest in one sitting and easier to review later.

The popular TED Talks are another good example of tailoring to a learning audience on the web. Although they are live audience lectures, they are rigorously prepared, edited with multiple camera angles, and limited to about 15 minutes.

Of course, not everyone has the budget for custom video. As a no-budget alternative at the university where I work, we're experimenting with training tutors to take automatically captured lecture videos and edit them down into a collection of highlights that learners can focus on during tutorials and that remain an asset for future use and review.

Demonstrational and other types of video also benefit from chunking, particularly when the task being presented is complex, important details are subtle, or the viewers are novices.

>> LET LEARNERS CONTROL PACING

One of the problems with video and animation is that it proceeds at a predetermined rate. This rate might be too fast or too slow for some learners. Fortunately, digital interfaces make it easy to provide controls for this. Ensure that learners can control how your media are played. They should be able to pause, rewind, and ideally make use of all the tools that users have gotten used to with YouTube, VLC, or iTunes. The 30-second Rewind button used by Apple comes in very handy when you just missed a point or phrase, for example.

>> USE VISUAL CUES

Lijia Lin and Robert Atkinson have shown that adding visual cues to animations like arrows, highlighting, and circles helps learners understand better and re-member more. This is essentially because educational animations can be highly complex, so learners can waste cognitive effort trying to figure out where to look as they try to keep up with the narration and the dynamic images. Visual cues guide learner attention to the correct spot, keeping them in sync with the animation and ensuring they don't focus on the wrong thing.

Slow motion, zooming, and highlighting are other types of cues that can help learn-ers discern important detail. As Daniel Schwartz and Kevin Hartman explain:

> Sometimes skills are quite complex so that replaying, zooming, and slowing the motion can be quite helpful … . Additionally, for some skills it is import-ant to help people see the critical components of the behavior. For example, novice tennis players may not see the key moves of the professional, in which case, they cannot possibly imitate it. Good procedural instruction makes sure that students can discern the behaviors of significance so they can imitate them.

Visual cues can aid in this discernment process.

>> USE ANIMATION FOR PHYSICAL PROCEDURES

There's very strong evidence that people learn physical procedures—such as how to do origami, assemble a piece of furniture, or tie a square knot—better by watching videos or animations than by viewing a series of still images. This is because, as explained earlier, humans are hardwired to learn motor skills by observation. Thus, a demonstrational video, even if humbly produced, will likely be the most helpful to your learners if the learning goals involve performing physical procedures (**FIGURE 8.5**).

FIGURE 8.5 Physical procedures involving motor skills are well supported by video and animation. How-to videos, like this one about cat grooming on YouTube, are incredibly popular on the web. (I admit that was a poorly veiled excuse to use a Grumpy Cat photo.)

>> USE STILL IMAGES FOR CONCEPTUAL PROCESSES

Although we learn physical skills best by observation, the same isn't true of complex cognitive tasks and nonhuman processes, such as how rain forms. Therefore, video and animation are not the best choice in these cases.

When it comes to conceptual processes, it turns out that animation and video do too much of the work for the learner. In contrast, a series of static images requires the learner to take the time to make logical connections between them, which helps her to learn, and to do so at her own pace. Thus conceptual processes are better learned when they're illustrated by a series of static images.

Caveats and considerations

While information on weather patterns and science processes have been found to be harder to learn when delivered via animation, this effect reverses when your learners are experts. Meteorologists are weather map experts and know what to focus on, thus they can learn from animated maps where novices would be overloaded. Furthermore, segmentation (breaking your content into chunks) has similarly been shown to work for novices but not for experts. Thus, you can't make an informed decision about when and how to use animation unless you know your audience.

Animation can be highly effective when used correctly, but it can also land you a post on FAIL blog. Excessive motion can be irritating, and ironically, can deflect learner attention. In *Designing with the Mind in Mind,* Jeff Johnson points out that when motion is overused, learners become blind to it, an effect known as *habituation:*

Our brain pays less and less attention to any stimulus that occurs frequently .... Overuse of strong attention-getting methods can cause important messages to be blocked by habituation.

Jakob Nielsen and Hoa Loranger sum it up like this: "Don't look like an ad." Their findings on banner blindness show that people have learned to totally ignore anything overly large or colorful, particularly if it includes animation. Just when you think you're getting their attention, you won't be.

Mathletics is a highly successful learning program, but at the time of this writing, the website for the product produces a bit of overload. It has multiple moving images and much of the page content is styled like an advertisement, presumably to grab attention. Combined with an unclear visual hierarchy, this makes it difficult to identify key information on the page. Although this is just a webpage, users might incorrectly assume their education software was designed the same way.

Think about movement like all other elements on a page. Does it serve an instructional or operational purpose, or is it simply attention-grabbing eye candy?

Strategies for models, games, and simulations

Let people learn through action and interaction, see experiences from angles they never could have in real life, and ask questions that would have been unanswerable in real situations.

—TONY BINGHAM AND MARCIA CONNER, *The New Social Learning*

>> DESIGN GAMES AND SIMULATIONS IN ALIGNMENT WITH LEARNING GOALS

Research has shown that learning does not improve when learner focus is placed on game goals rather than learning goals. For example, a virtual quiz show, or "frame game," decontextualizes knowledge, making it unlikely to transfer to real life.

Many skill and practice games for kids have them selecting correct answers from a list to earn rewards. As already discussed in Chapter 7, when extrinsic motivators are separated from learning objectives, they can encourage learners to focus on the wrong things, like "gaming the system," and can undermine intrinsic motivation.

>> FIND THE GAME IN YOUR LEARNING

We discussed the value of tapping into intrinsic motivation in Chapter 7 and the pitfalls of shallow gamification are now widely acknowledged. The alternative, therefore, is not to layer a façade of game mechanics onto the learning, but to find the core challenge already in the learning and help it emerge. Stephen Anderson says it best, although not in the context of learning: "Find the game that's already in your design. If engaging users is an important part of our job, we should be looking to surface the games and motivations already inherent in the activities we're designing for."

Use the "five whys" interview technique to get to the heart of what experts love about a topic. Ask enthusiastic students what they enjoy most. Think creatively until you tap into the heart of what makes the learning intrinsically exciting.

>> OPTIMIZE THE VISUALIZATION OF MODELS FOR CLARITY AND VISUAL THINKING

Chapter 5 explored strategies for creating educational graphics that communicate clearly in a way that's both cognitively efficient and appealing. Specifically, we looked at strategies to reduce overload, guide attention, support visual perception, and promote visual thinking and learning. While the educational graphics discussed in the chapter were static, all of these strategies can be applied to the visualization of dynamic and interactive visual media as well.

>> KEEP IT SIMPLE, AT FIRST

Popular games frequently present a staggering number of choices and functionalities. Game players love this, but only because these choices aren't presented all at once. Gamers and learners alike will head for the door if welcomed by a screen cluttered with options and controls. So how to strike the balance?

Have interface complexity evolve with learner progress. Games have nearly perfected the art of *progressive disclosure*. This means they introduce options and rules gradually, only after a learner is comfortable with the current state. Not only does this help prevent her from being scared off by an overwhelming interface, but it also has another key advantage: it lets her jump right in (see next strategy).

>> INTEGRATE LEARNABILITY INTO THE GAME: LET LEARNERS JUMP RIGHT IN

Look up. Now look down.
This completes the gymnastics portion of your exercise.
There is a painting on the wall. Walk over to the painting.
This is art.
Stare at the art.
You should now feel mentally invigorated.
If you suspect that staring at art has not provided the appropriate mental
sustenance, contemplate briefly on this piece of classical music ...

—PORTAL 2

The dialogue above, from the opening sequence of the award-winning game Portal 2 is just one of thousands of examples of the clever and sometimes humorous ways that learnability is integrated into gameplay. In this example, by looking up and down and interacting with an object in a short introductory sequence, the user learns which keystrokes and mouse interactions to use to control her character.

Games have to captivate users instantly if they're to be successful, so they don't have the luxury of simply throwing a manual at players or expecting them to patiently sit through some sterile training session before getting started. And yet their interfaces are often highly specialized or operate in unique ways while imposing a significant learning curve. One of the ways games manage this is by working gradual training into the gameplay itself. So integrated is the training, players often don't realize they're learning to use the controls.

The way in which games successfully integrate interface-based learning objectives into the game itself should inspire eLearning. When you have no choice but to teach the user how to use your interface, how can you integrate this training into the program, aligning it with progress and achievements, instead of treating it as separate?

What if you were to move this principle beyond learnability? How could you better integrate training into work itself? When can you allow learners to get something real done in the context of their learning activity? You might consider how your learning game can let players complete real work tasks as they learn, create reusable tools, portfolio pieces, or other artifacts of practical and lasting value, instead of just having their efforts disappear into fictional ephemera.

>> INTEGRATE THE GAME INTO LIFE: CONTEXTUALIZE LEARNING THROUGH INTERFACE DESIGN

As mentioned previously, quiz show games have proven ineffective because presenting knowledge out of its context can render it useless in real life. Therefore, think carefully about the relevance of your "set design" or the environment and tools that you provide.

When considering interface metaphors for a game, seek out designs that provide relevant situations and contextual cues. Are learners engaged in practicing spelling to write a story or to kill a robot? Are they solving geometry problems in order to build a more structurally sound spaceship, or just to collect coins? Are corporate learners experimenting with different sales strategies in a variety of real-world scenarios or in a wild fantasy world?

Whether it's history, chemistry, leadership skills, or accounting, there are captivating settings that are relevant (dinosaurs, explosives, the White House, and Wall Street, respectively) as opposed to irrelevant settings (aliens, large-breasted artillery experts, orcs—you get the idea.) If you need ideas, talk to the people who live and love what's being learned (historians, chemists, managers, accountants). Relevance itself is captivating for learners.

As Sara DeWitt says of the work done at PBS KIDS

We are committed to helping kids recognize the real-world applications of the skills they learn through our content. Our apps and the characters in them model positive behaviors and skills that children can apply beyond the screen. And many of our games are launched with offline activities that kids can play with their peers, parents, and educators.

For examples of their work, visit www.pbskids.org/lab.

>> EMBED FEEDBACK INTO THE GAME

Feedback is at the heart of good interfaces, successful games, and effective learning. It comes in many forms, from a bing sound, to a level up, to constructive criticism. When it comes to games, how you deliver the feedback is important too. Rather than interrupting a learning experience with, "That answer is incorrect," include the feedback as part of the game itself. As Julie Dirksen puts it in *Design for How People Learn*, "Use consequences, not feedback, when people make choices in a learning scenario." In practice this means that feedback for an incorrect choice could come in the form of a customer pulling out of a sale, or a dangerous accident onsite (**FIGURE 8.6**). If a richer explanation is required, consider how a character in the game might communicate it.

FIGURE 8.6
This simulation is designed to help prepare miners to respond to emergencies they may encounter working at a mine. In realistic simulations, the consequences of poor decisions can be embedded into the game realistically but safely. (Images courtesy of Leonard D. Brown and Michael Peltier, University of Arizona, Arizona MineSAFE, "Harry's Hard Choices.")

Three-dimensional virtual worlds don't in themselves ensure better learning outcomes, and creating them can be costly. Therefore, as with video, the best time to use immersive environments is when they provide something only that medium can. The following are some of the features of 3-D worlds that can lead to positive learning outcomes (as proposed by Tassos Mikropoulos and Antonis Natsis):

- First-order experiences (experience things, even dangerous things, firsthand)
- Natural semantics (manipulate real-world objects intuitively in a realistic way instead of working with symbolic representations)
- Scale (experience things that are out of scale, like an atom or the solar system)
- Make the abstract concrete (take an abstract concept and make it experienceable and perceptible)
- Presence (get a sense of being present in an authentic experience)

A Slower Speed of Light, created by the MIT Game Lab, lets learners experience the abstract concepts described by the theory of relativity in a directly perceptible way. According to Creative Director Philip Tan, "It's a game about something very complex made very tangible. It conveys some of the joy that theoretical physicists experience every day when they're dealing with these very, very interesting issues about the real world" (http://gamelab.mit.edu).

Atlantis Remixed (previously Quest Atlantis) is a multiuser, 3-D virtual environment that combines play, learning, and attitude change to engage children in social action in the real world. As described by the makers: "Central to our work ... has been designing a context for learning, which sits at the intersection of education, entertainment, and social action. Designed to support social commitment and real-world action, our designs provide an immersive context with over 60,000 players worldwide."

Leveraging gameplay effectively for learning means tapping not only into engaging emotions like curiosity and joy, but also a way of learning that's evolved over millions of years. But what happens when all this playing to learn goes mobile? We'll look at that in the next chapter.

Go further

While much is written about games for learning and gamification, there is still, unfortunately, a paucity of hard research about when and how to use them effectively for learning. This is bound to change, and if you're designing learning games, you're part of an ongoing experiment that's taking our field forward. So whatever you create, test it with users, measure the learning gains, and share your findings with the community.

Many of the books available on learning games are written for instructional designers, trainers, or teachers, but here are some helpful resources for learning more about multimedia and games:

- While decidedly geared toward commerce rather than learning, *Gamification by Design* by Gabe Zichermann and Christopher Cunningham is a good guide to interface features and mechanics for games.

- KinderTown is both a site and an app run by tech-savvy educators that consolidates and reviews educational apps for young children. As a bonus, they often link apps to real-world games that address the same learning goals.

- If you want to be inspired, check out *Reality Is Broken,* game designer Jane McGonigal's manifesto on how games can be used to change the world.

SOURCES

Crow, Tracy. 2010. "Learning, No Matter Where You Are: Q&A with Chris Dede." *Journal of Staff Development* 31 (1): 10–12.

Dirksen, Julie. 2011. *Design for How People Learn*. Berkeley, CA: New Riders.

Ito, Mizuko, Heather Horst, Matteo Bittanti, danah boyd, Becky Herr-Stephenson, Patricia G. Lange, C. J. Pascoe, and Laura Robinson. 2009. *Living and Learning with New Media: Summary of Findings from the Digital Youth Project*. Cambridge, MA: MIT Press.

Lin, Lijia, and Robert K. Atkinson. 2011. "Using Animations and Visual Cueing to Support Learning of Scientific Concepts and Processes." *Computers & Education* 56 (3), 650–58. doi:10.1016/j.compedu.2010.10.007.

Mikropoulos, Tassos A., and Antonis Natsis. 2011. "Educational Virtual Environments: A Ten-Year Review of Empirical Research (1999–2009)." *Computers & Education* 56 (3), 769–80. doi:10.1016/j.compedu.2010.10.020.

Nielsen, Jakob, and Hoa Loranger. 2006. *Prioritizing Web Usability*. Berkeley, CA: New Riders.

Schwartz, Daniel L., and Kevin Hartman. 2007. "It Is Not Television Anymore: Designing Digital Video for Learning and Assessment." In *Video Research in the Learning Sciences,* edited by Ricki Goldman, Roy Pea, Brigid Barron, and Sharon J. Derry, 335–48. Mahwah, NJ: Erlbaum.

Wright, Will. 2007. "Spore, Birth of a Game." TED. http://www.ted.com/talks/will_wright_makes_toys_that_make_worlds.html.

9

Learning Is Mobile

How to design effective learning interfaces for mobile environments

❮❮ The Backstory

Mobile learning has made many appearances throughout this book, and indeed, it's difficult to discuss digital learning without giving mobile apps ample attention (see the discussion of games in Chapter 8, "Multimedia and Games").

There's no shortage of professional guidance on mobile design. Excellent resources like *Designing Mobile Interfaces* and *Mobile Design Pattern Gallery* from O'Reilly Media, as well as official developer guides from Apple, IBM, and Android, offer an excellent foundation in interface best practices. I won't rehash what those resources have already done well. Instead, I'll highlight some interface design issues specific to learning experiences in mobile contexts.

Also, since mobile interface strategies have near a six-month expiration date, I've aimed to include higher-level strategies that remain relevant even as the specifics of technologies change.

Mobile learning: A rainbow of flavors

One thing to remember is that mobile isn't just for reference apps or games. Mobile learning (sometimes called mLearning) includes a wide range of scenarios and strategies that include augmented multimedia adventures, text message-based learning campaigns, co-present device sharing, and much more. Mobile devices like tablets and handheld game consoles can be used by multiple people at once and can support face-to-face interactions in offices, museums, and playgrounds. Mobile devices are by no means restricted to phones and tablets. Although less common, wearable devices like Google Glass and the SixthSense wearable gestural interface add a layer of information to the physical world as the user moves around in space-time.

So how do you corral this array of potential learning experiences into a manageable collection of options? Read on for some approaches.

15 APPROACHES TO MOBILE LEARNING

Different professionals explain the many approaches to using mobile devices in learning in different ways. Researchers Leonard Low and Margaret O'Connell describe the building blocks of mobile learning activity as the four Rs: record, reinterpret, recall, and relate. Connie Malamed presents some of the most common corporate mobile strategies in her article "It's Not eLearning on a Phone." The following list combines elements of these into a larger set that includes formal education and training as well as informal lifelong learning and social change.

1. Skills practice and review

If you're drilling math problems to shoot space invaders or answering quiz questions to collect coins, then you're probably munching on what some have called "chocolate-covered broccoli." Many apps package drill-and-practice tasks (broccoli) into an arcade game (chocolate) for an easier sell. While there's a place for these types of practice apps, the real potential of mobile learning is not so much in putting old-school strategies into new packaging, but about creating seriously integrated and enhanced experiences that leverage what mobile has to offer.

Moreover, not all skill and practice learning is chocolate-covered broccoli. Both the Numbers League and LetterSchool apps mentioned in previous chapters support practice in ways that are strategic, focused, and go well beyond gamified drilling.

Mobile devices can also be used to review information, procedures, and experiences after the fact when it's most convenient or most needed. For example, a learner who's captured video of a procedure being carried out by an expert can review this procedure later in preparation for performance or assessment.

2. Learning in bursts

Many mLearning experts advise instructional designers to write mini lessons that can be completed during a short break between activities and in a distracting environment. The MindSnacks apps, for example, provide a framework for foreign-language practice that relies on short games and activities that let learners engage in short bursts of practice over time. Lynda (www.lynda.com) provides an app that makes high-quality video tutorial content available on mobile devices, so learners can make progress through segmented courses one chunk at a time. Of course, in these cases we're assuming the learning content and objectives are not so complex as to require extended focus, deep analysis, or synthesis, for which other strategies would be required.

3. Mental calisthenics

Some games promise to make learners smarter by exercising their most important muscle: the brain. Adults hoping to keep their cognition fit in pursuit of lifelong learning turn to these types of apps for a mental workout as well as for entertainment. Nintendo's Brain Age series for the DS and the Lumosity site (which includes a Brain Trainer app) are popular examples of these.

Games like these will certainly hone your skills at playing them, but it's currently an open question whether or not those skills will transfer to real life or to improved cognition. However, there's some evidence that taking part in cognitive training exercises (what one group of researchers calls *neurobics*) slows cognitive decline and, according to Kurt Samson in *Neurology Today,* "can help seniors maintain higher levels of cognition and function better in their daily lives."

4. Performance support

Digital job aids, demonstrational videos, audio instructions, and reference apps are examples of performance support used on the job. Workers also use social media to tap their social network for just-in-time help. This enables them to get advice in the field by sharing imagery and information as situations arise. Connie Malamed's Instructional Design Guru lets users look up unfamiliar instructional design terms as needed. YouTube is full of how-to videos that people everywhere access via mobile devices to support them as they attempt an almost infinite number of activities, from assembling equipment to cooking, using software, or applying makeup.

5. Access to news and information

People keep up-to-date via continuous data streaming in from social networks, blogs, and news apps. Apps like Zite, FlipBook, and HootSuite help them customize and organize news. Tweets, posts, and articles lead to new discoveries, discussions, and knowledge sharing. The value in helping one another stay informed is one of the reasons so many workplaces now encourage the use of enterprise social networks.

Mobile devices also provide easy access to educational content for all topics and all ages, whether it's Wikipedia or Wikiversity, Udemy or Udacity, dictionaries, translators, or other references. The International Children's Library makes digital books in the world's languages available to children anywhere for free. Information has never been so liberated.

6. Motivation and engagement

Many motivational drivers, like connecting with others, competition, self-expression, and gameplay, are made widely available by mobile phones. When integrated with learning goals, these can help encourage learners to engage.

7. Capture and participation

Mobile devices can facilitate data collection and participation by making it easier to contribute. With mobile devices, learners can easily take photos, handle text input, and record audio and video that lets them capture data in the field and share it with others. For example, the Project Noah app mentioned previously allows learners to capture images of plants and wildlife and share them with members of the community, as well as with scientists who can use that data for research.

Teachers can also fuel participation in face-to-face sessions by having learners vote or contribute information using their mobile devices, using apps like ResponseWare or eClicker Presenter.

8. Content creation and mashup

The photo, text, audio, and video capabilities of mobile devices can be used to create original learner- or instructor-generated content from which other learners can benefit. Learners can create concept maps and sketches or annotate photos and videos directly from their devices. These artifacts can then be shared online as points of discussion or as instructional resources for the future.

9. Assessment

Multiple methods of assessment can be carried out via mobile devices, including simple quizzes, submission of learner-generated content, recordings of performance in situ, and peer reviews. In addition to survey services like Google Forms and SurveyMonkey, dedicated learning platforms like Blackboard let users create and take mobile tests.

Apps also give learners the opportunity to assess themselves, receive feedback from others, or submit formal assessment material to remote assessors. Tappestry is an educational social network and app that lets learners organize and record what they've learned informally. The resulting collection, like an ePortfolio, can be used for feedback or assessment.

10. Meeting and learning in teams

Video-conferencing apps like Skype and Google Hangout allow synchronous online collaboration by taking advantage of text, audio, and video input. Furthermore, many gaming apps let players "play co-op," that is, work in teams to pull together resources and skills in order to solve quests.

In addition to virtual collaboration, mobiles can support face-to-face teams. They can be passed around a group, and individual learners can send digital resources to others in the same room via Bluetooth or wireless and share screens during classes or meetings.

For example, Pass-Them-Around, an experimental app designed by Andrés Lucero and his colleagues for research into collocated mobile interactions supports face-to-face photo sharing. The app "allows people to create group 'huddles' and discuss photos by tiling devices to create larger displays." Similarly, educational apps like Operation Math Code Squad and digital versions of familiar tabletop games like Monopoly enable co-present users to "pass-and-play" around a tablet as they would around a game board.

11. Asynchronous collaboration

Mobile devices can support asynchronous collaboration via social media services, text messaging, forums, or e-mail. Learners can use these methods to get advice, share ideas, provide feedback, or problem solve with others over a period of time and in alignment with their individual schedules and time zones.

Alternate reality games (ARGs) blend real-world activity with digital communication. According to the designers of World Without Oil, ARGs can "engage large numbers of players in collaborative efforts to solve very difficult puzzles and challenges." Over an extended but predetermined period of time, ARG players in disparate locations engage in the game by communicating and coordinating with one another using various types of technology that can include mobile devices.

12. Situated learning

Mobile devices are great for supporting situated learning, or learning that occurs within the authentic context to which it applies, be that the forest, the office, the factory, or somewhere else. Scavenger hunts, augmented field investigation, and supported role-playing allow learning to be thoroughly situated in the real world, and there are distinct advantages to including the physical world in the learning experience. Scott Klemmer and colleagues point out that "interfaces that are the real world can obviate many of the difficulties of attempting to model all of the salient characteristics of a work process as practiced."

For example, learners are physically, intellectually, and emotionally involved in the real-world ecological fieldwork experience supported by the Project Noah app. The mobile device is not at the center of their experience, but becomes an extension of their capabilities and a way to connect with others.

13. Augmented reality

Mobile learning design has the power to respond to context and augment learners' experience of physical objects and places. Among the most popular examples are the star map apps like Sky Map on Android and NightSky on iOS, which let the user point his phone upward and see the names of the stars and planets mapped onto the sky.

Paul Milgram and Fumio Kishino developed a "mixed reality" scale that goes from the completely virtual environment at one end, to the exclusively real-world environment at the other end. Everything else is on a continuum somewhere in between. In his book *Augmented Learning,* MIT's Eric Klopfer explains the difference in terms of virtual information access:

A heavily augmented environment relies on frequent access to virtual information. That information may be accessed on the order of seconds or even continuously …. A lightly augmented world, which is designed around periodic access to virtual information, relies on players making much greater use of the real-world information and accessing the virtual information when certain events happen. Players move about in real space but get information when they move to certain locations or trigger points.

You might think of virtual-reality goggles and helmets at the heavy end of the spectrum, digital glasses a bit further down, and QR codes that provide access to specific information only periodically at the lighter end. QR codes can be a practical method for embedding learning opportunities into the physical environment since codes can link to information about a particular object or place. For example, learners can access instructions or task support by scanning an object in situ.

14. Embodied learning

Augmented reality handheld games can also support embodied learning in which players physically enact, feel, or experience abstract phenomena in direct and tangible ways. For example, Paul Gee describes the potential for learners to experience "embodied empathy for a complex system." The idea is that people can better understand complex systems by taking on the role of a part of that system.

Compare, for example, reading a textbook chapter on supply and demand to taking part in a mobile-supported, face-to-face role-playing game in which the learner becomes an agent in a commodities market, physically buying and selling goods with others in a shared space. By embodying part of the system, the learner can directly and personally experience the laws of supply and demand, as well as the effects of forces like monopolies or price fixing.

As Klopfer explains, embodying an experience makes it personal: "Attaining that sense of embodiment connects students emotionally to the game, which results in their significant investment in solving the problem at hand. They care about the answer to the problem because it concerns them."

At the other end of the mixed-reality scale, the MIT Game Lab's A Slower Speed of Light immerses players in an entirely virtual world in which the speed of light is gradually reduced so that players can experience firsthand the theory of special relativity in a much more tangible way.

National health, safety, and social initiatives employ mobile games to educate the broader public on issues to do with well-being or social responsibility. Recycle Hero, for example, is a game app for kids that encourages recycling. The app 9 Minutes "plays out the adventure of pregnancy" and rewards pregnant women and their spouses for keeping both mother and baby healthy and happy. An evaluation of the app showed measurable improvements in knowledge, attitude, and behavioral intentions regarding safer pregnancy and delivery.

Lower-tech examples are education campaigns that use text messages to disseminate health information and support healthy changes in behavior related to smoking cessation, diabetes, and AIDS treatment. For example, ZMQ Software Systems in India, a technology social enterprise, has created mobile phone games to fight HIV through education. The learning games have reached over 60 million subscribers in multiple languages in India and Africa (www.zmqsoft.com).

This list of mobile educational strategies is not exhaustive. Disruptive and exciting innovations will continue in this area, but I hope I've at least hinted at the wide range of technical and pedagogical approaches available for handheld digital technologies.

Design principles for mobile learning

By grounding interface design in principles and best practices, you can be far more confident in your results. Following are principles in the areas of instructional and universal design that are relevant to mobile learning interface design.

INSTRUCTIONAL DESIGN PRINCIPLES FOR MOBILE LEARNING

In "Design Principles for Mobile Learning," Anthony Herrington and his colleagues provide a set of foundational principles of instructional design for mobile learning. You're probably already familiar with many of these principles, and although most relate more to the work of educators and instructional designers, they can still inform interface design:

- **Real-world relevance:** Use mobile learning in authentic contexts.

- **Mobile contexts:** Use mobile learning in contexts where learners are actually mobile.
- **Exploration:** Provide time for exploration of mobile technologies.
- **Blended:** Blend mobile and nonmobile technologies.
- **Whenever:** Use mobile learning spontaneously.
- **Wherever:** Use mobile learning in nontraditional learning spaces.
- **Whomsoever:** Use mobile learning both individually and collaboratively.
- **Affordances:** Exploit the affordances of mobile technologies.
- **Personalize:** Employ learners' own mobile devices.
- **Mediation:** Use mobile learning to mediate knowledge construction.
- **Produse:** Use mobile learning to produce and consume knowledge.

MOBILE LEARNING AS INCLUSIVE

Mobile learning arguably holds the most powerful promise for learners in developing countries, as well as for learners in the developed world who, because of age, disability, socioeconomics or limited access, use and benefit from devices in unique ways.

For example, multitouch interfaces have opened the door to the very young, the very old, and those with physical and cognitive disabilities. Older adults can use iPads to maintain social connections, browse photo albums, shop online, read large-print books, play online games with their grandchildren, and, of course, pursue lifelong learning.

Those with autism spectrum disorder have access to a growing number of specialty apps that support learning in areas like emotion recognition and communication. The Grace app, for example, is one of many designed to help less verbal people, such as those with autism, stroke, or cerebral palsy, communicate through pictures. soundAMP turns up the volume for the hearing impaired, and Aurifi is an audio-only game in which players progress through a soundscape adventure by tilting and tapping the device when prompted.

Mobile devices can also help reduce the access gap between higher- and lower-income students. Carly Shuler at the Sesame Workshop has pointed to the potential for these devices to reach underserved children: "Because of their relatively low cost and accessibility in low-income communities, handheld devices can help advance digital equity, reaching and inspiring populations 'at the edges'—children from economically disadvantaged communities and those from developing countries."

Considering that there are more mobile devices than people on this planet and that mobile penetration in developing countries is rapidly approaching 100 percent, the opportunity is hard to overlook. (Note: The International Telecommunication Union's 2013 report reported mobile penetration at over 100 percent in developed countries and at 89 percent in developing nations.)

UNESCO focuses on the potential of mobile learning to bring education to everyone with its annual Mobile Learning Week event. The organization reports, "As the cost of mobile phone ownership declines, mobile devices are being adopted in areas of great poverty, where even schools, books and computers are scarce. The opportunities presented by mobile learning, particularly for learners who lack access to high quality education, is immense."

For example, the UNESCO Mobile Phone Literacy Project in rural Pakistan uses mobile phones to enhance a face-to-face literacy course for adolescent girls. The results are inspiring, with the number of girls receiving an "A" leaping from 28 percent to 60 percent. While the potential for mobile devices to dramatically expand access to educational opportunities for billions of people globally is compelling, this potential can be reached only if we design mobile learning interfaces with accessibility, diversity, and inclusivity in mind.

Universal design principles for mobile learning

While many of the design principles we've already looked at apply to inclusive contexts, there are also principles specific to inclusive design, and these tend to target simpler technology features, encourage greater flexibility, and account for greater user and access diversity. Sheryl Burgstahler provides a set of universal design principles for all technology and Tanya Elias has interpreted these in the context of mobile learning. **TABLE 9.1** includes these principles together with Elias's suggestions for how they might be applied in the mobile learning context. I then propose an additional three principles based on the work of other researchers in this area.

TABLE 9.1 Universal design principles for technology, interpreted for mobile learning.

UNIVERSAL DESIGN PRINCIPLE	DESCRIPTION	MOBILE LEARNING EXAMPLE
	(1–7 from Burgstahler 2007)	(1–9 from Elias 2011)
1. Equitable use	The design is useful and marketable to people with diverse abilities. Example: A professor's website is designed to be accessible to everyone, including students who are blind and using text-to-speech software.	Use cloud storage to compensate for the small memory capacity of lower-tech phones; select the simplest possible format for content.
2. Flexibility in use	The design accommodates a wide range of individual preferences and abilities. Example: A museum, visited on a field trip for a course, lets each student choose to read or listen to a description of the contents of display cases.	Package content in small chunks.
3. Simple and intuitive use	Use of the design is easy to understand, regardless of the user's experience, knowledge, language skills, or current concentration level. Example: Control buttons on science equipment are labeled with text and symbols that are simple and intuitive to understand.	Consider text messaging.
4. Perceptible information	The design communicates necessary information effectively to the user, regardless of ambient conditions or the user's sensory abilities. Example: A video presentation projected in a course includes captions.	Include captions, descriptions, and transcriptions.
5. Tolerance for error	The design minimizes hazards and the adverse consequences of accidental or unintended actions. Example: Educational software provides guidance and background information when the student gives an inappropriate response.	Scaffold and support situated learning methods; issue warnings with sound and text.
6. Low physical effort	The design can be used efficiently, comfortably, and with a minimum of fatigue. Example: Doors to a lecture hall open automatically for people with a wide variety of physical characteristics.	Use available assistive technologies such as SMS readers; consider issues of physical effort.
7. Size and space for approach and use	Appropriate size and space is provided for approach, reach, manipulation, and use, regardless of the user's body size, posture, or mobility. Example: A flexible science lab work area has adequate workspace for students who are left- or right-handed and for those who need to work from a standing or seated position.	
8. Community of learners and support	Community support for learning is facilitated through the development of groups and support from appropriate tools.	Encourage multiple methods of communication; support study groups and tools.
9. Instructional climate	The instructor makes contact and stays involved.	Push reminders, quizzes, and questions to students; pull in learner-generated content.
10. Suitability of tool to cognitive task	Different physical interface tools (pen, keyboard, multimodal, for example) can help or hinder learning depending on the context and the group. Use the interface best suited to the cognitive task and to the user group.	Avoid relying on digital keyboard input for nonlinguistic tasks or for speakers of non-Roman alphabetic languages.
11. Adaptability and empowerment	Design tools are flexible and adaptable to unanticipated use; design tools allow user groups to build and customize their own tools.	Avoid designs that are rigidly customized to a specific use context; support customization.
12. Compliance with international standards of accessibility	Designs comply with relevant standards for technical accessibility and inclusivity.	Validate your designs against the W3C's WCAG guidelines.

Sheryl Burgstahler proposed the first seven principles in the table, along with the associated descriptions, as general principles of universal design. Later, Tanya Elias added principles 8 and 9 as specific to the context of mobile learning. I have added 10, 11, and 12 to complete the list. Principle 10 is based on the work of Sharon Oviatt, who found that the use of some types of physical interfaces (due to the additional cognitive load they impose) increases the achievement gap between higher- and lower-income students. In addition, keyboard input measurably disadvantages indigenous, Asian, and other learners whose native language does not employ the Roman alphabet.

Principle 11 is based on work by several human-computer interaction researchers who advocate for learner autonomy. Thomas Reitmaier and his colleagues encourage researchers supporting learners in developing countries to design "flexible technologies that people can use in ways that they deem appropriate for themselves, their context, and their culture." Moreover, Yvonne Rogers and Gary Marsden suggest that designers move away from designing technologies that "augment frailty" or simply compensate for a lack of ability as perceived by the designers, and move toward designing tools that allow communities of users to create their own technologies, based on their own values and needs. Finally, principle 12 acknowledges that accessibility compliance supports all the other principles and universality more generally.

The Engineering Design Centre at the University of Cambridge provides free access to inclusive design cards to support designers in this area (www.eng.cam. ac.uk/inclusivedesign/dtisurvey/cards.php).

›› The Strategies
for designing interfaces for mobile learning

Design for mobile learning must take into account not only the software environment, but also varied and dynamic physical and social contexts. The following strategies will help you design for the unique advantages and challenges associated with this kind of learning in the wild.

›› DESIGN FOR MICROLEARNING

Experts suggest that mobile learning is best suited to short bursts of activity because this is so frequently how learners use their devices. Clearly, this is more true for phones (which are ubiquitous and small-screened) than it might be for tablets, and learning in bursts won't apply to all learning scenarios, but it's certainly a sensible way to think about performance support. When a learner needs help mid-task (or between tasks), he needs something that doesn't take him completely out of play. There are also good examples of skill practice sessions that are short enough to do on the train, at lunchtime, or in other in-between times. As mentioned above, apps like MindSnacks (short language games), Instructional Design Guru (reference app), and sites like Lynda.com (video tutorials) are good examples of chunked, quick access learning.

›› DESIGN FOR THE BROADER ENVIRONMENT

Play to the strengths of this platform—its portability, context sensitivity, connectivity, and ubiquity. Well-designed mobile games can use the physical and social context of the player as integral components to the game, creating a rich playing and learning environment.

—ERIC KLOPFER, *Augmented Learning*

Mobile devices can sense where a learner is in space and time as well as who else is nearby. Geomapping APIs can indicate which services, natural features, businesses, or other people are near a user and tailor learning accordingly. For example, in an article in *Interactive Learning Environments*, Chen and Li describe an app that suggests foreign-language vocabulary based on a learner's physical location and fluency level. (At the bakery? You might need the word *baguette*.)

Accelerometers and gyroscopes can tell us about a user's position in space; the GPS for the Soul app even uses the flash to detect the user's heartbeat and stress levels. Plugging into data via mobile device sensors where appropriate has the potential to help support learners in a more targeted and seamless way.

PARE DOWN FEATURES

What's the *least* I can do for you?

—CLARK QUINN, ASTD Tech Knowledge 2013 Conference

In a workshop on mobile learning, industry leader Clark Quinn discouraged the common tendency to overdesign and overdevelop, and challenged designers to ask of their learners: "What's the least I can do to get you over the hump?" He then cautioned: "Don't try to put everything in a mobile world. Focus on 20% of the features that give you 80% of the value."

With their miniature screens, smaller memory, and limited processing power, mobile environments forcibly push minimalism on users. So aim to design around just one or a few simple and focused tasks. Many children's apps focus on a particular activity (drawing pictures, writing your name, pattern matching).

Other kids' apps like Super Why! and Word Spinner combine a few activities into one app. Super Why! provides access to tasks from a simple home menu, whereas Word Spinner employs a game board interface with randomized access to activities. In contrast, MyMathBook arguably puts a bit too much in one menu system, which compromises usability for a preschool audience (**FIGURE 9.1**).

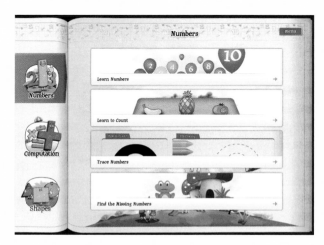

FIGURE 9.1 MyMathBook combines a number of math exercises for kids into one app. Combining many tasks into one app (and on one screen) can be tricky business for a small screen and a young audience. A separate initial menu screen might have worked better.

It's better to do one thing really well than several things poorly—this is especially true with apps. Users don't expect one app to solve all their problems. In fact, most will happily accrue and curate their own collections as part of personal learning and entertainment environments. Someone wanting to learn Spanish might have a translator app, a Spanish dictionary app, a practice game, and a podcast all rolled into one "Learning Spanish" folder for anywhere learning on the go.

APPLY FITTS'S LAW

Fitts's Law states that the time required to rapidly move to a target area is a function of the distance to the target and the size of the target. Translation: Make buttons and other graphical user interface controls big, because it's hard to click on small ones. Again, this might seem obvious, but learning environments are no strangers to finicky buttons and controls.

Many commercial websites have perfected the art of honoring Fitts's Law. Sites like Dropbox use it to its fullest to increase conversions. It's hard not to click on the gigantic box in the middle of the screen (**FIGURE 9.2**).

Programs and mobile apps designed for children are also good at keeping interactive elements nice and big, probably because they're guided by toy design, which knows to accommodate underdeveloped motor control. Ironically, the fact is that mobile devices can be harder for adults to use than they are for children, especially those with big hands, poor vision, arthritis, tremors, or any of the other goodies that come with aging. So why as designers do we often drop the "big and easy" approaches we apply to the design of children's software when it comes to apps for adults?

FIGURE 9.2 Dropbox applies Fitts's Law to its fullest to make clicking the sign-up button as easy and enticing as possible.

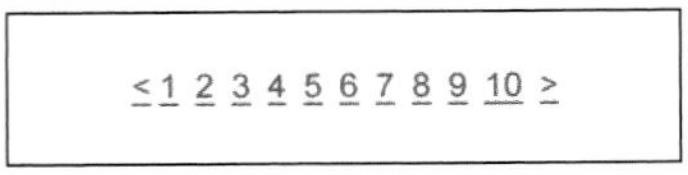

≤ 1 2 3 4 5 6 7 8 9 10 ≥

FIGURE 9.3 Links like those in a series of pages are often difficult to target on multitouch devices. Fitts's Law tells us that making these bigger and putting more space between them will make users lives easier.

One of the most common offenders is the underlined number. It's usually found in a list at the bottom of search results pages (**FIGURE 9.3**). It's not easy to target one character in a 10-point font, especially when it's wedged among five others of exactly the same diminutive size.

Apple's *iOS Human Interface Guidelines* suggest that designers give elements a target area of about 44 x 44 points. They point to the iPhone's calculator app as a good example of fingertip size controls. Of course, if you can be even more generous, consider it.

And finally, white space is as important as size. Surround buttons and controls with as much space as you can to avoid slips.

>> USE ANIMATED TRANSITIONS TO COMMUNICATE INTERFACE LOGIC

Owing to the considerable challenge of communicating the architecture of a complex space on a small screen, the mobile universe has spawned a slew of screen transitions to help users understand the digital space. Using the right transitions at the right time can be critical to mobile usability and learnability.

In a helpful article with video demos on some of these transitions and when they're most suitable, Cennydd Bowles writes, "When on-screen territory is at a premium, the gaps between screens become far more interesting." It's like scene changes in a play. Why have crew members run across stage pretending no one's looking when you can turn these transitions into part of the action? Smooth transitions support continuity and add value.

Here's a quick summary of the four transitions Bowles expands on, together with others that are useful for learning applications:

- **Horizontal transitions (left to right) for communicating hierarchy.** In iTunes, when a user clicks on an artist, he moves to the right to see albums, then right again to the song list, then right again to the song. To go "back" up the tree, he moves left. Horizontal movement to the right is a well-established way of communicating the hierarchical organization of information.

- **Vertical pop-ins for disruptive interactions.** When windows pop up from the bottom or down from the top, they're perceived as separate from the information and useful for login requests or calling on separate system controls.

- **Flips and page curls for settings and preferences.** When a user wants to change the city in a weather app, it flips around to take him "around the back," or perhaps lets him "lift" a map up by the corner to see behind it. Users expect to find background controls like settings and preferences around the back of an application and assume they can get there with flips and curls.

- **Card swap for changing frame of reference.** When a user switches apps on an iPad, the current screen sails behind the new one, which slots into place in front of him. This indicates a large change—he's changing the frame of reference and entering a new hierarchy. An even higher-level swap occurs when he changes user accounts on a computer. Apple handles this with a cube rotation effect.

- **Animated zoom for scale, distance, and hierarchy.** Zooming in on a photo or world map is a fairly intuitive process. In general, the difference in scale from one step to the next leaves the user with some common frames of reference (for example, he can continue to see the shape of Australia as he zooms in on it). In Powers of Negative Ten, however, the differences in scale are so massive that there's no visible relationship between one view and the next. In this case, the app includes a brief but smooth zoom-style blur transition to communicate that the view is becoming increasingly microscopic. Solar Walk does this in the opposite direction and to astonishing effect as zooming in and out allows the user to travel at light speeds through the galaxy. While zooming generally indicates a change of reference in physical space, Prezi uses zooming to organize conceptual hierarchy.

- **Slide-ins for menu anchoring.** Some apps provide controls in a persistent control panel on one edge of the screen. If content slides in and out from this same side of the screen, it seems to be connected or anchored to the menu that's docked there. This communicates how to access related controls. The NatGeo app uses a slide-in transition with its dock of controls.

- **Gradual build to minimize cognitive load.** An opening screen can be a lot for a user to take in at once, especially if it's highly detailed and graphical. Transitions can help him manage the load by having elements slide in one at a time, gradually building to the full screen. Amazing Alex, a physics game by the makers of Angry Birds, animates a gradual but still very fast build of the opening screen. The movement guides focus to each of the critical elements of the interface one at a time.

Few rules that deal with relatively new, constantly changing, and device-dependent interactions are carved in stone. As always, test to find out how your particular audience understands transitions for optimal results.

>> LEVERAGE INTERACTIONS UNIQUE TO MOBILE DEVICES

100 Floors is a puzzle app designed to use as many mobile gestures as possible. The user has to tilt and flip his phone to nudge objects, pinch, double-tap, swipe, and rub things to open doors and solve escape puzzles. Some apps require the user to blow on the screen to put out fires, inflate balloons, or blow glass, as in the glass-blowing Chihuly App (blowing is detected with the microphone). Mobile devices are utterly playful gadgets owing to all the direct manipulation and intuitive interaction they offer.

Carly Shuler of the Sesame Workshop created a diagram highlighting some of the unique learning affordances of handheld gaming devices for the *Pockets of Potential* report.

Intuitive interactions can also be used to reference the physical world that can improve the usability of an app. Take, for example, apps that act as compasses or spirit levels and are designed to look and behave like their real-world counterparts. Apple's *iOS Human Interface Guidelines* point out that apps like these provide "a lovely example of combining appropriate metaphor with direct manipulation for an intuitive design" (**FIGURE 9.4**).

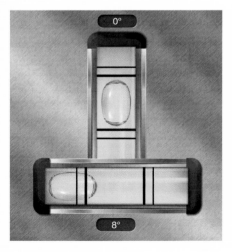

FIGURE 9.4 The Bubble Level app by Mogoco displays leveling information, not only in degrees by number, but also as liquid in a vial, a well-understood metaphor that also makes the app easier to use.

The Touch Gesture Reference Guide

The *Touch Gesture Reference Guide* is an excellent resource for the various touch interactions available to mobile devices and trackpads. Created by a team of veteran designers, the guide is also available as a set of elegant printable cards. You can download the guide for free from Luke Wroblewski's website at www.lukew.com/ff/entry.asp?1370.

The guide contains:

- An overview of the core gestures used for most touch commands
- How to utilize these gestures to support major user actions
- Visual representations of each gesture to use in design documentation and deliverables
- An outline of how popular software platforms support core touch gestures

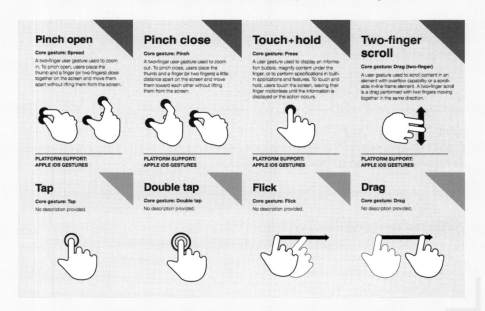

Caveats and considerations

Recreating real-world devices won't always be the best solution, and there are mobile-specific interactions that require special care, such as the following examples:

- Users may expect app orientation to change seamlessly, which may affect your interface strategy.
- Users can interact with only one app at a time.
- Hover/mouseover triggers don't apply for mobile devices. This means that if you're targeting mobile through the web instead of via an app, web interactions designed with these interactions will be unavailable to mobile users.

Furthermore, different learners will have different levels of mobile interface literacy. In other words, not everyone knows how to pinch and shake. So if you're designing for tech heads, live it up, but you might want to stick with taps and swipes for a broader audience.

If a particular gesture that goes beyond tap and swipe is especially well-suited for a learning interaction, for example, because it matches real-world context, then you might integrate it with the use of metaphor, on-screen cues, or a simple practice screen to ensure that users understand how to interact.

>> DESIGN FOR BEHAVIORS UNIQUE TO MOBILE LEARNERS

The fact that mobile users may be standing, walking, running, swimming, or talking opens up many possibilities. For example, the Nike+ Running app has features for use specifically while running. The Sleep Cycle alarm clock gets to work while users are fast asleep. These possibilities are undoubtedly exciting, but the side effects of users' contexts can be hard to predict.

Context impacts how people use their devices. Andrés Lucero and his colleagues point out that "when using their mobile phones, people have a tendency to hold their devices with one or two hands, with the screen facing toward them. People will usually adopt a particular device position, combined even with a second hand to cover the screen, either to browse private content, such as a confidential email, or to avoid glare." So consider how your app will be used and design for that use context—especially if it's meant to support performance or augment a real-world activity.

Context also impacts how people use devices socially. Consider medical students, for example. Unsurprisingly, these learners often access reference materials and resources on their mobile devices as they accompany doctors to see patients in clinical settings. The problem is that it looks terribly rude. Patients think these interns are chatting to friends instead of displaying proper bedside manner.

Desktop computers apply use constraints that small portables simply don't have, but the contextual variety that results means there's even less we can assume about use. This, of course, just places greater imperative on user research and testing. As a quick way to find out what doesn't work early, you can create a web prototype first. For more on that technique, see "Conducting Usability Research for Mobile" by Jared M. Spool (www.uie.com/articles/usability_research_for_mobile).

>> APPLY STRATEGIES TO SUPPORT VISUAL LEARNING

The smaller screen available on mobile devices, and the varied lighting conditions in which they're used, makes designing to support visual clarity even more critical. Review Chapter 5, "Learning Is Visual" for details on thoughtful reduction, contrast, information visualization, and other strategies to support visual clarity.

>> TAILOR INTERFACE DESIGN TO TASK TYPE

Different task types lend themselves to different interface styles. Apple provides the following useful examples in its *iOS Human Interface Guidelines:*

- If your app enables a productive task that involves the manipulation of a lot of detailed data, users are likely to appreciate an understated, mostly standard UI and streamlined navigation.

- If your app is a game or provides an immersive, story-driven experience, users expect to enter a unique world filled with rich graphics and innovative interactions.

- If your app helps users view content, they generally don't appreciate a UI that competes with it.

That final point is especially familiar to the learning context as it's also good advice for reducing extraneous cognitive load. All the strategies for quiet interfaces apply, so using controls that fade out or hide can help keep learning front and center.

>> TAILOR INTERFACE DESIGN TO MOBILE LEARNER AGE

Adults, teens, and children use mobile devices in different ways based on various physical, cognitive, social, and emotional factors. In addition, how they use them changes throughout the day and depends on where they are and who they're with.

PBS KIDS's Sara DeWitt advises designers that apps should "account for children's developing motor skills. All of our apps are tested to be sure they meet developmentally appropriate standards." For example, Alex Kuhn and colleagues improved their design of the StoryTime! app after multiple rounds of testing with primary school children. Their improved design removed the use of the double-tap action, which children found difficult; placed learning in context, which increased motivation; made the selection of features more precise; and favored the selection of higher-level features, that is, words rather than letters.

Rock Leung and his colleagues recommend a multilayer interface design for supporting older adults (age 65 and over) with the learnability of mobile devices. They found that presenting a reduced functionality interface first, then transitioning to a full-featured interface when learners were ready was particularly helpful in terms of "task completion time during initial learning, perceived complexity, and preference."

Research on teen use of mobile devices by Hilary Coolidge reveals that they frequently use these devices in groups. Furthermore, "When they are with their peers, teens' use of their mobile devices can change dramatically from the ways they use them when they are alone." Device use is also impacted by socioeconomic factors.

In short, expect age to matter to your interface design, so research and test to find out how it does.

PBS KIDS and mobile learning

In an interview with *Wired* magazine, Sara DeWitt of PBS KIDS described the nonprofit's unique and committed approach to creating genuinely educational media for children. "Just as we did with television in the 1960s, PBS KIDS is now looking at new platforms and saying, 'How can we use this to create age-appropriate, educational content to engage kids and help them prepare for success in school and in life?'"

PBS KIDS offers nearly thirty apps—available for download from its website—on learning in areas like math, literacy, and science, as well as educational party games and an app for parents with ideas for keeping kids entertained on the go.

Augmented, situated, and embodied. For a long-established company, PBS doesn't shy away from experimenting with new technologies. Its apps Fetch! Lunch Rush and Dinosaur Train Camera Catch employ different augmented reality techniques. Games like Going Batty and Caracal Leap in the Wild Kratts series rely on the device camera to encourage kids to get physical by jumping up and down to mimic animals, a strategy more often found in games for the Wii or Kinect.

Research and testing. DeWitt is quick to emphasize that PBS's work is always based on solid research evidence, and that its team tests not only for usability, but also for learning gains. "We do a great deal of testing in the development process of our apps, and have also done some of the earliest studies in the kids mobile apps space to test our apps for educational impact … . Many of our games are included in rigorous formative and summative evaluations, including pre- and post-tests to understand what children may have learned from playing with our content." One of the most recent studies showed impressive learning gains in vocabulary with the Martha Speaks Dog Party app. Some of the team's research (some of which is conducted by The Annenberg School for Communication at the University of Pennsylvania) is available online at pbskids.org/read/research.

Motivation. As it has for decades on television, PBS draws on children's intrinsic love of story and character in order to engage kids in learning experiences that are also entertainment experiences with their mobile apps. Characters that kids have come to know and love through television programming and books provide an engaging world in which learning can occur.

So take an online field trip to the PBS KIDS Lab (pbskids.org/lab). It's a great place to check out new developments in educational mobile apps created by some longtime leaders in children's educational entertainment.

>> DESIGN FOR SOCIAL MOBILE LEARNING

Mobile devices are personal devices, but people use them to connect with others. The *Washington Post* reported in 2012 that teens send an average of seven texts per waking hour. Studies and experience also show that teens often engage with media in groups and while interacting with others.

Not only is mobile use often very social, in some cultures an individualistic approach to mobile use can be an absolute faux pas. Thomas Reitmaier and his colleagues field-tested digital storytelling with mobile phones in Kenya and found that they were far from personal in this context:

Contrary to mobile phone use in Western contexts, in Adiedo the mobile phone is not a personal device. This could clearly be seen by the surprising comfort of our storyteller participants, when a cluster of sometimes 15 people—all trying to catch a glimpse of the mobile's screen—formed around them during story playback.

Aside from sharing one device, multiple devices are also increasingly linking up over networks. Links for sharing via e-mail or social media are commonplace and wireless connections can link devices in close proximity. For example, Nintendogs+cats StreetPass for the 3DS lets virtual dogs have play dates and share toys automatically with other virtual dogs and cats (without their "owners" even knowing!). When one device detects another in the vicinity, it shares pet information with the other device. The next time the player opens the game, he finds that his virtual Golden Retriever received a virtual squeaky toy from a virtual Maltese that passed by on the actual street. And they had a play date. So from group huddles to virtual animal play dates, the mobile and the social are inextricable.

Design for mobile-supported, face-to-face interactions

Mobile learning doesn't have to exclude real human contact. Tablets and even smartphones can support face-to-face collaboration. They can be passed around, used as game boards or controllers, or tiled together for collaborative sharing.

PicoTales lets multiple learners project creations onto a wall, allowing collaborative projections to interact for shared storymaking. Below are some practical recommendations based on research and general practice supporting real-life activity with handheld devices:

- Limit group size to between two and ten people for an effective experience.
- For larger groups of collocated learners, Andrés Lucero and his colleagues recommend designing for projection onto large screens and walls to create "broader ecosystems of mobile interaction."
- Design tablet apps as game boards for shared tabletop use.
- Design apps for pass-and-play, giving clear instruction to each player whose turn is active, and when it's time to pass to the next player.
- Design so that users can tile multiple devices together to create larger shared areas of interaction.
- Make the process of joining and exiting a collocated group intuitive and seamless. As Lucero and his colleagues put it: "People don't want to think about the hassles of setting up a group, but rather about the potential joys of repeatedly sharing and interacting with others in mobile collocated interactions."

Because social interaction is critical to learning, particularly in light of social constructivist and situated learning theories, it's worth thinking about how your learning experience might be enhanced by adding social connection features that support virtual or face-to-face collaboration.

>> PROTOTYPE, TEST, AND EVALUATE IN SITU

Whether you prototype with a website, paper, or an emulator, the important thing is that you do it, and that you do it with users in authentic, real-world contexts. Test not only for usability and learnability obstacles, but also for learning gains. Numerous studies indicate that you'll be surprised by what you find. Furthermore, including users in the design process can tap culturally specific solutions.

Where you can't realistically anticipate how users will come to use the learning environment, consider designing for flexibility and customization. For example, in the field study on mobile storytelling in rural Kenya mentioned earlier, Reitmaier and colleagues uncovered cultural surprises galore and concluded that for designers of mobile learning, particularly for learners in developing areas, "It is important to evaluate and test technologies in situ," and to create designs flexible enough to adapt to context and culturally specific use.

While we believe that we should emphasize understanding users and their needs, we should also accept that in [HCI for Development] our user understanding is often incomplete and unfinalized, and design flexible technologies that users can appropriate according to their needs, even if we do not know these a-priori.

Don't forget to share your findings with the community. You can team up with researchers who can run experiments and publish results in academic journals or share your experience via trade publications like *UX Magazine,* the eLearning Guild's Learning Solutions, or the ACM's *eLearn Magazine.* Together we can build best practices in design for mobile learning that gives everyone, everywhere a chance to learn and grow.

Go further

- Explore Apple's *iOS Human Interface Guidelines,* available for free from developer.apple.com.
- Read *Designing Mobile Interfaces* by Steven Hoober and Eric Berkman.
- Check out the continually updated reports on digital learning available from the Joan Ganz Cooney Center at the Sesame Workshop at www.joanganzcooneycenter.org.

SOURCES

Apple, Inc. n.d. *iOS Human Interface Guidelines.* https://developer.apple.com/library/ios/ documentation/UserExperience/Conceptual/MobileHIG.

Bean, Cammy. 2013. Clark Quinn Mobile Learning Design #astdtk13: *Cammy Bean's Learning Visions.* http://cammybean.kineo.com/2013/01/clark-quinn-mobile-learning-design.html.

Bowles, Cennydd. 2013. "Better Navigation through Proprioception." *A List Apart.* www.alistapart.com/ column/better-navigation-through-proprioception.

Burgstahler, Sheryl. 2012. *Universal Design of Instruction (UDI): Definition, Principles, Guidelines, and Examples.* Seattle: University of Washington. http://www.washington.edu/doit/Brochures/ PDF/instruction.pdf.

Donahoo, Daniel. 2012. "PBS' Quest to Build a Better Kids' App." *Wired,* July 27. http://www.wired. com/geekdad/2012/07/profile-pbs-kids-apps.

Elias, Tanya. 2011. "Universal Instructional Design Principles for Mobile Learning." *International Review of Research in Open and Distance Learning* 12 (2). http://www.irrodl.org/index.php/irrodl/ article/view/965/1675.

Fjeldsoe, Brianna S., Alison L. Marshall, and Yvette D. Miller. 2009. "Behavior Change Interventions Delivered by Mobile Telephone Short-Message Service." *American Journal of Preventive Medicine* 36 (2), 165–73. doi:10.1016/j.amepre.2008.09.040.

Gee, James Paul. 2010. *New Digital Media and Learning as an Emerging Area and "Worked Examples" as One Way Forward.* Cambridge, MA: MIT Press.

Herrington, Anthony, Jan Herrington, and Jessica Mantei. 2009. "Design Principles for Mobile Learning." http://researchrepository.murdoch.edu.au/5229.

Klemmer, Scott R., Bjorn Hartmann, and Leila Takayama. 2006. "How Bodies Matter: Five Themes for Interaction Design." In *Proceedings of the 6th Conference on Designing Interactive Systems.* ACM. http://hci.stanford.edu/publications/2006/HowBodiesMatter-DIS2006.pdf.

Klopfer, Eric. 2011. *Augmented Learning: Research and Design of Mobile Educational Games.* Cambridge, MA: MIT Press.

Kuhn, Alex, Chris Quintana, and Elliot Soloway. 2009. "StoryTime: A New Way for Children to Write." In *Proceedings of the 8th International Conference on Interaction Design and Children.* ACM.

Leung, Rock, Leah Findlater, Joanna McGrenere, Peter Graf, and Justine Yang. 2010. "Multi-Layered Interfaces to Improve Older Adults' Initial Learnability of Mobile Applications." *ACM Transactions on Accessible Computing* 3 (1), 1–30.

Low, Leonard, and Margaret O'Connell. 2006. "Learner-Centric Design of Digital Mobile Learning." *Proceedings of the OLT Conference.*

Lucero, Andrés, Matt Jones, Tero Jokela, and Simon Robinson. 2013. "Mobile Collocated Interactions: Taking an Offline Break Together." *Interactions* 20 (2), 26–32.

Malamed, Connie. n.d. "It's Not eLearning on a Phone." *The eLearning Coach*. http://theelearningcoach. com/mobile/its-not-elearning-on-a-phone/.

Malamed, Connie. n.d. "10 Tips for Designing mLearning and Support Apps." *The eLearning Coach*. http://theelearningcoach.com/mobile/mobile-learning-and-support-app-design/.

Milgram, Paul, and Fumio Kishino. 1994. "A Taxonomy of Mixed Reality Visual Displays." *IEICE Transactions on Information Systems* E77-D (12), 1–15.

Oviatt, Sharon. 2013. *The Design of Future Educational Interfaces*. New York: Routledge.

Reitmaier, Thomas, Nicola J. Bidwell, and Gary Marsden. 2010. "Field Testing Mobile Digital Storytelling Software in Rural Kenya." In *Proceedings of the 12th International Conference on Human Computer Interaction with Mobile Devices and Services*. ACM.

Rogers, Yvonne, and Gary Marsden. 2013. "Does He Take Sugar? Moving Beyond the Rhetoric of Compassion." *Interactions* 20 (4), 48–57. doi:10.1145/2486227.2486238.

Shuler, Carly. 2009. *Pockets of Potential: Using Mobile Technologies to Promote Children's Learning*. New York: The Joan Ganz Cooney Center. http://www.joanganzcooneycenter.org/wp-content/uploads/2010/03/pockets_of_potential_1_.pdf.

Samson, Kurt. 2007. "Mental Calisthenics Training Slows Cognitive Decline, Helps Seniors Stay Independent, Five-Year Trial Finds." *Neurology Today* 7 (3), 3–4. doi:10.1097/00132985-200702060-00003.

UNESCO. 2013. "Mobile Learning: 'We Cannot Continue to Live in the Pre-Digital Era.'" http://www.unesco.org/new/en/media-services/single-view/news/mobile_learning_we_cannot_continue_to_live_in_the_pre_digital_era/#.UiPpP2SSC70.

10

Designing the Space

The interior design of digital learning spaces,
including layout, navigation, and architecture

⟪ The Backstory

Designing educational space

In "Learning Environments for the 21st Century," Christian Kühn argues that learning space should be adaptable and agnostic—amenable to a natural evolution, to discovery, and to teamwork:

> Regarding learning environments as 'spaces for teams may well turn out to be the major paradigm shift in the design of educational facilities today … . For the time being, architects should refrain from the impulse to design the perfect learning environment but rather try to envision the infrastructure that enables effective learning environments to develop over time.

He's talking about schools, but the message is no less valid for our digital lives. He goes on to say that learning infrastructures should "offer options to create micro-environments which are easily appropriated and controlled by their user, while at the same time give a feeling of connectedness to a greater whole." The key elements are clear: learner autonomy and connectedness, two of the three components critical to motivation (as discussed in Chapter 7, "Learning Is Emotional").

And yet, how many educational technologies can you think of that allow learners to recreate the space as needed? How many environments have the capacity to evolve as learners needs change within the space?

In Chapter 6, "Learning Is Social," I used the design of a virtual design studio as an example of aggregating tools into a community environment instead of building an integrated whole from scratch. Sometimes this is the best (or only) way to keep a learning space adaptable over time, since tools can be added and removed as the community evolves. At an individual level, this is how a personal learning environment works: the learner compiles a unique combination of resources and human connections that adapt and evolve as required and as her expertise grows.

The downside to a multiple tool environment is, of course, a lack of coherence. Ironically, many universities suffer from the problems of both an overly rigid integrated system and a lack of coherence from multiple tools. The university where I work uses an industry-standard LMS that feels incredibly rigid and disconnected from the social learning that occurs organically outside of it. At the same time, the university supports sixty other tools to meet various needs from lecture recording to portfolios to synchronous meetings. Add to that the numerous administrative systems required to support an organization of over 50,000 students and it's no wonder the overwhelming response from students via user surveys and focus groups is always the same: There are too many different tools to deal with.

Currently, we address this fragmentation problem in fairly standard ways, namely, by encouraging staff to use one tool as an entry point from which other tools launch, and by providing a set of flexible templates with a consistent design. Many corporate organizations have more control over branding and tool use but face similar dilemmas. The challenges facing the design of coherent yet flexible and evolving learning environments are formidable.

Furthermore, learning environments function at many levels: tool, activity, learner, instructor, course, platform, and organization, as well as different combinations of these, and even the larger, more amorphous network of connected people and spaces that link across a web of social learning.

You can target your responsibilities as a designer to any of these levels. This chapter provides some insights that can help you design interfaces for spaces at multiple levels in order to foster coherent, adaptable, effective, and inspiring learning experiences.

The hardware interface

While designing digital screens may be your bread and butter as a designer, it's easy to forget that the tangible interface precedes all else: keyboard, mouse, touchscreen, goggles, glove, joystick, wand, body movement, gesture, and myriad experimental forays into tangible and embodied interaction.

Even if you're not involved in innovating these hardware interfaces, the "simple" decision of what hardware interface to design for is essential to learning. In fact, you should be looking both forward and backward when assembling your toolbox.

WHEN PAPER IS THE CUTTING EDGE

Amid the carnival of EdTech excitement, you'd be forgiven for forgetting that digital technologies are still just tools, added to a bag of tricks that has accumulated over many years. Sure, there are some tools we'll probably never go back to (punch cards? slide rules?), but then there are the workhorses that have survived for a reason, like pencil and paper.

Sharon Oviatt and her colleagues presented a study in which students working on math problems worked faster, remembered more, and made fewer errors on paper (both regular and digital paper) than they did on tablet-based UIs. The difference was most dramatic for low-performing students. Some of those students' comments are telling:

- "I was focusing on the computer, not the problem."
- "I knew I could do it, but it was just faster to write."
- "I'm a visual learner. I like to draw pictures to help me think clearly."
- "I need visualizations to figure out the problems."

This study was published more than seven years ago, yet it's still easier to quickly sketch, diagram, and think visually on paper than on a mobile device (digital pens and paper still aren't widespread among learners). As user experience designers, we know the value of thinking visually with paper and pencil all too well. Our processes and deliverables still include paper, marker, pencil, sticky notes, and napkins when creativity and big-picture thinking are called upon. On the plus side, digital capture of these old-school tools is now a cinch with mobile phone cameras at hand.

The problem with keyboard and mouse input is that they're suited to a particular kind of input (alphanumeric typing). It's not easy to draw math formulas, work with geometric shapes, write in languages for which the keyboard is not suited, create diagrams, or sketch and map ideas quickly with a keyboard. Many learning areas require all of these in combination and easy switching between them—it's hard to beat paper for its flexibility.

Furthermore, pen-based interfaces (whether paper or digital) align with the way things work in many real-world contexts, so imposing keyboard input removes the learners from real-world practice. It's also a lot easier to huddle and collaborate around a piece of paper than around a desktop computer, which makes paper better for supporting social learning. Multitouch tabletops provide some of the benefits of paper combined with the benefits of digital input, but they're still uncommon and aren't as easily adapted and rearranged as paper and pen. Multitouch tablets do allow sketching, but not with the same precision as pen interfaces and with greater limits on paper size.

Oviatt suggests that to optimize learning gains we match the physical interface with the task, such as writing or diagramming, as well as with the domain (the tools used by professionals).

BACK TO COGNITIVE LOAD

Of course, pen-based interfaces aren't always better, and certainly for Roman alphabetic input it's hard to beat a keyboard. There are also user groups for whom pencil and paper mechanics add cognitive load, for example, young children and those with disabilities. In their StoryTime! app project, Alex Kuhn and his colleagues removed the need for primary students to handwrite full sentences, thus helping the children focus on sentence construction. Kuhn's studies showed that using a mobile app that let students create and complete sentences using their fingers to move words around (like magnetic poetry) helped them to stay engaged and maintain focus on the learning objectives.

The bottom line is this: Before you think about software technologies, consider how the needs of a learning activity match up most effectively with the affordances of available technologies.

» The Strategies
for the design of learning spaces

The strategies in this section are broken down into two subcategories:

- Strategies for layout, navigation, and screen design
- Strategies for the design and configuration of learning spaces

Strategies for layout, navigation, and screen design

The general principles of good information architecture and effective page layout apply to all digital design, but learning experiences bring additional considerations into the mix. The strategies below provide guidance on layout and navigation issues specific to learning, including tips for displaying feedback and supporting learnability.

» PLACE POP-UP FEEDBACK NEAR QUESTIONS

Proximity is a critical and easily applied principle for learning interfaces. Research has proven that people learn better when text relating to an image is placed near that image. So the gist is this: Don't separate related text and visuals.

As obvious as that sounds, this guideline is frequently violated. For example, diagram labels are often corralled into a caption instead of distributed onto the diagram (as in the horse anatomy example in Chapter 5, "Learning Is Visual").

Another learning situation where the proximity principle is often neglected is in multiple-choice question feedback. I recently viewed an eLearning program about occupational health and safety. It was well-designed, but the answer feedback came up on the bottom of the screen, far away from the quiz questions. This is very common, usually for practical reasons having to do with prebuilt templates and skeletons that automatically place feedback at the bottom. Yet, research indicates that learners will get more from feedback if it's near the item it refers to (**FIGURE 10.1**).

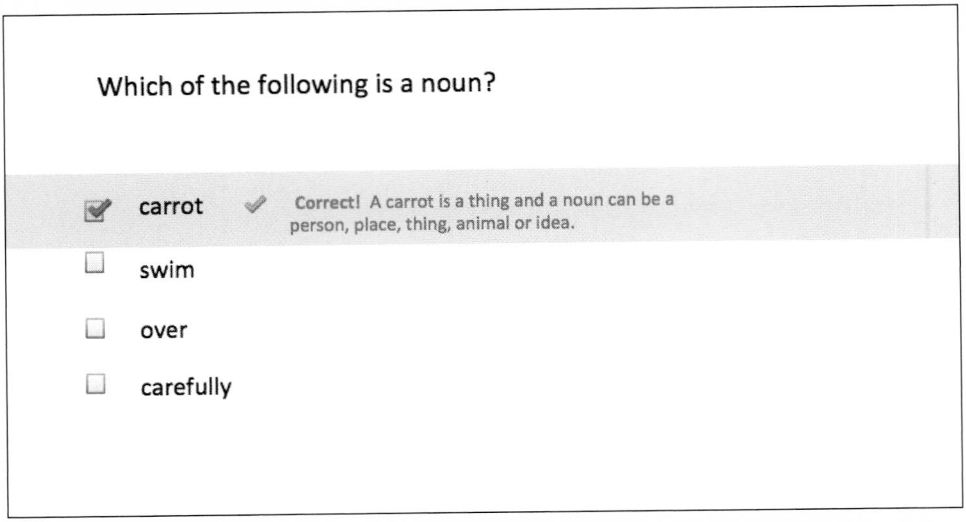

Which of the following is a noun?

☑ carrot ✓ Correct! A carrot is a thing and a noun can be a
              person, place, thing, animal or idea.

☐ swim

☐ over

☐ carefully

FIGURE 10.1 Users learn better from feedback when it's placed near the item it refers to, as in this image.

So, whenever you can, rather than including feedback for an incorrect answer at the bottom of the screen, include it beside the answer. Likewise, if you're designing a template, design spaces for feedback next to spaces for answers.

Caveats and considerations

If you have a video or animation that requires explanation, include the explanation as audio narration—learners will thank you for it. If you can't use narration, let learners read the written explanation first and then play the video, rather than including the text *within* the video or having it play in parallel. In this case, placing explanatory text on the same screen as the video or animation means your learners will have to process them at the same time, which is too much to take in at once.

>> DESIGN TO ACCOMMODATE RICH FEEDBACK

Learners value and learn more from teachers who give them helpful feedback. It's the difference between simply being told your answer is wrong, and being told *why* your answer is wrong and receiving suggestions for what to do next. While many eLearning programs still slap their learners with just a green tick or a red *X*, as designers we should generally be aiming for better.

Formative feedback is given throughout a lesson or course, while *summative feedback* is given at the end of a course. Feedback can be delivered by e-mail, presented directly on-screen, or presented as direct consequences to action embedded within a game or virtual environment. (This is intrinsic feedback, which was discussed in Chapter 8, "Multimedia and Games.")

Intrinsic feedback is worked into the program as real-life consequences to user actions. Whether it's an explosion in a virtual chemistry lab or an angry customer, digital environments are the best place for this kind of authentic feedback based on the real world.

But feedback isn't always intrinsic. It also comes in the form of extrinsic feedback, like test answer support, or explanatory text following an incorrect decision. ELearning industry leader Michael Allen suggests that designers use a unique visual identity for extrinsic feedback, such as a virtual advisor. He also reminds us that "feedback should be displayed in close proximity to either the action taken, the consequences, or preferably both."

One of the major disadvantages of massive open online courses (MOOCs) at the time of this writing is that there's no way to scale expert feedback for every learner enrolled in the course. No teacher could possibly respond individually to 20,000 students and provide the rich feedback that is so beneficial to learners. Instead, MOOCs currently rely on peer feedback and on modeling examples of good work.

While feedback itself will be written by the instructional designer, as the interface designer, you'll need to design space for rich feedback, remembering to place it near the answer it refers to and thinking creatively to ensure that it's given intrinsically where possible.

>> USE DEFAULTS AND SUGGESTIONS TO MANAGE CHOICE

Learners like choices, but as Barry Schwartz argues in *The Paradox of Choice*, too much choice makes people unhappy. In a learning environment, too much choice becomes overwhelming, discouraging, and, paradoxically, makes it difficult for learners to maintain the sense of autonomy necessary to motivate them.

Furthermore, in learning scenarios, it's important to remember that experts can handle more choice than novices. What do you do when your interface has to cater to both? One solution is to use defaults and suggestions. In other words, when you have to provide four or more options to learners, make one stand

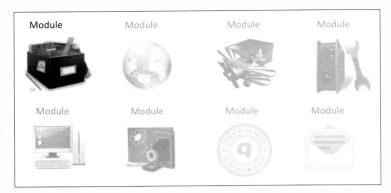

FIGURE 10.2 To help learners manage choice and prevent them from feeling overwhelmed, make one option stand out in a selection of four or more items.

out (**FIGURE 10.2**). In this way, you'll guide novices' attention to optimal choices without removing options for experts.

>> INTRODUCE FEATURES GRADUALLY TO MANAGE CHOICE

Another stellar approach to offering choice but keeping learners from feeling overwhelmed is exemplified by game interfaces. In many adventure games, the interface becomes gradually more complex as the user builds familiarity with existing options. An advanced user might have access to hundreds of features and options, while a beginner might start with just two or three.

This is an excellent principle to carry over to interface design for learning, as it not only helps learners manage choice, but also lets new users jump right into the action and bypass tedious instructions—a clear boost to motivation and engagement, as well as a good way to manage cognitive load. (Refer to Chapter 8 for more on this topic.)

>> SHAPE THE PATH

Suggest a particular course of action, nudge people to take a first step, set up defaults, get a small initial commitment—these are the kinds of little details that can shape the path.

—STEPHEN ANDERSON, *Seductive Interaction Design*

The two previous strategies for managing user choice are related to the notion of "shaping the path." Shaping the path can be thought of as making small changes that guide users in a particular direction.

Interface design can shape the path in many ways. For example, when the learner first logs in to a program, rather than showing her an empty screen (as my human resources system does, which still confounds me even though I've used it dozens of times), the interface should offer simple choices that keep her moving toward her goal.

The research-sharing service Mendeley handles this well. When the user first opens the program, her library is naturally empty. Instead of being faced with an empty box labeled "zero documents" (or, at the opposite extreme, an overwhelming list of features), the software gently shapes the user's path. It guides her to the next step and provides a very simple set of options that keeps the process flowing without removing control (**FIGURE 10.3**). This simple design detail keeps the user engaged in her task, establishes trust, and increases the chance that she'll come back.

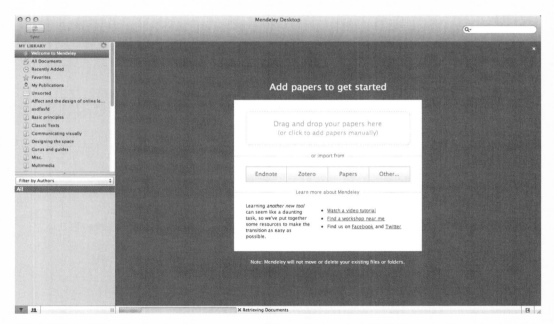

FIGURE 10.3 Rather than confronting a new user with an empty screen, Mendeley provides a simple set of options that help her learn how to use the program and guides her in the right direction.

You don't need research proof to know that nobody likes to RTFM (read the *** manual). In Chapter 8, we looked at how games incorporate learnability into gameplay itself so that users can jump right in. The next step is to extend this principle of cleverly using context to replace written instructions to the learning activity itself.

Allen provides an excellent example:

Use context visuals to imply the challenge and controls. For example, the image of a disassembled device with pieces randomly scattered about expresses the challenge and the controls nonverbally...with proper invitations for action, such as changing cursor shapes, learners will experiment and learn faster than through reading instructions. And they'll enjoy figuring things out more than following a set of instructions that lay it all out for them.

William Lidwell, Kritina Holden, and Jill Butler put it another way in *The Universal Principles of Design*:

If you find you're needing to provide instructions, redesign the screen ... . The amount of help necessary to successfully interact with a design is inversely proportional to the quality of the design—if a lot of help is needed, the design is poor.

Sound a bit extreme? Perhaps. But this is a genuinely valuable way to scrutinize learning interfaces. For example, if you have the words "Click the button at right to continue," do you need that extra text? If the button at right is big and labeled "Continue," then the text is probably superfluous and distracting. On the other hand, if the button at right is a tiny gray arrow, and that's why you need to put the text there, then the text is still superfluous because it's the button that needs to be redesigned.

AVOID MINESWEEPING

It's tempting to think that creating a navigation scheme that requires people to explore unguided will be fun or delightful, but then you're forgetting that people come to software for a reason, and Easter egg hunting is not usually the reason. Research indicates that people are extremely task-oriented online. They engage in information foraging and exhibit behaviors not unlike animals foraging for food. More importantly, they're impatient. They're primed to filter, click, skip, take the shortest route, and above all, to act. Minesweeping—that is, making them click at random to find controls or answers hidden on a screen—gets in their way and wastes their time. In fact, usability research shows that people over the age of 12 do not like this kind of interaction. This is understandable, as it wastes precious time without a purpose.

Caveats and considerations

There are two caveats about the no minesweeping rule. First, the rule doesn't necessarily extend past navigation. Learners are likely to be more tolerant of "click to find out" exercises that are guided, relevant to the learning, and not simply part of navigation. Second, the rule applies to adults—learners over 12 years old to be more precise. Young children are much more open to this kind of hunt-and-peck approach. Still, take care to ensure that it doesn't become an obstacle rather than a motivator.

Strategies for the design and configuration of learning spaces

The strategies below will help you better design your learning environments, whether they're custom-built or specially configured spaces based on standard technologies.

>> DESIGN FOR VARIOUS FORMS OF ASSESSMENT

Assessment is the weak link in e-learning systems. E-learning designers have relied predominantly on tools that are directed at the construction of test items. The disadvantage of such items is that they tend to focus on the measurement of low-level retention of isolated facts, rather than on the application of knowledge to solve ill-structured problems.

—WIM JOCHEMS, JEROEN VAN MERRIËNBOER, AND ROB KOPER,
   Integrated E-Learning

Assessment holds so much sway within formal learning environments that I'd be remiss if I didn't mention it at least once. Even informal learning environments may benefit from offering methods by which learners can assess their own progress, or review the work of others.

Interface designers don't design assessment, but if you're involved in designing an environment that will need to account for it, the core principle is to consider assessment in all its variety. It's easy to think that all testing and evaluation come as multiple-choice questions, which are among the easiest to automatically deliver. However, pedagogically speaking, there are far more authentic and effective ways of evaluating the capabilities of a learner. This is where some believe eLearning technology designers can do better than we have.

Assessment often meets practical needs like certification, promotion, graduation, and so on. However, it should also always be looked upon as part of the learning itself. Rich feedback, trial and error, and self-reflection are just some of the ways in which testing is an incredible learning opportunity.

Item-based testing can be personalized with adaptive and interactive technologies that tailor question delivery to the learner's individual level of mastery. But beyond that, assessment, both formative (during a course) and summative (at the end of a course), can involve a wide variety of approaches and tools, including screen capture, peer review, learner-produced video of performance, learner-produced artifacts presented in portfolios, scenario-based challenges that let learners apply their learning, and much more.

In the assessment category, there's also the ongoing issue of plagiarism and cheating. Technology has made this both easier to do and easier to detect. Software like TurnItIn lets instructors check essays for plagiarized text. Beyond acting as a policing tool, it can also provide information to students before they submit their work, for example, by highlighting bits of text with large similarities to other work and saying, "This text (link) looks similar to this (link). Need help with referencing your sources?" For more information about how companies manage risk in this area, see Nikki Shepherd Eatchel's article "Online Testing: Making It Count" (http://elearnmag.acm.org/featured.cfm?aid=1266889).

>> SELECT TOOLS BASED ON THE LEARNING DOMAIN AND ACTIVITY

When it comes to learning, finding a good fit between learning outcomes and the hardware interface (as mentioned in the first section), software interactions, and software tools can lead to real learning gains.

Aim to design software interactions that seek to match real-world activity. As Allen advises

Match behavioral modalities. If the real-world activity would require moving something, have learners drag objects. If they would have to type a message, have them type one. If they'd have to tell a caller his credit application is being denied, have them record what they would say.

Furthermore, different software tools are more or less effective for different types of learning activities. *Asynchronous communication tools* that allow for interaction over time, such as discussion forums, are well suited to learning experiences that require reflection or independent research. *Synchronous tools,* such as chat or live online classroom sessions, are well suited to experiences that benefit from group synergy and social presence.

Finally, as mentioned above, consider the affordances and limitations of the hardware interfaces that learners work with. A keyboard and mouse are good at certain types of input, like letters and numbers; touchscreens are good at others, like intuitive object manipulation. Paper and pen are still better for sketching out ideas or creating symbols and diagrams. Therefore, you can choose the right tool (or combination of tools) for the task when there's a choice, or aim to meet the same needs via design when there isn't.

>> SET LEARNING IN REAL-WORLD CONTEXT TO PROMOTE TRANSFER

As education researchers say, learning is situated. Context matters. In the instructional design world this relates to transfer. One of the biggest challenges for education and training is ensuring that what learners learn in the classroom actually transfers to real life, or that they can take what they learned in one context and transfer it to other contexts. The closer the learning experience is to the real-world context, the more likely learners will be able to transfer what they've learned to the real world. Thus, the message is to set learning activity within real-world contexts. The importance of authentic context for educational games was discussed in Chapter 8.

A second important point is that you can support transfer by setting practice and examples in multiple contexts. According to Ruth Clark and Richard Mayer, "When you expose learners to multiple contexts, they are better able to extract essential principles and transfer them to various real-world scenarios." So consider placing that course for vet nurses in the surgery room as well as at the farm, or provide examples for that math program that take place at the shop, on the construction site, and in the playground. Context variety supports transfer.

>> GIVE LEARNERS CONTROL APPROPRIATE TO THEIR LEVEL OF EXPERTISE

Much like choice, having control is something that isn't always good for learners. Despite their hankering to be in control, they're not always fit for the job. An important distinction here is that expert learners can successfully handle much more control over their learning than beginners.

This has implications for professional development, where it's often the case that nonmandatory learning is provided to experts in a particular field, for example, a course for medical practitioners on new strategies for diagnosing autism. This kind of program is better suited to an approach that gives learners plenty of freedom to pick and choose what they want to learn. As experts, they have well-established mental models and very stringent time limits. It will likely benefit them to be selective about which modules or topics they focus on and when.

In contrast, the same learning program created for first-year medical students might look very different. These beginners have less previous knowledge in the topic and are thus less equipped to select an effective learning path through content and activities. They might choose to skip practice exercises they need or topics they're less interested in. In this case, decisions about the information architecture and navigation will be shaped by decisions about learner control.

Learning designers will generally be making decisions about learner control and the structure of the experience, but as an interface designer you should have strategies they can draw from to implement these designs effectively.

Here are some general principles:

Let learners control their pace through a learning experience. Provide video and animation controls, let learners review previous content, and always permit them to exit. But you'll have to be more careful with giving them control of the sequence of instruction.

Give beginners less control and more guidance, but give experts more control. Novices are frequently unable to effectively design their own path through nonlinear content, or to decide how much practice they require. Therefore, you should allow learners choices over which topics and activities to do only *if:*

- They have prior knowledge, for example, in advanced courses or professional development.
- The chunks of content are not interdependent.
- The learning experience is designed to be supportive and informational rather than skill building.

Along these same lines, research shows that unguided exploratory learning is not the most effective approach if used on its own for achieving specific learning outcomes.

>> SUPPORT EXPERIMENTATION AND PLAY

Mitchel Resnick at the MIT Media Lab is a proponent of what he calls "lifelong kindergarten." He recommends that education be inspired by the way children learn in kindergarten, where they move through a spiral of activities in which they imagine → create → play → share → reflect.

How can interface designers create environments that allow learners to imagine, create, play, share, and reflect? The most obvious guides are those educational technologies designed to assist learners in "making and doing," such as Scratch, created by Resnick. Scratch effectively supports every step in the spiral.

The key to play is that it's a safe way to engage in experimentation. When Resnick and his team spoke with children as part of research studies on this process, the kids themselves left the researchers with sound tips, and four out of six of these tips were about being free to make mistakes.

Adults want to know that it's safe to make mistakes, too. Interfaces must be mistake-friendly if they're to support experimentation and creative thinking. Mistakes are also excellent learning opportunities. Allen reminds us to "allow learners to step back and make corrections. This rewards learners for continuously evaluating their work—an outcome we could prize."

This relates to learnability, but indirectly works its way into the instructional design itself as well. A forgiving interface lets users easily go back, undo, and retry multiple pathways.

WELCOME MISTAKES: DESIGN FOR RETRIES AND DO-OVERS

Many interactive systems make it too easy for users to make mistakes, do not allow users to correct mistakes, or make it costly or time-consuming to correct mistakes. Even more important than the impact on time is the impact on learning. When exploration is discouraged and anxiety is high, learning is severely hampered.

—JEFF JOHNSON, *Designing with the Mind in Mind*

Making your program a safe place for users to make mistakes has benefits at the user experience, pedagogical, and practical levels. It allows for safe exploration, which is critical to learning, but also the learners are often "performing" within learning environments, which means the stakes are high. They might be testing out ideas or demonstrating their knowledge in front of peers and assessors—scenarios that involve judging, grading, evaluation, and reporting. A random association game quickly leads to graduation, job, failure, or unemployment.

Of course, at the basic level, the error-friendly environment aligns with a graphical user interface *error recovery* principle. Some of the additional reasons a mistake-friendly environment is critical for learning are

- **Pedagogical:** When learners are able to edit, reformulate, and refine what they're working on, opportunities for reflection and learning are increased.
- **User experience:** Learners get frustrated when they feel like they can do better but can't show it by changing or improving their input.
- **Practical:** When the technology fails learners, or they perform badly due to an interface-based slip or mistake, you'll get lots of angry e-mails unless they can do-over without penalty.

Whether learners submit input to teachers, competitive peers, parents, or employers, the stakes are high. Giving them ways to edit, delete, undo, go back, try without committing, and so on are essential to creating an atmosphere of safe exploration. But what can we do to prevent errors? Jeff Johnson reminds designers to prevent errors as much as possible by:

- Deactivating invalid commands (using negative affordances)
- Making errors easy to spot by showing users what they've done, for example, deleting a paragraph by mistake, posting the same message twice
- Always allowing users to easily undo, reverse, or correct their actions

Although good error prevention is not entirely in the hands of interface designers, many decisions lie in our hands. For example, we should

Design good signifiers. Make things *look* like they're going to do what they do. The design of objects on the screen should communicate how learners can interact with them and what they can do.

Make actions reversible. For example, always keep the Back button working. The Back button is one of the most commonly used tools online. Knowing that they can explore and try different options but hit the Back button if they want to makes learners feel comfortable. Learners are also generally more likely to use the Back button than buttons you put on the screen to do the same thing, so honor it.

Provide safety nets. Include safety nets like automatic saves or repeat tries in case something fails. If that's impossible, consider reminding learners to save work themselves.

Confirm important actions first. Before deleting that essay forever, or publishing it to all users, make sure your learner didn't just hit Delete or Publish by mistake.

Give warnings. Remember to provide warnings like "Are you sure you want to exit?" or "Are you sure you want to submit your assignment?" and you will prevent a whole lot of learner strife.

Provide help. Help, of course, works best when it's contextualized, so try to replace or supplement a separate manual with on-screen help that appears next to the item to which it refers.

Both warnings and help should be secondary resorts. Ideally, you do so well with the first four that the last two become largely unnecessary or redundant.

But what about examples more specific to learning? Learners who run into technical problems when trying to complete a quiz are often condemned to freaking out and spamming a forum. How many times have you accidentally clicked the wrong answer in an online quiz, only to find there was no going back. (Flashbacks of an early version of the computerized GRE haunt me to this day.)

Systems like Coursera and Moodle handle this scenario by allowing learners to take a quiz multiple times (instructor willing). That may strike you as a bit nutty, because how could a student not score 100 percent by the fifth time around? But it's not so nutty if you consider that what really matters about these quizzes is student learning.

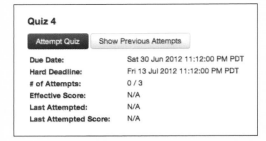

FIGURE 10.4 The three-try quiz is forgiving of technical errors and of student misunderstandings and slips.

There are also a few interface tricks you can keep up your sleeve to ensure that anyone who passes the quiz does so because they *learned* from their mistakes, not just because they memorized the correct answers. For example, in the Stanford HCI course at Coursera, in addition to a three-try limit, there's a clever 10-minute interval between quiz-taking sessions (**FIGURE 10.4**). To do better next time, a learner's understanding will have to have gone further than short-term memory. Secondly, the order of answer choices is randomized, so the learner can't just memorize a series of letters (a, c, b, c) to get by. Small interaction design changes can make a big difference.

Another forgiving design decision offered by the Coursera example is that assignment resubmission is allowed up until a deadline. In the case of the HCI course, assignment content is entered into a long web form and the learner can save her work or submit the form when she's done. How many students of the thousands each term have accidentally pressed Submit before they were ready? I don't have the numbers, but I'll bet it's a lot. The tutors were never bothered, however, by these thousands of errors because the software lets learners *resubmit* as many times as they like, until the deadline for that assignment is reached. (They even incorporate a silent grace period after the published deadline.) Submission doesn't actually close until half an hour *after* it was meant to, further preventing mass catastrophe. They really thought of just about everything.

>> ACT LIKE YOU'RE LISTENING

How fast did you want your university entrance exam scores back? If you asked your professor a question and she stared back at you blankly for one or two minutes, how would you feel? If you told a classmate you discovered a cure for acne, and she told you to wait a second then spun a rainbow wheel in front of your face while doing something else, would that fill you with goodwill? And yet, this is precisely what interfaces do to us all the time.

Researchers consistently find that system responsiveness is the *number one most important* determining factor of user happiness (you read that right)—it's even more important than factors like usability and learnability. Interfaces need to keep up with learners and let them know what's going on; if learners have to wait, interfaces need to tell them why, for how long, and how they're getting on with things in the meantime. If they don't, learners will simply abandon them if they can, or become resentful and ineffective if they can't.

Here again, we can thank Jeff Johnson for an excellent summary of ways to ensure that interfaces are responsive (adapted from *Designing with the Mind in Mind*):

- Let learners know when the system is busy and what it's doing.
- Immediately acknowledge learners' actions and input.
- Indicate how long operations will take.
- Preserve learners' perception of cause and effect.
- Let learners do other things while they're waiting.
- Animate movement smoothly and clearly.
- Allow learners to cancel or delay long operations.

>> DESIGN FOR SOCIOCULTURAL CONTEXT

As mentioned in Chapter 5, small design decisions can have very different effects across cultures. While we tend to think of nationality when it comes to cross-cultural design, this also applies to subcultures arising from things like age, interest, profession, or socioeconomics. A troll is a fantasy creature to most adults, but an internet annoyance to the net generation. Sixties chic is nostalgic to baby boomers and ultra-modern to hipsters. Kids don't know what CD stands for and don't recognize drawings of typewriters and rotary dial telephones (these still show up on primary school worksheets, much to the bewilderment of 6-year-olds). Using red in a visual denotes sexiness in the fashion industry but failure in finance. Cute and pink may appeal more to teen girls in Seoul than to teen girls in Los Angeles. Informality prized in Australia could be totally offensive in Taiwan. And these are just a few examples.

The message here is to take the time to learn about your audience, especially if you're designing for a culture or subgroup different from your own. Do ethnographic research, and ensure that representative learners review the content with a view to cultural appropriateness.

Technology in schools

Kent Rahman, user experience consultant at ThoughtWorks, leverages ethnographic research methods to better understand school users of educational technology (both students and teachers). Ethnographic research provides a unique window into real-world behavior that can't typically be captured by surveys or self-reporting. It also allows designers to gain a broader and more sophisticated understanding of the larger learning ecosystem in which technology plays a part. Rahman offers the following insights gleaned from his research on tech use in schools:

- One size does not fit all. User interfaces (UIs) and workflows need to be tailored by subject. In other words, what works well in social studies won't work in math.
- Understand the context: classroom environment, desk real estate, movement from class to class, at home versus in class, unpredictable Wi-Fi, and so on.
- Understand that every school is different; some are better prepared to adopt new technologies than others.
- Offering students new ways to communicate with teachers and other students increases participation among students who are less likely to participate normally. For example, when allowed to ask teachers questions via direct message, students who normally wouldn't ask questions or participate were more likely to do so.
- Failure is not an option. If one student is unable to participate due to technical failure, a confusing workflow, or a confusing UI, then the whole digital classroom breaks down. Potential emotional fallout with the student who feels alienated contributes to teacher frustration with the technology.
- Understand and respect the limitations of technology. Sometimes a paper and pencil is better (and more efficient)!

>> DESIGN FOR AGE-SPECIFIC LEARNING NEEDS

There are important differences between how learners of different ages use technologies and react to design decisions. For example, kids love minesweeping while those over age 12 hate it. Teens use digital devices differently than adults do. If you design at a university, don't forget that most undergraduate learners and many corporate recruits are closer to the teenage bracket, so their experience and tech habits could be firmly placed in the adolescent zone and not in the adult one. This changes their expectations about the web and how well it can support their learning. Knowing the difference means knowing your learners.

Furthermore, research has busted some key stereotypes about teen web use:

- **Teens love the internet, but browse only half as much as the average adult.** They don't do a whole lot of tweeting. They talk on the phone less, but watch more video on their mobiles and out-text everyone else.

- **They're not technology experts.** Jakob Nielsen's work shows that, while there will always be that kid who handles desktop support for the family, on average, teens are no more able to fix or solve computer problems than adults.

- **They're less successful with websites than adults.** They'll give up on a website rather than try to solve technical problems, because they have less patience—no surprise there. So consider carefully any interface elements that might load up bandwidth or slow down the task.

- **They're unlikely to have the latest technology.** Studies show that teens often use secondhand hardware. It may not have audio, and even if it does, it's probably busy playing their music. They often have trouble with plug-ins such as Acrobat and Flash, and refrain from downloading things because they don't know how, don't want to wait for the download, are scared of viruses, or are thwarted by parental controls.

- **They don't all have the same experience.** Teen users are no less diverse than adult users and it's important to acknowledge the diversity of exposure to the web within this group. For example, Christine Greenhow and her colleagues found that even within wealthier countries like the United States, low-income teens made up 30 percent of the high school population, they had less access to the internet than their wealthier counterparts, and they were more likely to go online from places other than home.

Clearly, when it comes to learning, overarching decisions about support for exploration, information architectures, managing choice, providing guidance, and shaping the learning space can all have measurable effects on learning outcomes. Considering design decisions at this higher level will mean better results and a better experience for learners.

Congratulations! You've made it to the end of the book, which means you're just about ready to get designing. But before you do, check out the next and final chapter, where I've collected all the strategies outlined in the book into a cheat sheet and combined it with a collection of resources and checklists as a handy toolkit to support your work on exceptional interface design for learning. Enjoy.

SOURCES

Allen, Michael W. 2011. *Successful e-Learning Interface: Making Learning Technology Polite, Effective, and Fun*. Michael Allen's E-Learning Library. San Francisco: Pfeiffer.

Clark, Ruth C., and Richard E. Mayer. 2008. *e-Learning and the Science of Instruction: Proven Guidelines for Consumers and Designers of Multimedia Learning*. San Francisco: Pfeiffer.

Coolidge, Hilary. 2007. "Mobile Usability for Teens Who Are Going Mobile." *UXmatters*. http://www.uxmatters.com/mt/archives/2007/12/mobile-usability-for-teens-who-are-going-mobile.php.

Covey, Nic. 2009. "Breaking Teen Myths." Nielsen Company. http://www.nielsen.com/us/en/newswire/2009/breaking-teen-myths.html.

Greenhow, Christine, J. D. Walker, and Seongdok Kim. 2009. "Millennial Learners and Net-Savvy Teens? Examining Internet Use among Low-Income Students." *Journal of Computing in Teacher Education* 26 (2): 63–68.

Jochems, Wim, Jeroen van Merriënboer, and Rob Koper. 2013. *Integrated E-Learning: Implications for Pedagogy, Technology, and Organization*. New York: Routledge.

Kuhn, Alex, Chris Quintana, and Elliot Soloway. 2009. "StoryTime: A New Way for Children to Write." In *Proceedings of the 8th International Conference on Interaction Design and Children*. New York: ACM.

Nielsen, Jakob, and Hoa Loranger. 2006. *Prioritizing Web Usability*. Berkeley, CA: New Riders.

Nielsen Company. 2011. "Kids Today: How the Class of 2011 Engages with Media." http://www.nielsen.com/us/en/newswire/2011/kids-today-how-the-class-of-2011-engages-with-media.html.

Oviatt, Sharon, Alex Arthur, and Julia Cohen. 2006. "Quiet Interfaces that Help Students Think." In *Proceedings of the 19th Annual ACM Symposium on User Interface Software and Technology*. New York: ACM.

Schwartz, Barry. 2005. *The Paradox of Choice: Why More Is Less*. New York: Harper Perennial.

11

The Learning Interface Designer's Toolkit

Bringing it all together into a kit of cheat sheets, evaluation heuristics, and a slew of other resources to help you bring better interface design for learning into your work environment

Strategies and heuristics for the design of learning interfaces

A consolidated list of the 104 strategies presented throughout the chapters of this book is provided for easy reference at: www.InterfaceDesignForLearning.com.

Usability is critical to a successful digital learning experience. In 1990, Jakob Nielsen and Rolf Molich released the first round of the now classic industry standard set of usability heuristics. They're called *heuristics* because they're more like rules of thumb than specific guidelines. Odds are, you're already well acquainted with these, and indeed, they should be part of any learning interface designer's toolkit.

Nielsen has since updated the set, and his ten general principles for user interface design, which are standard for the evaluation of websites and software, are listed below. According to his evaluation method, "violations" of these heuristics are identified and assigned a level of severity to guide redesign.

NIELSEN'S 10 USABILITY HEURISTICS FOR USER INTERFACE DESIGN

1. Visibility of system status

2. Match between system and the real world

3. User control and freedom

4. Consistency and standards

5. Error prevention

6. Recognition rather than recall

7. Flexibility and efficiency of use

8. Aesthetic and minimalist design

9. Help users recognize, diagnose, and recover from errors

10. Help and documentation

See the full description for each at www.nngroup.com/articles/ten-usability-heuristics. For other sets of guidelines and heuristics, see Bruce Tognazzini's list of first principles of interaction design at www.asktog.com/basics/firstPrinciples.html. If you're really keen, the Nielsen Norman Group makes over 2,000 usability guidelines available as part of both free and paid reports on different topics at www.nngroup.com/reports.

Nielsen has based his evolving set of usability heuristics on years of ongoing user research studies. Without the kind of testing and polishing only years of crash-testing in a maturing field can provide, a new list of heuristics for the design of learning interfaces could never claim to be as solid or resilient as the well-established usability set.

Nevertheless, there's a need for guidance to support evaluation in this area, and I believe we have enough research from which to draw an initial set.

The heuristics below are informed by guidelines for the evaluation of online instruction available in the educational research and human-computer interaction literature. These will be refined as research findings grow and the field matures, but to get things started, here's a first set of eleven heuristics for the design and evaluation of learning interfaces.

11 HEURISTICS FOR THE DESIGN OF LEARNING INTERFACES

1. Relevance of media and reduction of extraneous load

Causes for extraneous cognitive load, such as imagery, visual and decorative detail, and other media elements that do not directly support the learning objective or required interactions should be avoided.

2. Learner control and freedom

The level of learner control afforded by navigation, architecture, and interaction design should be appropriate to audience characteristics and pedagogical approach.

3. Support for learning objective(s)

Interface graphics, content graphics, and interaction design should support the learning objectives as defined by educational designers or instructors.

4. Alignment with specific learner needs

The design should be influenced by specific audience characteristics such as prior knowledge, culture, literacy, computer literacy, visual literacy, age, professional, or subgroup culture, and any other aspects that can affect design decisions.

5. Appropriateness of look and feel

The look and feel should reflect an image appropriate to the audience, message, and content of the learning experience (for example, neither too childlike to be patronizing to experts, too serious to depress engagement in children, nor too lighthearted to be offensive for serious subjects).

6. Support for the cognitive aspects of learning

The design should support the cognitive aspects of learning relevant to the experience (for example, reasoning, cognitive load, problem solving, social interaction) as defined by one or more theories of learning psychology. Obstacles to the cognitive aspects of learning should be treated as errors in learning interface design.

7. Support for the affective aspects of learning

The design should support the affective aspects of learning relevant to the learning objectives within the constraints of available research evidence. Obstacles to the affective aspects of learning should be treated as errors in learning interface design.

8. Appropriateness of media and tools

The design should use media, devices, and tools appropriate to the type of learning or activity.

9. Accessibility

The design should be accessible to all learners within its scope, regardless of disability, device type, or technological literacy.

10. Usability

The design should conform to usability guidelines and best practices.

11. Feedback and responsiveness

The design should permit both operational and instructional feedback. Feedback should be intrinsic where possible and, when extrinsic, it should be placed near the relevant item and leave room for instructionally "rich" responses. Operational feedback should be provided instantaneously.

Learner-centered design principles

A workshop on learner-centered design held at the respected Computer Human Interaction Conference in 1998 produced some guidelines central to graphical user interfaces for learners. Remarkably, because these guidelines were based on basic principles rather than technology-dependent factors, every single one of them is still relevant today. Here's the list created by workshop experts (as reported by Sherry Hsi and Elliot Soloway in 1998):

- Provide feedback.
- Focus on cognitive goals.
- Automate routing or irrelevant tasks.
- Have a "theory of learning" or a model of the learner.
- Provide multiple representations and links between them.
- Use multiple formats and media types to address diversity.
- Include subject matter content.
- Recognize the agency of learners and the locus of control.
- Include the teacher as a local designer and learner, too.

- Include ways to see the history of interactions and user progress.
- Recognize that learning occurs not just in schools.
- Consider the prior knowledge of users.
- Recognize that students are diverse culturally, linguistically, motivationally, and developmentally.
- Facilitate mobility from screen to floor.
- Design for prior knowledge and diversity.

Educational design patterns

If you're an interface designer, you're probably acquainted with the glory of design patterns via splendid books like Jennifer Tidwell's *Designing Interfaces*. The idea that rigorously tested and proven "recipes" for effective design strategies can be used over and over again for reliable results is a mainstay of best practices in software and systems design. So what if you could have recipes like these for digital learning design?

Well, a number of researchers are attempting to do just that. Generally, they're education researchers and, as such, they've created patterns for *educational* design (the design of learning tasks and activities) and not for *interface* design. But many of these educational design patterns have implications for how a supporting interface should be designed.

For example, there are patterns for the effective design of online debates, brainstorming sessions, and synchronous online discussions. Patterns like these have been collected into libraries like the Design Principles Database (www.edu-design-principles.org) and Pedagogical Patterns (www.pedagogicalpatterns.org).

While *interface design* patterns specific to learning are still a bit pie in the sky, a few studies have provided us with a start. Christian Kohls and Tobias Windbrake surveyed 600 different interactive learning graphics and extracted four widely established patterns from their findings. These tackle interface interactions at a very detailed granularity (for example, click and drag patterns). Specifically, they are:

- **Active areas** change a dragged element to indicate it is selected and being dragged.
- **Activators** change the areas in the background.

- **No-go areas** define negative areas, that is, areas that cannot be entered.
- **Sandbox** defines positive areas that cannot be exited.

While this provides just a tantalizing taste of what might be, I hope to one day see educational design patterns and interface design patterns come together and have happy "learning interface design pattern" babies. This will make our jobs infinitely easier and better grounded, but until then, we toil on with what we have. And that ain't so bad, considering.

Process: User research and evaluation

How do we evaluate a user interface for learning? Standard usability testing is critical but not enough. Sherry Hsi and Elliot Soloway suggest that "traditional UCD task analytic methodologies (such as goals, operators, methods, and selector rules—or GOMS—analysis) work well when a task or domain is well specified. In the case of learning, goals not only differ across learners (both students and teachers) who have different intentions, but also across content domains and pedagogical approaches." We need ways to combine user-experience research methods with education and psychology methods. I hope that the heuristics I've provided above can be of assistance, but they're a set of guides rather than a process. For process inspiration, you might turn to some of the evaluation studies and strategies presented by researchers.

For example, Sharon Oviatt and her colleagues describe a study in which "performance was assessed using convergent metrics of dynamic information processing, including speed, attentional focus, metacognitive control, correctness of solutions, and memory."

Raquel Prates and her colleagues propose a new version of the traditional human-computer interaction task model enriched for education, including the specific analysis and needs of educational experiences and contexts. In her paper "Interface Design for Web Learning," Lorna Uden presents a methodology that she calls the Web User Object Modeling method to guide designers in the development of highly usable web learning environments.

Finally, as mentioned earlier, commercial developers like the professionals at PBS KIDS include educational measures to evaluate learning gains before and after use as part of their user experience evaluation repertoire.

Process is easily an area large enough for several libraries of books and certainly out of scope for this book, but I wanted to touch on it here if only to point a finger in some directions previous designers have taken, raise awareness of how learning experience has unique research and evaluation requirements, and to highlight just some of the many things we need to work on in the coming decade.

Join the community

Don't just read the book—join the community. To grow the field, we need to plant the seeds, but we also need to show up and garden together. There's a growing community of interface and user experience designers sharing their experiences at places like Mendeley and Twitter. Join us and be a part of the revolution.

MENDELEY GROUP

Have a great project, question, study, article, or idea you want to share? Join over a hundred other designers sharing books, websites, articles, and research findings together at our Interface Design for Learning Group on Mendeley at www.mendeley.com/groups/778381. (I've also added a link to every source used for this book there.)

TWITTER

Tweet with #UX4L (user experience for learning) to reach the community.

The way ahead

As Jeff Johnson says, "Interaction design is a skill, not something that anyone can do by following a recipe. Learning that skill amounts to learning not only what the design guidelines are but also how to recognize which rules to follow in each design situation." I hope the theory, principles, and strategies in this book will help you make more effective design decisions and expand your expertise in design for learning. Please share your case studies and experiences with the community. Together we can fill the digital future with magical learning experiences.

SOURCES

Johnson, Jeff. 2010. *Designing with the Mind in Mind: Simple Guide to Understanding User Interface Design Rules*. Amsterdam/Boston: Morgan Kaufmann Publishers/Elsevier.

Hsi, Sherry, and Elliot Soloway. 1998. "Learner-Centered Design: Addressing, Finally, the Unique Needs of Learners." In *CHI 98 Conference Summary on Human Factors in Computing Systems*. ACM. http://portal.acm.org/citation.cfm?id=286697.

Kohls, Christian, and Tobias Windbrake. 2007. "Where to Go and What to Show." In *Proceedings of the 14th Conference on Pattern Languages of Programs*. New York: ACM Press.

Nielsen, Jakob. 1995. "10 Heuristics for User Interface Design." http://www.nngroup.com/articles/ten-usability-heuristics.

Oviatt, Sharon, Alex Arthur, and Julia Cohen. 2006. "Quiet Interfaces that Help Students Think." In *Proceedings of the 19th Annual ACM Symposium on User Interface Software and Technology*. New York: ACM Press.

Prates, Raquel Oliveira, R. S. F. Xavier, R. De Janeiro, R. Maria, and Rosa Maria Videira de Figueiredo. 2005. "An Experience with an Enriched Task Model for Educational Software." In *Extended Abstracts on Human Factors in Computing Systems*, 1721–24. ACM.

Uden, Lorna. 2007. "Interface Design for Web Learning." In *Flexible Learning in an Information Society*, edited by Badrul H. Khan, 178–85. Hershey, PA: Information Science Publishing.

Index